The Story of
ASIA'S LIONS

The Story of
ASIA'S LIONS

Divyabhanusinh

Marg publications

General Editor Pratapaditya Pal
Research Editor Annapurna Garimella
Executive Editors Savita Chandiramani, Rivka Israel
Senior Editorial Executive Biswajeet Rath
Editorial Executive Arnavaz K. Bhansali

Senior Production Executive Gautam V. Jadhav
Production Executive Vidyadhar R. Sawant

Design concept, jacket design Roma Sinai Mukherjee

Design Execution Marg
Designed by Naju Hirani *based on the concept*

ISBN: 81-85026-66-1
Library of Congress Catalog Card Number: 2004-326003
Price: Rs 1850 / US$ 49 / UK£ 30

The Gir Welfare Fund will receive 5% of the net sales value of each copy sold.

Published by J.J. Bhabha for Marg Publications on behalf of the
National Centre for the Performing Arts, 24, Homi Mody Street, Mumbai 400 001.

Colour and black and white processing by Reproscan, Mumbai 400 013.

Printed at Silverpoint Press Private Limited, Mumbai 400 013, India.

For

Asia's Lions
who survive in spite of us

&

D.D. Kosambi, 1907–1966
Guide, Friend, Teacher, Benefactor

contents:

Pages 2–3, 5 ■ A pride in a grassland, Gir.
Photographs: Divyabhanusinh.

Pages 8–9 ■ Lioness and cubs, Gir.
Photograph: Divyabhanusinh.

Page 5 ■ Portrait of D.D. Kosambi by Jatin Das.
Author's collection.

*Marg acknowledges the generous support
of The Indian Hotels Company Limited
and The Pirojsha Godrej Foundation
in the publication of this book.*

preface

THE LION IS so deeply ingrained in the human psyche that the impulse to write a book about this magnificent animal is not unique. However, two additional reasons propelled me to write this one. First, a history of the interaction of the lions of Asia with man over the ages has not yet been attempted fully in English, or for that matter in any other language. Second, my ancestor Vanraj Chavda, the founder of the principality of Anhilwad Patan in north Gujarat in the 8th century, was born in the Gir forest, now the last home of Asia's lions, and was therefore christened "king of the jungle" according to the popular tradition of Gujarat. The suffix to my own name, "sinh", also means lion. It was thus natural that I had a large dose of lion stories in my childhood, far more than most children would have had even in Gujarat where the animal thrives in folklore and literature. Moreover, I studied at Rajkumar College, Rajkot, at a time when M.A. Wynter-Blyth, the pioneer of large mammal census in independent India and an authority on the Gir and its lions, was its principal. This happy happenstance had its own impact on my young mind.

With such antecedents, I should have written about lions much earlier. This did not happen, again for two reasons. First, there was the matter of earning a living, a must for the cadets of small principalities which in any case had disappeared into the cauldron of republican India. Second, the cheetah problem engaged my attention unexpectedly and dramatically, which kept me busy researching the subject from 1984 to 1994 resulting in a book the following year. A vague idea of writing a history of the lion had come to me as far back as the 1960s, when I re-read with fascination the articles on the Gir Forest and its lions by M.A. Wynter-Blyth and R.S. Dharmakumarsinhji in the journals of the Bombay Natural History Society. I started collecting data haphazardly and fitfully from then on but other preoccupations intervened. I have often wondered how differently I would have written the lion story if I had done it more than three decades ago when there were still scores of eyewitnesses who had lived in princely India, experienced lion and other shikar, and survived the upheavals of 1947. It was however only in the 1980s that I encountered the historical lion in a big way, as I dug deep into Indian history's sources for my cheetah work. It was after the cheetah manuscript went to the publishers in 1994 that the lion engaged my attention as fully as is possible for a senior executive in the corporate world, and only after my retirement in 2001 that I finally began writing it all down. Normally, an author should not find it necessary to give such a lengthy background to his work, but after the cheetah book was published, readers wondered how this interloper, neither of the academic world, nor a field scientist or forest officer, came to write about cheetahs. Almost a decade later I find I am still explaining myself.

The sources for the history of the lion are remarkably similar to, and in some cases the same as, those for the cheetah. This helped insofar as collecting research material goes, since my job was partially done during collection of the cheetah data. I believe that there is nothing like visual material to illustrate fine nuances of the past or present; here too illustrations tell their story wherever possible as in the earlier book. And yet there are major differences between the two works. The cheetah is so difficult to find among historical sources and the references are so few that I had to use almost all the material I had unearthed to put the story together. In the case of the lion, the opposite is true. There was often so much material that I was confronted with the dilemma of what I should choose and what I should reject. I beg the indulgence of my readers if I have left out any of their favourite sources or stories. While the size of the cheetah book was limited by the material available, I have deliberately limited the length of this one in order not to make it into an unwieldy tome, for it is possible to expand almost each of the chapters into a book by itself. Besides, the cheetah is dead and gone from India, its story has ended here as far as I can tell. The lion on the other hand has hung on by a thread. The last chapter here deals with the threats it faces from us. I had planned to write two chapters on the subject but soon I realized that this animal and its problems have been the subject of our scrutiny ad infinitum. The Central and Gujarat state governments have initiated some schemes for its preservation, but only time will tell if they have succeeded or have remained on paper as many others have. What is required is not suggestions for solutions – of which there are plenty – but action.

The British period saw crucial developments in the "sport" of hunting the lion as well as in its protection. What is often referred to as the "British administration" or simply "the British" by many an author, consisted of individuals with very different personalities who acted differently and quite often uniquely. It is simply not on to convert the lot into a faceless mass. I have tried to give full names and designations of the dramatis personae of the time wherever possible, also to retain some of the flavour of the past. For the very same reason, I have used place names as they were known then rather than those in use today. The word "Pakistan" appears rarely in the text as lions had disappeared from the area that was to be the new country even before its idea had found political expression and long before it became a political reality.

I must make a special mention of the princely order from whom I am fortunate in having received a fund of inside information. But I have been careful to present the facts – warts and all – for the reader to judge; however, no apology is called for. Persons who have at their command surplus resources and time (Indian princes had plenty of both since the imperial government had taken away from them the bothersome and resource crunching responsibility for external relations of their states) indulge themselves lavishly and often publicly without concern for others' judgements and feelings. It is a pattern of behaviour as old as history itself, and is not unique to the Indian princes. One has only to look at their predecessors and more to the point, their successors – industrialists and politicians – to test the veracity of the statement. It is easy to pass judgement on the past; it is more important however, to build on what the present has inherited from it.

I have adhered to the narrative style and have kept analysis to the minimum to try and make the history accessible and compelling for even the reader with but a passing interest. I have no doubt though, that if a lion could write a history of its relationship with humans and their depredations, it would be very different and illuminating, *the* definitive work.

Suryodaya, 310 Gom Defence Colony
Vaishali Marg, Jaipur
sawaj_cheetah@rediffmail.com

CHAPTER 1

Asia's Lions Today

Birds of the Gir
■ The many species of birds include the crested serpent eagle, Indian peafowl, painted sandgrouse, and purple sunbird.
Photographs: Divyabhanusinh.

THERE WAS A TIME when the lion roamed Asia from Palestine in the west to Palamau in eastern India. It was the most visible of the large cats and it struck awe in its human observers as no other animal did.

Yet, today this magnificent animal has become extinct in Asia but for a small population hanging on by a thread in a corner of India. To most Asians the lion survives only in vague memory or in fairy tales. Few of them outside Gujarat are aware of its existence on the continent. How this sorry state came to pass is the story of this book. But first, let us briefly look at the lion's last home in Asia and how lions here differ from those of Africa, and recount some of the close relationships humans have had with the lion which remains an active presence in the culture of Gujarat.

The remote region in which Asia's lions survive is the isolated Saurashtra peninsula. It is bound by the Gulf of Kutch in the north, the Arabian Sea in the south and west, and to the east by the Gulf of Cambay (Khambhat). To the northeast of Saurashtra lie the Little Rann of Kutch and the flat sedimentary lowlands of Nal and the Bhal. Here is a peninsula with a difference, physically almost cut off even on the fourth side from the mainland of the Indian subcontinent. Both human and animal populations have been isolated over the millennia, and among the former, though the language they speak is a distinct dialect of Gujarati, the dress, folklore, and the way of life is noticeably different from the rest of Gujarat even today.

The surface of the peninsula is a sheet of Deccan lava interspersed by trap dykes which are the peculiarities of the region. While most of Saurashtra is low-lying, there are two prominent hill masses. One occupies an area east of Rajkot and much of the middle of the peninsula, with Chotila being its highest peak at 357 metres. The other one is a higher and bolder mass centring on the Gir range with Sarkala the highest peak, at 641 metres. Its eastern offshoot is the Mytiala hill which is 471 metres high, and further east the 498-metre-high Shetrunjay.[1]

The Gir forest, the last home of the Asiatic lion (the term commonly used for Asia's last surviving lion), surrounds the Gir hill system with an area of approximately 1,800 square kilometres, of which a little over 1,400 form the Gir National Park and Sanctuary. Mytiala forest to the east is cut off from the Gir as are the Girnar mountains to the northwest, which are weathered volcanic remains with the highest peak of Goraknath standing at 1,117 metres. The forest is a haven for a variety of flora with 448 flowering plants and 96 tree species being recorded here. *Sag* or teak is the commonest and forms over 31 per cent of the tree cover, followed by *dudhalo, khair, bor*, and other species.[2] The western area of Gir is dominated by teak whereas in the eastern parts of the forest, *Acacia* species are more prominent. There are areas in the central portion which are thick jungle with semi-evergreen riverine tracts going through the forest. *Khakhro* or flame of the forest trees are a riot of colour at the onset of summer while the stately *vad* or banyan and occasional stands of bamboo are sentinels of the pleasing prospect, interspersed with *bor, jambudo, sawar*, and many other tree species.

This forest is also haven to some 290 species of birds. From the peacock to the grey partridge, and the crested serpent eagle to the king vulture, it provides them all a habitat to survive and prosper. It has lost only one species of bird in recent times – the grey hornbill which has become locally extinct. The Gir is reputed to have six species of amphibians and 24 species of reptiles, the mugger or marsh crocodile being the largest with a population of some 700 individuals. The forest was at the forefront of the crocodile conservation programme and today it has one of its largest

On the road

■ Lions prefer to walk on the soft road surfaces. Here the adult male is heading straight for the photographer, though there is no malice in his expression.
Photograph: Divyabhanusinh.

Some predators of the Gir
(clockwise from right)

■ The rusty spotted cat is rare, and difficult to spot.
Photograph: Bharat Pathak.

■ The jungle cat's small size and nocturnal habits make it rarely visible.

■ The leopard is the second largest predator of the Gir. Very adaptable in its habits, it does not easily show itself.

■ The striped hyena, earlier called the laughing hyena because of its peculiar call, is a carrion eater and a shy animal rarely seen in daytime.
Photographs: Divyabhanusinh.

populations in the country. It is a habitat rich in mammals as well, with 32 species being found there, from the musk shrew to chital, wildboar, sambar, and nilgai which form the prey base for the carnivores which include the tiny rusty-spotted cat which was recorded in the Gir forest for the first time as late as in 1989,[3] jungle cat, jackal, hyena, and leopard, the lion itself being at the top of the food chain.

The forest is studded with human settlements too. There are 14 forest villages and 54 Maldhari nesses (cattle pens of herdsmen) with a total population of approximately 2,500 and a livestock population of 13,000 heads according to the 2004 figures.[4] The three Hindu pilgrimage sites of Tulshishyam, Banej, and Kankai located in the forest cause a human influx during festivals whereas cattle from outside the protected areas invade it annually, particularly during years of scarcity. The forest is important for humans for yet another reason. Four major rivers of Saurashtra – the Rawal, Machundri, Singhavdo, and Hiran – issue forth from the Gir, apart from the Shetrunji whose main source is the eastern Gir and the Ojhat whose tributaries are from the Gir and the Girnar mountains. This then, is the mixed bag kingdom of the *sawaj* – the Asiatic lion, *Panthera leo persica.*

A common question is: how are these lions different from the African lions? One distinguishing morphological feature is the abdominal or belly fold of loose skin which is clearly noticeable both among males and females but somewhat more prominent in the males. This feature is rare among African lions. The tuft of the tail in both males and females is somewhat more pronounced than among African lions but the distinction between the two is not sharp. Male lions have a more pronounced tuft of hair at the elbow than their counterparts in Africa; here too the distinction is not sharp. The male Asiatic lion grows a luxuriant mane surrounding the face, covering the throat and upper parts of the front legs, somewhat halo-like as seen from the front of the animal. However, the mane is not as full or long as that of the African lion and unlike the latter it is not prominent at the top of the head, making the ears of the Asiatic lion very visible. A thin strip of hair grows from the back of the head, past the shoulder blades onto a part of the back of the animal. The skulls of lions collected from Gir often have a bifurcation of the infra-orbital foramen. While this is not a universal feature, it has not been recorded at all in African lions.[5]

Dr Stephen J. O'Brien and his team of scientists who have examined the genetic profile of Asiatic lions have found that their DNA fingerprint patterns are so uniform that: "the Gir lions were all identical.... It was as if they were all clones or identical twins.... The Gir lions had even less variation and were more severely inbred than [even] cheetahs." They concluded that the male lions of Gir who had "dramatically" undersized manes in comparison with African male lions had become "feminized" because of inbreeding caused by a bottleneck which was also the cause of the belly fold and the infraorbital foramen bifurcation.[6]

Lions with manes of different colours are so well known in the Gir that the *pagi*s of old and Maldharis today have a name for each shade of the mane.[7] For example a full grown lion with a light brown mane is called *bhurio*, a lion with a light coloured (yellowish) mane a *pilo*, and a black maned lion a *kalio* or *kamho*. In fact, in the stories and folklore of Saurashtra and Gujarat a lion with a luxuriant mane is called a *kesarisinh*. The Sanskrit word *kesarin* is a name for the lion and means "one who has a mane",[8] whereas *keshwari* is the Gujarati word for mane, of a lion or of a horse.

There is a twist in the tale. In spite of such a range of well defined manes, the lions from India were considered "maneless" for several decades in the 19th century

Prey
■ Chital or spotted deer, and sambar, two of the species which form part of the prey base of the lion in the Gir.
Photographs: Divyabhanusinh.

The Maldharis

■ An old Maldhari walks through the Gir forest in the monsoon.
■ An extended family in a ness in the forest.
■ Women churn curds to separate butter.
Photographs: Bhushan Pandya.

The Sidis

■ Sidi women resting by the roadside with their pickings of jamun to be sold in the nearby markets.
Photograph: Bhushan Pandya.

and in the early part of the 20th. In the 1830s, a Captain Walter Smee described the lions shot by him near Ahmedabad as "maneless", since the manes of these animals were very scanty and did not cover their shoulders.[9] Such lions are indeed known of in the Gir and we have a special name for them, *untio*, but they appear to be very rare with few such specimens seen. In lion populations elsewhere too, maneless or scantily maned lions are not unknown. The Maneaters of Tsavo who played havoc with the railway track layers on the Mombasa to Nairobi railway in Kenya in 1898, were both "maneless".[10] Such lions occur even today in Tsavo National Park, Kenya[11] and they appear to be a variant of the better known forms of the animals from say Kenya's Masai Mara or Tanzania's Serengeti. The "maneless" tag does not apply to the lions of Gir at all.

Unfortunately, in India sufficient data is not available to establish local morphological variations of lions from different regions as they disappeared from the rest of the country before naturalists got down to describing them. Other felines such as tigers and leopards from different regions show noticeable local variations which are well recorded. The cheetahs of India too had three different variations according to Mughal chroniclers: the cheetah of the Deccan, the cheetah of the mountainous regions of the north, and the cheetah of Gujarat – the last-mentioned being the largest and best for coursing antelope. Since cheetahs were used for sport, Mughal chroniclers observed these animals closely and provided this information for the benefit of those who would need to know. But no such descriptions of lions are available.

Even so, the earliest visual records of lions from India which are accurate enough for us to draw conclusions, are those of the Mughals whose paintings do give us a glimpse of what they must have seen. The paintings with lions may be classified as three types: those that depict lions and other animals as part of a story or a fable, those that are studies of lions per se, and those that depict lions as a part of a hunting scene. Some of these paintings are illustrated in Chapter 6, but here we may make some observations on the accuracy of depiction.

The first category of paintings includes the following:

"Noah's Ark" by Miskin, circa 1595.[12] The lion is shown in profile with a thin dark line of a mane around the face and above the head as well. A "smiling" lioness faces the viewer; she too has a dark circle around the face.

"The Raven Addressing the Animals" ascribed to Miskin, circa 1595–1600.[13] The lion listens attentively to the bird along with other animals both real and imaginary. The lion's neck and back are dark brown with barely a suggestion of a mane.

"A Lion's Court" by Farrukh Chela, from the *Anwar-i-Suhaili*, 1595–96.[14] Here the lion holds court from a raised position. All the animals sit below and listen attentively. The lion has no mane but the neck, chest, and front of the legs are rendered in dark brown.

In all the above pictures the animals are accurately enough drawn to be individually recognizable, even the cheetah and the leopard which are often mixed up are distinguishable, but the lions have almost no manes.

In the second category of paintings are the following:

"Animals", circa 1610. This page from the *St Petersburg Muraqqa*[15] is remarkable insofar as it appears to be a collage of unconnected subjects. It has a cat with kittens, a hound bitch with pups, also a urial, nilgai, and other animals. At the top of the painting in the middle, is a lion; at the top left-hand corner is a lion killing a nilgai, while at the top right-hand corner is a lion killing a chital. The lion in the middle is

The Maldharis
- A girl fetches water.
- With a herd of buffaloes at a water trough near a ness.
Photographs: Bhushan Pandya.

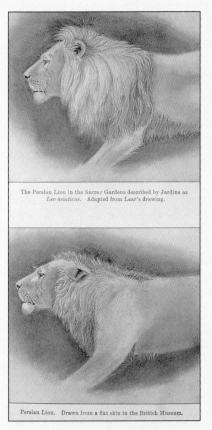

The Persian Lion in the Surrey Gardens described by Jardine as *Leo asiaticus*.   Adapted from Lear's drawing.

Persian Lion.   Drawn from a flat skin in the British Museum.

A Persian lion
■ The one on top was drawn from a specimen living in Surrey Gardens in the 1830s. The other was drawn from a flat skin in the British Museum (Natural History section).
From Pocock, 1930.

Pair of African lions
■ No bigger than an Indian lion, the male has a far more luxuriant mane which covers its ears and shoulders unlike the Indian lion. This pair is from Ngorongoro Crater, Tanzania, whose population went through a bottleneck some years ago, as had the Gir lions.
Photograph: Divyabhanusinh.

Colourful lions
■ A fully grown lion with a dark brown mane and the same body colour – such specimens are uncommon.
Photograph: Divyabhanusinh.

Hurriana Lion in the Tower Menagerie described by Bennett as *Felis leo bengalensis*. Adapted from the original woodcut.

Gujarat Lion. Drawn from Capt. Smee's skin in the British Museum.

A "Hurriana" lion and a "Gujarat" lion

■ The former was drawn from a specimen living in the Tower Menagerie, London in the 1820s. The British encountered many lions in the environs of Delhi at that time, hence the name. The latter was drawn from a flat skin of Capt. W. Smee's lion in the British Museum (Natural History section). The animal appears to be a sub-adult specimen, hence the scanty mane and the myth of the "maneless" lion of Gujarat.

From Pocock, 1930.

Colourful lions

■ *A* kamho lion. A black-maned lion whose body sports a dark greyish tinge, it could also be called a *jamwo*.

■ *A* fully grown lion. It has a mane of light brown colour – too dark to be called a *pilo*, but not dark enough to be called a *kamho*.

Photographs: Divyabhanusinh.

A mock charge
■ Disturbed by the photographer's arrival, the lion charged him. Such charges are warnings not usually pressed home. Of note is the abdominal fold, so prominent in Asian lions.
Photograph: Divyabhanusinh.

imperial entourage and observed wild animals at first hand. It is possible that in this category of paintings, they were showing animals only as symbols of the story they told rather than depicting them realistically as they would do elsewhere. Inaccurate renderings are certainly not because of ignorance.

But when it came to animal studies or hunting scenes involving the imperial family, the artists were careful enough as a rule to make accurate renderings of lions with proper manes and of different colours. Most of the Mughal hunts of lions are depicted in open country or grasslands, areas which were very easily accessible from the enormous camps which the great Mughals set up when they went hunting. The manes of the lions in these paintings are usually brown.

With the decline of Mughal power, patronage at small courts assumed importance where subsidiary schools of painting developed. This brings us to the paintings of the Kotah and Bundi schools from present day Rajasthan. While they were stylized to a degree, yet they hold some interesting information. All the lion hunts depicted are in jungles as against the open terrain seen in Mughal paintings. The painting titled "Maharaja Ram Singh I of Kotah (1695–1707) Hunting Lions at Mukundgarh", Kotah, circa 1695–1700,[22] has two male lions in it, both with well defined and accurate manes of a dark brown colour. "Rao Bhoj Singh of Bundi Slays a Lion", Kotah, circa 1720, attributed to Kotah Master,[23] has very stylized animals, extremely light coloured, and yet with well defined black manes. A hunting scene attributed to Joshi Hathuwa, 1784,[24] shows Maharao Umed Singh I (1770–1819) hunting lions. There are in all nine lions in the picture within a stockade in a jungle, not one has a mane. The lions depicted appear to be of a pride with lionesses and sub-adult males which would explain the absence of the manes.

There is a striking contrast between the "Kotah lions" and the earlier Mughal paintings. When the Kotah artists painted manes they were usually dark brown or black suggesting a variation in the colour of the lions found in jungles as opposed to

Lions at rest
■ A *belad* of two brothers gets disturbed, they wake up and watch the photographer, then one of them decides to move on. Their body colour has a greyish tinge – such lions are called *jamwo*.
Photographs: Divyabhanusinh.

those found in open grasslands. (But some of the darkest maned lions are found in African savannah.) Did the scrubland where the Mughals hunted have an effect on the colour of its lions' manes, or deprive them of some of their hair over the millennia? We cannot say for sure. But the paintings of the Mughal and the Kotah schools must surely be true enough to depict the commonest types of manes of lions seen in their respective regions.

By the time T.C. Jerdon's *Mammals of India* was published in 1867, lions had virtually disappeared from the subcontinent with the exception of Gir and its environs. It was the first "scientific" work of its kind in the empire but it came too late to note local variations in lion populations based on empirical evidence. Jerdon described the animals from hearsay, as is clear from the text.[25]

Apart from the manes of lions, there is the question of their size. The *pagi*s of the Gir suggest two variations found in the forest: the short-bodied or stockily built lion known as the *gadhio,* and the lion with a longer body called *velar.* The etymologies of these terms are not clear, they are colloquial and are used among the small band of persons whose traditional occupation was tracking. It appears that the word *gadhio* comes from *gadhedo,* donkey, and hence may mean ass-like, that is short or small in comparison with a *velar* which may well have derived from the "waler" breed of Australian horses from New South Wales which were used by princes in Saurashtra in the first half of the 20th century. Two *pagi*s of the old school who had followed their fathers' profession, Bhanabha Kathalbha and Abhlabha Jafarbha, the latter a Sidi of remarkable talent, informed me that the lions of eastern Gir are larger animals. This belief is based on tradition and ocular observation rather than on actual measurement of lengths and weights of animals.

The size of Asiatic lions in comparison with the animals from Africa has also been commented upon throughout the British period and later. The accepted position today is that the average length of the two is the same.[26] But R.I. Pocock, writing in 1930, records that African animals were bigger on the basis of *Rowland Ward's Records of Big Game.*[27] However, this conclusion is based on a very narrow base of information he was working on. After an extensive search in the shikar literature of the British period, journals, unpublished shikar diaries of hunters, and interviews with former hunters, I have been able to compile a list of 73 measurements from Gir and its surrounding areas.[28] While these are hunters' records and are subject to several inaccuracies, they are at least roughly indicative of the length of the dead animals measured. From the present compilation it will be seen that the largest lion (not skin) from India was 10 feet 6 inches long, while the second largest was 10 feet 2 inches. A total of 37 animals were more than 9 feet in length. Captain Walter Smee's lions do not feature among these. It is quite possible that the animals he shot were young lions whose manes had not fully grown. Rowland Ward's records of the twelve largest lions from Africa shows that the largest was 10 feet 11 inches long while the smallest was 8 feet 2 inches long.[29] We may allow for the fact that this record was compiled in 1935 after Pocock's analysis was done and there may have been additions since, which may have shown more lions from Africa at the top end of the scale. In the meantime the method of measuring trophies has changed and we have no comparative data from India.[30] We may still conclude that sizewise, the populations are comparable. It must also be remembered that all the lions from India for whom we have measurements came from one small pocket, as against those of Africa which came from several different areas spread over a vast region, from far larger population bases, and yielded far more measurements.

Many accounts refer to a population bottleneck in the Gir with lions almost dying out in the late 19th century. Several alarming reports were circulating then and one making the rounds was that the total number of lions was as low as a dozen. That there was a drastic reduction in their numbers is certain, but the figure of twelve lions was certainly an exaggeration.[31] There is also the physical bottleneck which usually escapes attention. The Saurashtra peninsula was till about 300 years ago separated from the rest of India by a strait, which can still be traced through the flat lowlands of the Bhal, the large lake of Nal, and the salt wastes between the lake and the Little Rann of Kutch. M.A. Wynter-Blyth was of the view that Saurashtra was possibly almost insular up to the 17th century.[32] What effect this had on the lions over the centuries is a matter of conjecture as there is no database of information. However, a study has been conducted which compares the pure-bred Asiatic lions from the Sakkarbag Zoo in Junagadh, which are descendants of wild animals captured from the Gir, with lions from Serengeti and the Ngorongoro crater in Tanzania. The last mentioned population too had gone through a severe bottleneck in 1962–63 from which they grew to a population of 100 in a restricted area of 260 square kilometres. The study found that the Gir lions had complete genetic monomorphism which had resulted in greater incidence of abnormal sperms (spermatozoa with deranged mid-piece) and lower number of motile sperms (those capable of independent locomotion) in comparison with the two African populations. Asiatic lions had also lower circulating levels of testosterone which could cause reproductive problems. While no such sign was visible in the Ngorongoro population, the Sakkarbag Zoo lions exhibited a similar abnormality. One male which had mated with oestrus females failed to produce any offspring and three of the other tested males produced only single-cub litters or stillborn cubs in 1985–87.[33]

Dr Stephen J. O'Brien and his team have concluded that the founders of the Gir lion population had become separated from the mainland population of the subcontinent as a result of the geographical isolation of the Kathiawar peninsula some three millennia earlier. These deformities are a result of this population bottleneck[34] and not the better known one at the beginning of the 20th century. Though the lion population has grown uninterruptedly from 1985 onwards, these deformities are a matter of grave concern for the long-term survival of this relict population as it would be premature to assume that all is well with the Gir lions.

A unique feature of the lions of Gir is the close relationship that has evolved between them and man. Lions are gregarious in nature and less prone to be shy than tigers; as a result, they have been more closely observed by man over the years. During the princely administration of Junagadh state prior to 1947, the Forest Department shikaris were expected to know the lions in their respective beats and they could recognize particularly males by their size, colour and size of manes, or distinguishing marks such as scars on the face usually acquired in fights. Those shikaris whose tracking skills were honed by generations of observations were unequalled at their job. Hebat of Jambuda ness, a Sidi shikari, was highly respected for his skills even among British hunters.[35] In the 1950s there was yet another shikari Haidu jamadar who was among the last of a long line of accomplished trackers, equally renowned.

A lioness with a cub at kill
- The mother and her young are on a natural kill of a domestic buffalo. The lioness's stomach is full. Her abdominal fold is noticeable.

Photograph: Divyabhanusinh.

In fact, there was such familiarity between the shikaris and lions that individual animals were given names by them, a practice that continues today.* A lioness who had lost an eye was called Badi, the one-eyed one. Another lioness was called Bandi, the one with tail cut, for she had lost part of her tail in a fight. Yet another was called Khari as she was very short-tempered. A large male lion of the late 1950s was called Tilio because he had a mark on his forehead like a tilak. This lion went on to adorn a postage stamp of India, and his death was reported on All India Radio![36] A pair of lions seen in the late 1960s were named Ubhdo for erect ears and Belio for a drooping ear. In the 1970s two magnificent males were named Akbar and Sultan. In the 1980s two were named Raj and Moti and another two were christened Dharam and Veero, after the Bollywood star Dharmendra and his role in *Sholay*. In 1997 a pair of Maldhari twins from Dudhala ness surprised two lions on a buffalo kill. The lions attacked the twins whose cries of distress brought others to the scene and they survived to recount the tale. The two lions were promptly named Natha and Amra after the Maldharis they had attacked!

During the rule of the nawabs, *pagi*s of the Koli tribe demonstrated their skill to important state guests by placing a handkerchief on the mane of a sleeping lion with the help of a stick, while another would go and retrieve it. However, the entertainment came to an abrupt stop when one of the *pagi*s met his end prematurely as the lion woke up in the middle of the proceedings.[37] I have been witness to some astounding encounters in Gir. Once I was sitting on the ground beside the experienced shikari Abhlabha Jafarbha, when Sultan, one of the pair of large lions well known at the time, approached us and sat barely 3 metres away

---

* Large carnivores have been named in the past elsewhere, but not with such regularity. For example, it was only from the late 1970s that several tigers were given names in Ranthambhore National Park, when they became very visible in daylight as a result of strict protection, and individuals became recognizable as a result.

Lion on a kill
■ A young male on a natural kill of a domestic cow which he dragged into the undergrowth to feed on.
Photograph: Divyabhanusinh.

waiting for a handout. On another occasion, one morning in July, on turning a corner in the road I came across two large lions sitting in a clearing. The lions were known to the shikari Bhanabha Kathalbha. Getting down from the vehicle he and I walked up to them and sat down barely 10 metres away. The lions who were full after a kill regarded us with calm curiosity for a while, but soon completely ignored us, lay down, and went to sleep. Once along with the shikaris, I was able to follow a lion on foot as he walked on the road. He moved apparently lazily but actually at fairly fast clip for 6 kilometres as he went along marking his territory. He would look back to make sure that a respectable distance of about 20 metres was maintained between him and us. That aside, he was quite unconcerned and the walk was abandoned only after he moved off into thick jungle away from the road. Even lionesses with cubs but a few weeks old, allow human presence at remarkably close quarters. Being able to watch a relaxed mother with her cubs gambolling around her, from just a few metres' distance, is a glorious experience which remains permanently etched in one's mind.

Such behavioural instances cannot be taken for tameness of lions. The animals are truly wild. In certain parts of Gir they have come to regard humans as no threat to themselves but rather as providers of food, as a result of baits given to them. To take liberties with these animals would be an act of utter foolishness as is illustrated by occasional but repeated attacks on humans in such situations.

The lions of the Gir are very different from wild tigers and leopards. M.K. Ranjitsinhji observes in the context of artificial feeding that, while there are several factors which militate against the practice, it does reveal certain patterns of behaviour of some species in the proximity of human beings. Leopards in Wankaner, Gujarat, and tigers in Dungarpur, Rajasthan, had been artificially fed for four to seven generations in the 1940s and each animal could be individually identified. He records that during darkness and in or near thick cover, the leopard revealed more tolerance, whereas in daylight and in open areas, the tiger was more tolerant. But in no circumstances or with any amount of inducement could the tiger or leopard ever be made to match the "incredible confidence that the Gir lion now exhibits to the close proximity of man on foot".[38]

The Gir lions' behaviour is obviously a result of generations of them having observed humans and what they mean to them. At the same time the lions are sharp enough to spot possible conflict and they react swiftly. On several occasions I have observed lions leaving their location abruptly on seeing or hearing a Maldhari with whom they have continuous conflict, for the latter's cattle form a sizeable proportion of their prey base!

If lions accept people at close proximity in Gir, local culture too accords the animal a central place. The lion is deeply embedded in the culture of Gujarat, and more so in the Saurashtra peninsula where it provides a continuing link with the past. It is interesting to note that there is a typical name for it in the Kathiawari dialect of Gujarati, *sawaj*, which is not known elsewhere even in Gujarat. Colonel J.W. Watson speculated that the word had an Arabic root.[39] This is highly unlikely. The Sanskrit word *swapado* stands for savage, ferocious, a wild beast[40] or a beast of prey and the word appears for the first time in the *Atharvaveda*.[41] The word *sawaj* appears to have roots in antiquity.

Lions are the subject of stories taught in schools or sung in folksongs, and they are immortalized in literature. The state textbook for teaching Gujarati in class 7 has a story titled "Lion's Friendship". It is a tale of a friendship between a local prince and a lion who together endured several vicissitudes, and they were parted only on the prince's death when the lion returned to the forest never to be seen again.[42]

Jhaverchand Meghani (1896–1947) the renowned storyteller and poet of Gujarat, recounted a traditional tale, "Gift of a Lion" in which God took the form of a lion to save the honour of a devotee prince who had promised to give a Charan supplicant any gift he desired. The latter having demanded a wild lion was humiliated when presented with one and he left in shame.[43] Among the most loved poems in Gujarati is "To a Charan Lass" in which Meghani recounts the bravery of a Maldhari girl who tried to save her favourite calf from the jaws of a lion.[44] This local incident has been immortalized in verse and song, and like many others concerning lions is taught in schools and is sung by bards. But lions had made an earlier appearance in Gujarati verse. Arguably the greatest romantic poet of Gujarat was Prince Sursinhji of Lathi (1874–1900) better known by his nom de plume, Kalapi. His romantic poetry born out of unfulfilled love attained a literary elegance unmatched since. His short poem "A Morning in a Forest" describes the peace and quiet of the dawn shattered by a lion's roar. All of a sudden

> A star broke from its moorings in the sky, a cannon ball was fired,
> Red hot streaking the sky it flew,
> River Ganga burst forth from her mountain fastness,
> Lord Ram's arrow flew from his bow string,

---

* Anyone interested in knowing how peaceful the lion–human relationship can be, ought to read the detailed account of Elizabeth Marshall Thomas (1994, pp. 109–86) of the Juwa tribesmen and lions living in the Kalahari where she herself stayed for extended periods in the early 1950s near the Gautscha waterhole. In an area of a few square miles lived a cheetah, a leopard, at least five spotted hyenas, ten lions, and thirty people. In other words there were in all fifty carnivorous creatures who shared the one and only waterhole in the region and hunted the same antelope population.

A pride at rest
■ Three *pathda*, sub-adult males, rest with their mothers near the Hiran dam.
Photograph: Divyabhanusinh.

As the antlered stag jumped across the river in fright.

Standing there was the lion roaring loudly,

Shaking mountains, even the sun was startled turning red like burning coal;

Birds would not flutter or sing, trees vibrated, the earth trembled!

The universe had burst open! Deluge! As if Lord Shiva had blown his conch![45]

The Gir is also sung of in folksongs all over the Sorath area of Saurashtra and elsewhere. The Charans of the forest have sung of the marriage of one hill Ghantulo with another Ghantuli when the rivers Hiran and Sarasvati were part of the bridegroom's party and the hill Vansadhol became the best man, causing happiness all over the Gir![46] One of my most enduring memories is that of a Maldhari performing *arti*, in the four cardinal directions of the earth from his ness where his cattle were penned for the night. When I asked the meaning of the ritual, he replied that it was a prayer to God to protect his wealth in the ness from lions. For beyond it, they were the lion's right!

Such noble sentiments are fast disappearing with increasing pressures on the environment.* The lion is a unique continuing tradition of Gujarat. The most precious gift the state can give to the rest of India and to the world is to allow this prized inhabitant to prosper in its present habitat, as it has done in the past, and also to be reintroduced elsewhere, to ensure its long-term survival.

Both lions and humans having evolved together over several millennia, saw no danger from each other. They scolded each other and stole each other's food, neither one was aggressive towards the other. By the 1980s large-scale farming and livestock breeding in the area changed all that. Farmers and sportsmen started shooting lions, the latter in turn became aggressive towards the former. The first step of aggression was taken by humans, not by lions. There is a lesson to be learnt here by everyone including field zoologists if we are to understand fully the genesis of lion behaviour.

CHAPTER 2

An Oriental Patrimony

To the ancient Persians too, lions were an important part of life, but they are best represented in art forms or rituals rather than in the realism of the hunting ground. Astronomical observations of the constellations of Leo and Taurus and their connection with the annual cycle or calendar were not confined to Persia. Thus we have the Lion and Bull combat on a relief from Persepolis as also the earlier Assyrian bronze disc of the 8th century BCE from Khorsabad with the same motif.[34] Persian kings appear to have maintained tame lions as well, as evident from a lifesize statue of a lioness with a chain round her neck found at Persepolis dated to the 5th century BCE and now preserved at the National Museum in Tehran.[35]

The lion came to symbolize royal power in Persia too, as in other regions. A rhyton in the form of a golden lion preserved at the Metropolitan Museum of Art, New York and the royal seal of Darius I (521–485 BCE) preserved at the British Museum, depict the lion with great delicacy of touch. The latter shows the king in his chariot shooting an arrow at a male lion who stands up on his hind legs in a position of attack while another lion lies pierced by an arrow, inert below the chariot horses.[36] This royal seal is in the same genre as the earlier Assyrian seals. More than a thousand years later in 590 CE, Bahram Gur is believed to have seized the throne of Persia, retrieving the crown after defeating the lions guarding it. There is an interesting painting by Sultan Muhammad from the *Khamsa* of Nizami from Tabriz painted between 1539 and 1543, depicting Bahram Gur hunting a lion which was itself in the process of killing an onager.[37] The lion, along with the rising sun, as a symbol of royalty survived the onslaught of Islam for centuries in Iran but was ultimately snuffed out in 1979 when it became an Islamic Republic. This may well have been on account of its pre-Islamic associations of royal power.

Empires came and went across Asia and fortunes changed beyond recognition. It is tempting to quote the words of Omar Khayyam who uses metaphors of a fox, a lion, and a Persian wild ass, the last two being important large mammals of Persia which were also predator and prey, to drive home his point of the ebb and flow of royal splendour:

> A Palace gorged in by gigantic Bahram
> The vixen whelps there and the lion nods.
> Bahram who hunted none but onagers,
> Lies tumbled in a pitfall called the grave.[38]

But even though Bahram Gur went and empires were reduced to dust, the lion continued to be relentlessly hunted through the ages. In medieval times the Arabs pursued the lion in the desert, river banks, and marshes, and devised several methods for the lion hunt. A lion would be induced to give chase to a rider on a horse. The horse, being swifter, remained out of reach until the lion was tired of running, whereupon the horseman would turn around and shoot an arrow into the lion's foot. This would

Lion attacking bull
■ Greek marble relief dated to the last quarter of the 6th century BCE.
Soon thereafter the lion became extinct in Europe, but lives on in art and culture to the present day.

Lion attacking bull
■ Palace of Darius, Shiraz, Persia, 6th–
5th century BCE.
This Achaemenian bas-relief is
symbolically related to the spring
equinox. The lion represents imperial
power and might.
Courtesy Khojeste P. Mistree.

infuriate the lion and the chase would be repeated until the lion was riddled with
arrows and died. Such a method of hunting required training of horses to face the
lions. Some rich persons kept caged lions in their palaces and the horses were
trained to get used to the lion's sight, smell, and roar. The horses were fed daily in
front of the caged cats until they lost their fear of the carnivores. Sometimes a
wooden dummy would be made and covered with a lion skin. It would then be
moved around by manipulating strings and horns would be blown to produce roar-
like sounds in the stables.[39]

On occasion two men would track down and hunt a lion, one working as a decoy
while the other surprised the lion from the left and pierced its heart. Or, a group of
men would form an ever-decreasing circle around a sleeping lion in the midday sun
and then spear it. To hunt a lion a man would carry a spear and a double-edged
sword in his hands, and daggers in his belt. If attacked he would plunge the spear in
the lion's throat and would try to strike it with the sword in the rear legs. Then he
would jump back, and if the lion pursued him, he would thrust the sword through
one of the lion's eyes into the mouth, or stick a dagger in its throat. The hunter
would then stand aside and watch the lion in the throes of death.[40]

Yet another method related by Arab writers was of a hunter approaching a lion's
den. The lion would be lured out by creating a commotion. The hunter would thrust
his left arm, padded securely in woollen cloth, towards the lion. As the animal
lunged at it, the hunter would plunge his sword into the lion's flank. A.H. Layard
who was in Mesopotamia in the middle of the 19th century reports this method of
hunting as well – with one difference in technique. Instead of covering the hand in

woollen cloth, he mentions hard wood sharpened at one end in one hand which would be thrust into the lion's mouth at the critical moment.[41]

Apart from being an object of sport, parts of the lion were used in traditional medicine in Arabia. Two grains of a lion's brain dissolved in an ounce of milk was an antidote for grey hair. An epileptic child was supposed to be cured of the malady if it was made to wear a piece of lion skin suspended from a hair round its neck. The gall bladder and fat of the lion were specially sought after, as anointing the eyelids with the lion's gall was supposed to give piercing eyesight while applying dry gall powder to a sword wound would help it heal speedily.[42] Such beliefs only added to the lion's woes.

Lions continued to be kept as pets till not so long ago. Henry Creswicke Rawlinson, orientalist and soldier who deciphered the Persian cuneiform, lived in Mesopotamia in the middle of the 19th century. He had a pet lion which was very attached to him. It followed him about like a tame dog and ultimately died of a disease at his feet.[43] General Omer Pasha the Turkish Governor of Hillah, presented a full-grown lion to A.H. Layard, which moved around the thoroughfares of Hillah near Babylon harming no one. Only the butchers had a tough time, for the lion would help himself to their meats until satisfied, whereupon he would lie down in the sun and "allow the Arab boys to take such liberties with him as in their mischief they might devise"![44]

There is one intriguing miniature painting in the *St Petersburg Murraqqa*.[45] It is a painting of the Isfahan school of the late 17th century, attributed to 'Ali Quli Jabbadar which shows the Shah, probably Sulaiman (1666–94), out hunting with lions. The Shah with a nimbus around the head is pictured towards the right-hand side of the painting astride a white horse, with a servant carrying a golden parasol for him. In the left foreground is an attendant with a hawk on his right hand and two dead birds in his left. Further left a lion has caught a wild boar, one attendant has sunk a dagger into the boar with his left hand while the right hand tries to restrain the lion. Another attendant approaches the lion with a chain as if to fasten it to the lion's collar and take it away. In the left middle portion two Asian elephants with their mahouts watch the proceedings. They have cages instead of howdahs, which were presumably used to bring the lions to the hunting grounds. In front of them a collared lion attacks another boar while further in the background a mounted hunter is about to spear a stag. It may be noted that the lion in the foreground has a dark brown colour on its neck and partly on the face, which is barely the suggestion of a mane, whereas the animal at the back has no such colour differentiation and therefore may be a lioness.

This is the only known painting of lions being used for the hunt and therefore merits some scrutiny. Dr A.H. Morton opines that hunting with lions was never a normal practice in Iran. He goes on to add that though Muslims would not eat the flesh of boar, it would not prevent them being killed in a hunt. He feels that wild boar would as a rule have been excluded from hunting scenes because of their unclean nature.[46] According to Dr Morton, the scene could have been set somewhere in the Caspian provinces where the Safavids had palaces. The miniature may not be entire fantasy as the likeness of the Shah and other courtiers is real enough. Morton goes on to add that training lions may be an experiment which may not have been much of a success and what one needs is confirmation from some other source.[47] The most intriguing part of the painting is that two keepers are trying to draw away one lion from the boar it has caught, just as a cheetah would be separated from an

antelope in order to perform halal on the latter to make it fit for consumption by the faithful. Since a boar was in any case not permissible food, what was the need to remove the lion? Why not let it eat the boar? However, the focus of the painting is on the trained lions hunting boars, so obviously the event was important enough for such a rendering, and not all fantasy. Thus the question were lions ever used for hunting, has no definite answer.

It appears that lions had already become extinct in the Trans-Caucasus region as early as the 10th century where these animals were not incidental "but rather an important member of the fauna".[48] As European powers extended their reach in continental Asia, records of local rulers gave way to those of conquering armies from across the oceans which give us more accurate information. According to recent sources, lions were still found in the northern and easterly direction of Tashkent around the 1880s and they were "heard" of in the hilly areas around Kabul in Afghanistan about the same time.[49] The last reported sighting of lions in Baluchistan at Bolan Pass was in 1921.[50] In Iran a lion was sighted in the southwest some 40 miles from Dizful in 1942,[51] and a British administrator, J. Trench reported seeing lions in 1943 on the border of Afghanistan.[52] Outside of India, the maximum number of sightings and reports of lions in Asia in this period was from Iran. And yet, almost no material remains by which the lion of Iran can be described – "no skin, skeletal material, photograph or detailed description" as noted by Fred A. Harrington in his

CHAPTER 3

A Search through Antiquity

Pataliputra, he described the country, its geography and climate which he observed in the course of his travels and recorded with remarkable accuracy in some instances and with equal fantasy in some others. It is unfortunate that his writings are fragmentary and have survived in classical literature only through other chroniclers. His observations of the animals he saw (and did not see) are illuminating. He accurately states that there were no hippopotamus in India. On the other hand, he has described some fantastic beasts such as winged scorpions and enormous flying snakes as well, which are difficult to explain. Megasthenes surely knew of both lions and tigers, indeed both these felines were found in substantial tracts of land between Anatolia and the Indus in his time. In fact, Iran and the Indus had both these animals up to the early part of the 20th century when they became extinct. His description of the size of the tiger is curious. Strabo states on the authority of Megasthenes that

> the largest tigers are found among the Prasii (easterners), being nearly twice the
> size of the lion, and [they are] so strong that a tame tiger led by four men having
> seized a mule by the hinder leg overpowered it and dragged it to him.[32]

Killing a mule is no difficult task for a normal sized tiger. However, the lion and the tiger, two of the largest felines, would be of near equal size, and Megasthenes is way off fact in this comparison. He has also recorded an interaction between dogs and a lion which is of particular interest to us. Strabo states on the authority of Megasthenes that

> There are also dogs of great strength and courage, which will not let go their hold
> till water is poured into their nostrils: they bite so eagerly that the eyes of some
> become distorted and the eyes of others fall out. Both a lion and a bull were held
> fast by a dog. The bull was seized by the muzzle and died before the dog could be
> taken out.[33]

We need to examine the dog and the lion episode further. Quintus Curtius Rufus is one of the chroniclers of Alexander's later campaigns leading to the invasion of India in 327 BCE. Not much is known of him though he is believed to have been a contemporary of Emperor Augustus (63 BCE to 14 CE) by some, while others believe that he was a contemporary of Emperor Vespasian (69–79 CE). His narrative is based on Ptolemy who accompanied Alexander to India, from Kleitarchos their contemporary, and from Timagenes who lived during the reign of Augustus. Another chronicler Diodorus the Sicilian was a contemporary of Julius Caesar and Augustus. His narrative of Alexander's invasion appears to have been based on the same sources as those of Quintus Curtius Rufus.[34] Both have described an incident which occurred when Alexander was met by King Sophites (Sobutha or Saubh?) whose kingdom lay to the west of the river Hyphasis (Beas). After initial suspicion Alexander and Sophites came to establish friendly relations with each other. The latter wishing to impress Alexander, gave a demonstration of the ferocity of his dogs and Quintus Curtius Rufus records:

> His country possesses a noble breed of dogs, used for hunting and said to refrain
> from barking when they sight their game which is chiefly the lion. Sophites wishing
> to show Alexander the strength and mettle of these dogs, caused a very large lion to
> be placed within an enclosure where four dogs in all were let loose upon him. The
> dogs at once fastened upon the wild beast, when one of the huntsmen who was
> accustomed to work of this kind tried to pull away by the leg one of the dogs which
> with the others had seized the lion, and when the limb would not come away, cut it

off with a knife. The dog could not even by this means be forced to let go his hold, and so the man proceeded to cut him in another place and finding him still clutching the lion as tenaciously as before, he continued cutting away with his knife one part of him after another. The brave dog however, even in dying kept his fangs fixed in the lion's flesh; so great is the eagerness for hunting which nature has implanted in these animals, as testified by the accounts transmitted to us.

I must observe, however, that I copy from preceding writers more than I myself believe, for I neither wish to guarantee statements of truth of which I am doubtful, nor yet to suppress what I find recorded. [35]

While Quintus Curtius Rufus claims to repeat faithfully what he has received and is not entirely convinced of the veracity of the episode, Diodorus the Sicilian records the same event with a few differences:

Among the many valuable presents which he (King Sophites) bestowed on Alexander were 150 dogs remarkable for their size and strength, and superior also in other points, and said to have been bred from tigresses. Being desirous that Alexander should have proof of their mettle by seeing them at work, he placed a full grown lion within an enclosure, and selecting two of the least valuable of the dogs included in the present, cast them to the lion. When these were likely to be vanquished by the wild beast he let loose two other dogs. Then when the four dogs together proved more than a match for the lion, a man who was sent into the ring with a knife cut away the right leg of one of the dogs. When the king (Alexander) loudly remonstrated, and his bodyguards rushed forward and arrested the hand of the Indian, Sophites announced that he would give three dogs instead of the one which was mutilated. Then the huntsman, taking hold of the leg, cut it away quietly bit by bit. The dog without uttering so much as a yell or a moan of pain, kept his fangs fixed in the bite, until all his blood being drained he drew his last breath on the body of the lion.[36]

A pack of hunting dogs can hold a large prey at bay. Indian wild dogs or dholes are known to hold the tiger at bay and even kill it, though some members of the pack are accounted for by the tiger in the process. Sindhi hounds of today are also fierce, large, and capable of such feats. Such breeds may have been known in Alexander's time, though to dispatch a lion, a large pack would have to attack it and surely several of them would meet their end before the cat was subdued. The accounts we have seen here are exaggerated, but pursuing a large carnivore with a pack of hunting dogs is distinctly possible and the Indians of the time appear to have done so. Actually, A.L. Basham points out that a large hill breed of dog perhaps resembling today's Tibetan mastiff, was famous beyond India, for Herodotus records that the Persian Emperor Artaxerxes I (465–425 BCE) exempted four Babylonian villages from taxation in return for their breeding Indian dogs for war and hunting. These dogs were also known in Egypt of the Ptolemies (304–30 BCE).[37]

Hunting with dogs was a common practice in India which continued up to the first half of the 20th century among the princes. For example, in Kolhapur state (in present-day Maharashtra) they were used for hunting wild boar and deer.[38] Till about the early 1950s some thirty to forty dogs were kept in a bastion of the fort in Karauli state (Rajasthan). Their keepers were the sweepers of the town who bred pigs to clean up municipal areas and they would also handle the unclean pig meat which was fed to the dogs. Tigers and leopards were run down with these packs. Often the prey was finished off by the royal hunter with a rifle shot

Coin of Nahapana
■ Western Kshatrapa ruler, circa 2nd century CE.
The coin is based on a Satavahana prototype. The obverse shows a lion with a prominent mane, standard (*yupa*), inscription above, and three-arched hill below; the reverse has a thunderbolt (*vajra*) and arrow.
Courtesy the Indian Institute of Research in Numismatic Studies, Anjaneri, Nashik.

towards the end of a chase.[39] Thus, the ancient Greek accounts were by no means far-fetched.

Let us now turn to Strabo the famous geographer of Ancient Roman times who was a contemporary of Emperor Augustus. He is believed to have lived long enough to see Tiberius succeed him and is believed to have died in the year 24 CE. He was a keen traveller who had voyaged to Egypt and as far east as Armenia. His knowledge of India is derived from contemporary and earlier sources and his *Geography* is a careful compilation of the history and commerce of the region. He described India's animals too, but what concerns us here is his description of a royal procession.

> When the king washes his hair, they celebrate a great festival and [his subjects] send him great presents.... In the processions at their festivals many elephants adorned with gold and silver are in the train, as well as four horse chariots and yokes of oxen. There comes a great host of attendants in their holiday attire, ... garments embroidered and interwoven with gold, wild beasts such as buffaloes, leopards (*pardalis*), tame lions (*leontes*) and a multitude of birds of variegated plumage and fine song.[40]

Strabo's *Geography* was written in the 1st century CE. But if the passage is based on a description by Kleitarchos who accompanied Alexander on his campaigns and to whom Strabo refers in the passage, he may be describing a royal procession of Poros or the Nandas of Magadha on the basis of what he may have heard or seen. On the other hand if he was describing a procession on the basis of information available to him in his own time, then of course, he could be describing the procession of a Maurya, Kushana, or Satavahana king. Such royal processions were a regular annual feature at Dussehra in Indian principalities large and small until 1947. Only one procession, at Mysore, continues today on a much reduced scale. Those who have seen such processions or read of them, would immediately feel the ring of veracity of Strabo's description. It may be noted that such processions were an annual feature in India unlike the coronation pageants in the tradition of European monarchies which took place but once on the accession of the king to the throne. Strabo records tame lions in a royal procession. Lions can be tamed and indeed they can withstand crowds. Emperor Haile Selassie's court at Addis Ababa is a recent example. In Kolhapur state lions and tigers were tamed to walk with their keepers in the early part of the 20th century[41] and Maharaja Kishen Singh of Bharatpur (Rajasthan) had a tame lion which was displayed on a special cart on occasions of state as was done for the visit to India of the Prince of Wales (later Edward VIII) in 1921.[42] Even the free-ranging wild lions of the Gir are extremely trusting of humans. As for *pardalis* mentioned in the text, the reference is probably to cheetahs rather than leopards which are the least tolerant of humans among the large cats.

This brings us to yet another authority somewhat later than Strabo. Claudius Aelianus who lived in Rome in the 2nd century CE, compiled a work called "On Peculiarities of Animals". His information as far as India is concerned was based on what he had heard or read. Two passages from his text are relevant to us here.

> The Indians bring to their king tigers made tame, domesticated panthers (*pantheras*), and oryxes with four horns.[43]

There is no doubt about the four-horned antelope, and cheetahs were more likely than leopards to be "domesticated". Coming to the tiger, it has to be said that they can be tamed, but to move around with them freely in a crowd would be more difficult than with a tame lion. It is possible that Aelianus could have mixed up the two but no definite conclusion is possible from this short sentence. In another passage he observes:

> I have no reasons whatsoever to doubt that the lions of the largest size are found in India, and what convinces me is that this country is such an excellent mother of other animals. But of all the beasts one can encounter these are the most savage and ferocious. The skins of these lions look black – the bristly hair of their mane stands erect, their very aspect strikes the soul with terror and dismay. If they can be captured before they are fully grown and not otherwise, they can be tamed, and they become so tractable and domestic that they are led by the leash, and with huntsmen and their hounds take part in hunting young deer and stags, and boars and buffaloes and wild asses, for, as I am told, they have a very keen scent.[44]

Some lions in India do have black manes. But there is no record of these animals being used for hunting by man except for the painting from Iran mentioned earlier.[45] Cheetahs and caracals were used for the purpose, but the caracal would find boars, buffaloes, and wild asses difficult to subdue, whereas the cheetah could possibly tackle their young. In all probability Aelianus has mixed up the cheetah with the lion. The point nonetheless is, that the Indians tamed lions by the 1st century CE.

As we shall see in the next chapter, the vedic people knew the lion. Over the centuries, environmental changes caused by prolonged drought as well as the impact of human settlement, had made tracts of Baluchistan, Sind, Punjab, and the Gangetic plain hospitable enough for the lion. Around the 3rd century BCE, about the time a strong monarchical power was evolving in eastern India, the lion assumed centrestage to symbolize royalty. Though large swathes of eastern India were tiger country, the lion became a symbol for the region's dynasties. It being the most visible of large cats it lent itself easily to such symbolism rather than the secretive tiger. In any case it had not represented any earlier cult and was available for its new role.

Unlike in ancient Egypt the lion was not worshipped, but it was tamed enough to be a part of royal processions. There are no signs of its being hunted or becoming royal game in the sources we have seen so far. For these we must look elsewhere.

CHAPTER 4

Mrigaraja: King of the Beasts

Gold coin of Chandra Gupta II (376–415)

■ A lion slayer type coin on the obverse of which the king slays a lion with an arrow, he has a foot on the animal as if to hold it in an advantageous position. On the reverse, the goddess Durga rides her proper mount, the lion. These coins were struck to commemorate the victory over Gujarat.

Courtesy Bharat Kala Bhavan, Varanasi.

Apollonius came across nomads who offered him wine made from dates and honey together with slices of lion and leopard meats which had been freshly skinned. Lions were also "served up whole". The biographer goes on to record a king's banquet:

> The king reclines on a couch and near him recline not more than five of his kindred, but all the other guests sit during the meal. A circular table is set in the midst, which is about knee high.... On [it] are scattered laurel leaves and another leaf like myrtle, which the Indians use as perfume. Fish and fowl are set on it, with lions, antelopes and swine, served up whole: but only the hind quarters of tigers, for they are unwilling to eat the rest of the animal, because they say that as soon as it is born, it lifts its forepaws to the rising sun.[13]

Both these sources are about 1,000 years after the *Rigveda* and therefore by themselves cannot be an indication of practices in earlier times. It would be difficult to conclude from these references when the practices noted by Sushruta and Apollonius started. But tribal peoples do eat meats of carnivores even today and Waghri tribals "relished" lion meat according to a British period source of the 19th century. Lion fat was also used as a cure for rheumatism.[14]

Shatapatha Brahmana has two stories of the origin of the lion. According to one, Indra emitted the *soma* he had forcibly drunk at a ritual Tvashtra sacrifice to which he was not invited. A part of it came out of his nose and that became a lion.[15] According to the other story, when Indra drank the *soma* at the sacrifice,

> his vital power flowed out of every limb. Along with his urine his vigour flowed forth and became a wolf. A wolf is the impetuous rush of wild animals; with the undigested contents of his bowels, fury flowed forth, that became a tiger. A tiger is a kind of wild animal; with his blood his power flowed, that became a lion. A lion is a ruler of all wild beasts....[16]

These two stories are a traditional interpretation of the origin of three major carnivores though it is not possible to trace the tradition to its source. It is significant that in the Rigvedic Sautramani sacrifice, the hair of the same three animals is used. The other interesting point is that both the tiger and the lion feature in this creation process and both are seen as paramount over other beasts.

Coming to the various names of the lion, the foremost are *hari, haryaksha,* and *kesarin*. All three are attested to since the time of the *Mahabharata*, the great epic said to have been composed between the 4th century BCE and 4th century CE. Hari is a descriptive word meaning brown, tawny, pale yellow, etc. and incidentally, it is also the word for a horse. *Haryaksha* stands for the one with *hari* coloured eyes and *kesarin* means the one who has a mane. The word *mrigendra*, king of "animals" or "beasts" (the word *mriga* is used in its generic sense to denote all animals) has been used in the *Harivamsha*. Similar words such as *mrigapati, mrigaraja, mrigadhipa,* etc. are used primarily for the lion though occasionally these names are used for a tiger.[17] This signifies a greater familiarity with the lion which as already mentioned is an animal more likely to be seen and observed by humans. There is however one word – *panchasya* and its synonyms *panchanana, panchamukha,* and *pancha-vaktra* – meaning "one who has five mouths". How this came about is quite unclear. Some ingenious explanations have been given by commentators,[18] but they are more imaginative than logical.

This brings us to the throne of rulers in ancient times. The vedic word for it is *asandi* and it occurs in connection with the ritual of royal coronation, the *rajasuya* ceremony.[19] The seat on which the ceremony is performed is the *asandi* and it is covered with a tigerskin (*vyaghracharma*).[20] According to the *Shatapatha Brahmana* the *asandi* is made of the wood of the *udumbara* tree (*gular* in Hindi, *umber* in Marathi and Gujarati) or *khadira* tree (*khair* in Hindi, Marathi, and Gujarati).[21] The *asandi*, according to this authority, is to be covered by a blackbuck skin (*krishnajina*).[22]

In the *Mahabharata* and the *Ramayana* (the second great epic believed to date between the 2nd century BCE and 2nd century CE) and later literature, the word *bhadrasana* or *bhadrapitha* is used for the seat on which the king is crowned. The word *simhasana* on the other hand is also current from the *Mahabharata* onwards. The *Shabdakalpadruma* of Radhakanta, the Sanskrit lexicon of the 19th century, explains the word as deriving from *simhachintam asanam* "a seat marked by a lion". This explanation is based on the fact that the throne has lion heads on the arm rests and clawed feet for its legs. But this obviously is a very late explanation as it represents the thrones of Indian princes in use in the 19th to mid-20th century. Dr Mehendale's view is that the *simhasana*, lion's seat, is derived from the words *simhasya asanam*. "Since the lion is looked upon as the chief among animals, and the king is considered chief among men, the seat of the king could be thought of as a seat of the lion among men or, in short, the seat of the lion."[23] This is a plausible explanation, as the roots of such equations go far back in time. In the *Mahabharata* the animals were divided into two categories: *gramya*, "domestic" and *aranya*, "wild". Man topped the former list; the lion, the latter.[24]

Simhavalokana means "viewing, observing like a lion". In the *Raghuvamsha* of Kalidasa, 5th century, there is a description of Raghu's conquest of the four cardinal directions. After defeating the Kambojas, Raghu mounted the Himalaya. It is said that the lions sat unperturbed in their den and viewed the panorama, turning their heads to survey the tumult of battle caused by Raghu's lion-like victorious army. Raghu marvelled at their calm demeanour. The actual words used are *simhanams parivritya avalokitam*, from which is derived *simhavalokita*.[25]

A king's appearance is also compared to that of a lion. Thus the kings who entered the gaming room for the famous dice game in the *Mahabharata* are described as "having necks (possibly manes?) like that of a lion (*simhagrivah*)".[26] Krishna with his awe-inspiring swagger is described as *simhakhelagati*, "one who has the stately walk of a lion".[27] The gait of other great figures of the epic such as Balarama, Duryodhana, and Karna is similarly described, whereas Bhimasena's walk is described as *simhakhela*, "lion's gait".[28]

Kautilya, the minister of Chandragupta Maurya who ruled from 324 to 300 BCE, is traditionally known as the author of the great work on statecraft, the *Artha-shastra*, though it is now clear that while the work's earliest portions may be that old, there are several later interpolations. The treatise gives a detailed description of, among other things, the organization of the state, how the land must be put to use, what the king must do, and so on. Among the departments of state enumerated in it, is that of forest produce. It requires the superintendent of the department to prepare

> ... an animal park for the king's recreation ... containing shrubs and bushes bearing
> sweet fruits, having trees without thorns, with shallow pools of water, and stocked
> with tamed deer and (other) animals, containing wild animals with their claws and
> teeth removed (and) having male and female elephants and cubs useful for hunting.
> And he should establish on its borders or in conformity with the (suitability of the)

Gold coin of Kumara Gupta I (415–455)

■ A lion slayer type coin on the obverse of which the king slays a lion with an arrow though he does not have his foot on the animal. On the reverse, the goddess Durga rides a lion.
Courtesy Bharat Kala Bhavan, Varanasi.

land, another animal park where all animals are (welcomed) as guests (and given full protection).[29]

From the foregoing two important points emerge. Firstly, the park to be set aside for the king's amusement should be such that it poses no danger to his person: the passage goes to the extent of saying that the wild animals' teeth and claws must be removed. This probably applied to large carnivores, most likely tigers, as the jungles in the Maurya kingdom of Magadha with their tall grasses and thick forest cover were more suitable for tigers than for lions. The second part mentions the creation of certain areas exclusively for the protection of wild animals, and this is the earliest record of sanctuaries for flora and fauna.

The Kandahar inscription of Emperor Ashoka informs us:

> Ten years being completed king Piyadassi showed piety (i.e. *dhamma*) to men. And from that time (onwards) he made men more pious. And all things prosper throughout the whole world. And the king refrains from (eating) living beings, and indeed other men and whosoever (were) the king's huntsmen and fishermen have ceased from hunting....[30]

The Rampurva pillar edict V of Ashoka declares:

> Thus speaks the beloved of the Gods, the king Piyadassi: when I had been consecrated twenty-six years I forbade the killing of the following species of animals namely: parrots, mainas, red-headed ducks, *chakravaka* geese, ... *nandi-mukha*s (birds encountered in rice fields?), pigeons, bats, ants, tortoises, boneless fish, *vedaveyaka*s (?), *puputaka*s of the Ganges (skate fish?), porcupine, squirrel, deer, lizards, domesticated animals, rhinoceroses, white pigeons, domestic pigeons, and all quadrupeds of no utility and are not eaten.... Forests must not be burned in order to kill living things or without any good reason....[31]

Such a change of heart is unique in the annals of history but hunting of wild animals continued after Ashoka and the Mauryas as we shall see below. Here we need to take a leap forward in time to make comparison with a 13th-century source. *Abhilashitarthachintamani* or *Manasollasa* (1129–30) is a treatise of encyclopaedic nature concerning among other things a king's sport and pastime at court. The work is from south India, attributed to the Chalukya king Someshvara III. Among the various types of hunting the work describes are *sarmeyavinoda,* hunting with dogs; *syenavinoda,* falconry; *matsyavinoda,* fishing; and *mrigyavinoda,* deer hunting. The treatise goes on to state that there are thirty different methods of hunting deer of which it describes twenty including *vyaghrajamrigya,* that is coursing *krishnasara*, blackbuck with *chitraka*, cheetahs.[32]

The *Manasollasa* is far more contemporaneous than the *Arthashastra* which anticipates several latter-day hunting practices, particularly those of the Mughals. Though the two works are possibly more than 1,000 years apart, they are at one insofar as neither specifically mentions the hunting of large carnivores. The *Arthashastra* says that the park for the king's recreation must have such animals minus their teeth and claws. It points out the benefits of hunting:

> there is exercise, getting rid of phlegm, bile, fat, and (a tendency to) perspiration, practice in hitting the targets of moving and stationary bodies, knowledge of the minds of animals in anger, fear, and condition of ease, and (only) occasional marching.[33]

In other words, the *Arthashastra* recommends hunting to keep the king and courtiers fit for battle and yet does not want them exposed to unnecessary danger.

Leogryph with rider
■ Panel from exterior of a temple, Chaukhandi near Sarnath, Gupta period, 5th century CE.
This is a good example of the lion taking variable forms in art. It acquired importance in regions way beyond its natural range.
Courtesy National Museum, New Delhi.

Lion sculpture in the Five Rathas complex at Mamallapuram
■ Pallava period, 7th century CE.
Photograph: V. Muthuraman.

As far as the *Manasollasa* is concerned, the treatise concentrates on pleasures, *vinoda*, and pastimes at the court of the king. Hunting large carnivores is not recommended by either text; yet it is known that Indian kings did pursue this sport with vigour, and celebrated their feats.

We have noted that a goddess riding a lion had already appeared on Kushana coins in the 1st century.[34] A similar device of a "goddess seated on lion, and holding a fillet or noose and a cornucopia" appears on the gold coins of Chandra Gupta I (320–)[35] the first king of the Gupta dynasty which restored the magnificence of the Mauryas in Magadha and beyond. However his son Samudra Gupta (335–376), the architect of the new empire, struck gold coins with six different devices, one of them being the tiger-slayer device[36] with the legend *vyaghraparakramah*, "bearing the strength of the tiger". The coin commemorates Samudra Gupta's consolidation of his hold over the Ganga valley,[37] and shows the tiger, the dominant carnivore of eastern India, being shot by the king with an arrow.[38]

Chandra Gupta II (376–415) who succeeded his father Samudra Gupta (or, according to some accounts, followed his brother Rama Gupta) continued the expansion of his empire westwards. His father is supposed to have received tributes from the Shakas who controlled Malwa and Kathiawar and they were finally defeated by him. To celebrate his victory over Kathiawar,[39] gold coins were struck with the lion-slayer device bearing the legend *simhavikramah*, "valorous like the lion".[40] While his father was depicted with the tiger, the animal Chandra Gupta II slays with an arrow is the lion, probably the dominant carnivore of Kathiawar even at the time.

The legend on the coin explains the significance of the portrayal.

Kumara Gupta I (415–455) who succeeded his father, struck fourteen known types of gold coins which included peacock, rhinoceros-slayer, tiger-slayer, elephant-rider-cum-lion-slayer and lion-slayer. The rhinoceros is shown being slain from horseback with a sword or short lance, whereas the lion and the tiger are being slain by bow and arrow and the king is on foot as in the earlier Chandra Gupta II coins. The depiction of the elephant-rider-cum-lion-slayer coin shows the elephant trampling the lion.[41]

The question arises as to whether these depictions are symbolic or an illustration of the royal hunting practice of the time. The coins depict three different modes of hunting. In the first, the lion or tiger is shot by an arrow, a perfectly feasible feat. Of course, it is probable that the king would be accompanied by courtiers who would follow suit with their arrows once the king let fly the first shaft from his bowstring. The second type of scene, with an elephant (with rider) trampling a lion or tiger, has been recorded in several sources. It was common practice to go after large carnivores on elephantback when hunting in tall grass or in thick forest cover. In the third instance, the rhinoceros is being attacked with a sword or a short lance by a horseback rider. This is likely to have been the preferred mode of hunting in such a case, since the thick hide of the animal would make an arrow less effective. In other words, the depictions are realistic enough to be considered authentic illustrations of various methods of hunting, in addition to being symbolic representations of a king's bravery and victory. These coins are an invaluable record as for the first time we see historical personalities hunting lions and other animals, we get a glimpse of their hunting methods and their sport.

At this point we must again leap forward in time to examine a document on hunting of the 16th century. Raja Rudradeva or Rudra Chand was king of Karmachala or Kumaon and a contemporary of Emperor Akbar. He wrote a treatise on hawking, *Shyainika Shastram*, in Sanskrit. The work discusses the various *vyasana*s, vices of men. According to some opinions, hunting is one of the vices, but this treatise also notes its advantages. It also makes a comprehensive survey of various hunting practices current then, which had probably changed little over the centuries. In fact, until the arrival of gunpowder and its use on the battlefield and hunting grounds, there was a remarkable continuity of hunting practices over the millennia from the time man mastered the elephant and the horse and had the use of the bow and arrow, sword, or lance. The third chapter of the work which surveys the extant practices during Rudradeva's time does not report the arrival of the gun on the hunting grounds.[42] Rudradeva records how rhinoceros and lion are to be hunted. For the latter, he says that expert archers on fleet-footed horses could strike an "infuriated" lion in an open field, or ambush it and kill it like a cat. He goes on to add that archers could hunt lions by lying in wait for them and then shooting them with poisoned darts, such a method being most successful at waterholes and in the vicinity of *Belleric myrobalan* trees or in cornfields. (The significance of this tree, called *bahera* in Hindi and Gujarati or *beheda* in Marathi, is not clear. It is a common enough tree found in deciduous mixed forests throughout India[43] and it does not have any special relationship with cornfields.) Another easy way of hunting ferocious animals was to attract them to the bait of a dead cow in a suitable place.[44]

The first method described by Rudradeva does not bear any resemblance to the depiction on Gupta coins we have seen, but it is curiously similar to an Arab practice

Lion pillar at entrance to temple near the Kiritiarjuniya relief at Mamallapuram
■ Pallava period, 7th century CE.
Photograph: V. Muthuraman.

CHAPTER 5

Under the Delhi Sultanate

Throughout its history India has been exposed to several foreign influences which manifested themselves in architecture, sculpture, coinage, and language. Simultaneously the traditional cultures and religious callings of the people of India continued to evolve and assimilate new ideas. Besides Hinduism and regional beliefs, two other major faiths, Jainism and Buddhism, were born and prospered on Indian soil. By the middle of the 7th century Islam had been established as a religion. The Arabs had traded with Indian ports for a long time prior to this; however, Islam as a political force was to enter India by way of the conquest of Sind by Muhammad bin Qasim in 712–713 who defeated Dhir, the son of Chach, the usurper brahman ruler of the region, and married the former's wife.[1]

While conquest of a portion of India by a foreign power was nothing new, there was a unique element here. This invasion marked the beginning of the establishment of a religion which had its origins outside India and which came to have a major influence on the subcontinent. Under Islamic rule, the lions of India encountered a new culture born in a foreign land but which had come to stay. To these rulers the lion was no stranger, as it flourished in their homelands. Arabic, Turki, and Persian cultures interacted with local traditions and as we shall discover, lion imagery evolved through synthesis over the centuries.

The period from the 11th century onwards saw the rise and fall of invaders, rulers, and dynasties – from Mahmud of Ghazni and Mohammed Ghori to the Delhi Sultanate founded by Qutb-ud-din Aybak, followed by the Khaljis, Tughluqs, and Lodis. Material relating to the lion from this period is scanty, most of it being from literary sources.

The Islamic invaders continued to hunt as they had done in their own countries, and as their pre-Islamic ancestors had. They even invoked God in their enterprise. 'Isami who wrote his history of India in the middle of the 14th century gives an account of a hunt of Mahmud of Ghazni who attacked India in 1000:

> One day, I am told, the king rode into the desert intending to hunt. In the course of his hunt ranging over a few *parasang*s (administrative units), he stripped mountains and deserts of wild animals. Then a deer sprang before him; and immediately on seeing it he left his troops and guards. In its pursuit he galloped his horse with lion-like boldness. On drawing close to the deer he pulled an arrow from his quiver and shot it.... Thereupon he dismounted from the horse and slaughtered the game citing the name of God. This done, he withdrew and rode back to his own camp.[2]

'Isami records that Qutb-ud-din Aybak who ruled Delhi from 1206 to 1210 rode out of his palace sometimes to go to the race ground or to hunt and

> It looked as if his polo-stick ball had consumed the ball of the earth and the surface of the earth had been stripped of Game.[3]

To the Sultans of Delhi, hunting was a normal royal activity. Iltutmish (1211–36), Balban (1266–87), and Ala-ud-din Khalji (1296–1316) were keen falconers and they went hawking with eagles in winter. They were said to be not fond of big game, while Kayqubad (1287–90) was known to be keen on the chase with his hounds.[4]

A hunt of Mubarak Khalji (1316–20) when he went in the direction of Badaon from Delhi which lasted two to three months is illustrative of the enterprise. He had with him sparrowhawks, kites, falcons, hawks, and "two to three thousand deer-hunting panthers".[5] The reference is obviously to cheetahs though their number is greatly exaggerated. Even the great emperor Akbar, who had far greater resources than the Khalji king, did not have more than a thousand cheetahs at the height of his reign. 'Isami who wrote about the hunt thirty years after the event recorded that the destruction of game was so complete that

> If today anybody visits that meadow where the emperor had hunted in those days, one would find the land, from end to end, to a distance of several *parasang*s full of bones. The royal troops hunted so much game, neither an animal will be born nor will a leaf of grass sprout in that hunting ground till the Day of Judgement.[6]

For elsewhere, in this case in the Deccan, Ala-ud-din Hasan Bahman Shah (1347–58) went on a hunting expedition on his march which continued for a month and which left "the desert and mountains stripped of game and heaven fell into a trance".[7]

Falconry and hunting with hounds were practices equally known in India earlier. However, total destruction of game appears to be the hallmark of this period, a new facet of the royal pastime. At the same time the keen sense of documentation which the Turki, Arabic, and Persian writers had, meant that their records were far clearer than most previous Indian sources. The latter were literary or generic, they were rarely factual or empirical in the strict sense.

From the records it appears that Firoz Shah Tughluq (1351–88) was the keenest hunter of the Sultanate period. He was particularly keen on big game such as tigers, lions, wolves, bears, various species of deer, wild dogs, and antelope.[8] *Tarikh-i Firuz Shahi* of Shams Siraj 'Afif, a contemporary writer, gives the following account:

> Since the monarch, the Elect of the Merciful Lord God, was interested in hunting matters, during his reign he took game of various sorts and devoted much effort to this, taking innumerable game of every kind. He had obtained beasts of prey of every variety. Of the single class of cheetahs and leopards (*yuz u palang*) [in all probability a manuscript error for *yuz palang* i.e. cheetah], he gathered so many that it is beyond computation, and of the class of caracal (*siyah gush*), so many that it cannot be stated in writing, and of the class of dogs so many that it surpassed all comparison. Indeed, during his reign, by the inspiration of the Lord God, Sultan Firoz Shah acquired a number of lions (*shir*).* And of the hawks (*baz*) [in this case the reference is likely to be to goshawks, *Accipiter gentilis* as other birds of prey have been identified separately], peregrine falcons (*bahri*) [*Falco peregrinus calidus*], red headed merlins (turumtay) [*Falco chiquera chiquera*], red-capped or barbary falcons (*Shahin*) [barbary falcon, *Falco peregrinus babylonicus* is a rare visitor, whereas *shahin*, *Falco peregrinus peregrinator* is the resident bird commonly used for falconry and is the bird referred to here], *simtans* [?silver-bodied hawks of some kind] and the like there came to be so many that it cannot be brought within the grasp of human comprehension or imagination. All these rending and rapacious animals were entrusted to servants (*bandagan*). Following each animal were two or three servants to take care of them, and all these animal keepers used to go on mounted horses.[9]

Firoz Shah's hunting establishment was large. The foregoing passage testifies to the fact that he was a keen falconer, he coursed blackbuck with cheetahs, and flushed birds of several species with the caracal. The presence of lions in his menagerie is undeniable; however they would have been a symbol of royalty, rather than serving

---

* The Persian word for lion is *shir* whereas the word for tiger is *babr*. In the India of today most people think the other way around. Maharaja Ranjit Singh was called *Sher-e-Punjab*, the lion, not tiger, of Punjab, and even the late Sheikh Abdullah, former Chief Minister of Jammu and Kashmir, was often styled *Sher-e-Kashmir*, the Lion of Kashmir, even though there were no lions in that state!

مشاهل کرد برجست و مرد

The Lion kills Shanzaba
■ Sultanate-Lodi period, 1492. An illustration from *Kalilah-wa-Dimnah*, the Arabic translation of the story of the Lion and the Bull from the *Panchatantra*.
Courtesy National Museum, New Delhi.

confusion of other animals and men, for they could attack the hunters at close quarters. Lions were royal game and could be hunted only by the emperor and with his permission by the notables in the empire. Thomas Roe had to take Jahangir's permission to tackle a troublesome lion[9] and Francois Bernier records from Aurangzeb's reign that

> ... of all the diversions of the field the hunting of the lion is not only the most perilous but is peculiarly royal; for except by special permission, the king and princes are the only persons who engage in the sport.[10]

Thomas Roe reports that the imperial standard sported a couchant lion and the rising sun.[11] A painting by Payag from the *Padshahnama*, the chronicle of Shah Jahan's reign by Abdul Hamid Lahawri preserved in the Royal Library, Windsor Castle, depicts the siege of Qandahar in the Deccan in 1631 by Shah Jahan's army led by Nasiri Khan. The imperial standards are scarlet pennants with green borders with a passant lion and a rising sun behind it in each of them.[12] Another *Padshahnama* painting by the "Kashmiri Painter", of Shah Jahan's royal procession in 1655, clearly shows pennants which have a field of green with a couchant lion and the sun rising behind it in each.[13] This symbolism is ancient and was common in older Persian imagery; it also has echoes of the Hindu sun worship and the lion's association with Hindu royalty and divinity. No doubt the Mughals took these symbols from their own cultural past, but they must have been aware that the lion and the sun held a special place in the tradition of royalty preceding them in India.

Emperor Akbar maintained an account of the game he had shot and even the records of the guns used for the hunt were kept.[14] Jahangir too was equally meticulous. In the eleventh year of his reign he records that in a span of 39 years, as many as 28,532 animals and birds were hunted in his presence of which he himself accounted for 17,167. Lions take pride of place for they appear at the top of the list of the tally and he records that he had shot 86 of them.[15] Not surprisingly, one of the finest studies of an animal in Mughal painting is a painting of the Jahangir period, "Lion drinking water after devouring its kill" attributed to Nanha circa 1618, preserved at the Sawai Man Singh II Museum, Jaipur.[16] The painting is realistic to a high degree in its depiction of the animal, its environment and its prey a bull, or a cow, the remnants of which are being sequestered by a jackal! But in the hunting field the animal was pursued with vigour and its successful shikar was a matter of good omen. Bernier records the following:

> You must know, then, that as it is considered a favourable omen when the king kills a lion, so is the escape of that animal portentous of infinite evil to the state. Accordingly the termination of the hunt is attended with much grave ceremony. The king being seated in the general assembly of the *Omrahs*, the dead lion is brought before him, and when the carcass has been accurately measured and minutely examined, it is recorded in the royal archives that such a king on such a day slew a lion of such a size and of such a skin, whose teeth were of such a length, and whose claws were of such dimensions, and so on down to the minutest detail.[17]

Though the weighing and measuring of lions with extreme care was the established Mughal practice, as reported by Bernier, just one record made by Jahangir survives. When the emperor encountered and shot an exceedingly large lion near Rahimabad between Delhi and Agra on December 22, 1623, he took great care to have it weighed and its length measured from the top of its head to the tip of its tail: He noted that in his entire hunting career he had not come across such a large, magnificent, or well proportioned animal. As was his practice he ordered the imperial painters to take its likeness,[18] as he had done several times before when he came across a rare or magnificent bird or animal, such as the turkey, the zebra, or barbary falcon.

It is regrettable that no other such records are available, as much information about these cats could have been extracted from them. The lion shot by Jahangir weighed eight and a half Jahangiri maunds or 255 kilograms (1 Jahangiri maund = 30.10 kilograms[19]). It was three and a half cubits (*zar-i-shari*) and two *tasu* long, i.e. 9 feet 4 inches or about 2.85 metres (1 cubit = 31.7 inches and 1 *tasu* = 1.33 inches[20]). The weight range of a lion is between 145 and 225 kilograms.[21] Jahangir's lion was obviously heavier than usual whereas in length it would be among the larger trophies recorded.[22] From Jahangir's description it is clear that he had the animal measured and not its skin which could have yielded a longer result.

Before we go further it is necessary to examine the words used for the lion and the tiger in the chronicles of the times. The Persian word for the lion is *shir* while it is *babr* for the tiger.[23] The two animals have distinct words, with no hint of confusion in the minds of Mughal emperors or their chroniclers. In India however, by the time the Urdu language got round to recognizing the big cats, the issue got mixed up. By the 19th century therefore the word *babbar* or *babbar sher* came to mean lion in Urdu/Hindustani, and the word *sher* meant tiger – in any case by the second half of the 19th century the latter was largely the only one to survive in the Hindi-speaking belt. (In Sanskritized Hindi the word is *simha* for lion, *bagh* for tiger.) The translators of the Mughal texts who were working in north India in the second half of the 19th century or later paid more attention to the political, social, and other aspects of what the texts contained as far as the accuracy of the translations was concerned. They simply translated *shir* as tiger without much ado.[24] They were also misled by their familiarity with Hindustani in which the word *sher* is used for both lion and tiger, such usage being common even today. In contrast, the Mughal emperors and their chroniclers were closer to nature than their British translators living in presidency towns such as Calcutta or smaller "stations" and they knew what they were seeing and recording.

If we look at the locations where Akbar or Jahangir came across the big cat the picture becomes clear. Akbar encountered it at Mathura and Mewat near Delhi; Jahangir records his encounters with it at Bak Bhal and Nag Thal near Bari, near Dholpur, Palam (the site of the international airport at Delhi), Rupbas near Agra, Ajmer, and Mandu where, as we shall see, Thomas Roe had his problems with a lion. These were all grassland and scrub at the time, which was the preferred habitat of the lion. There may have been stray tigers but they were not likely to have been encountered in groups as described by the Mughals. Of the 33 wild species of the family *Felidae*[25] the lion is the only gregarious cat; the tiger is a solitary creature as a rule except when a female is with cubs.

Another noteworthy fact is that there are no known Mughal paintings in the public domain depicting a tiger hunt or the study of the tiger as an animal per se, except for one which records the chance encounter of Akbar in 1561 near Narwar in central India when a family of five tigers, two of which were "white", attacked his cavalcade. The event is recorded for all time with a double-page illustration in the *Akbarnama* and Abul Fazl uses the correct Persian word for them, *babri* in the text.[26] Dr Asok Kumar Das has shown that there are more than thirty paintings of the Mughal period in the public domain depicting a lion, a lion hunt, or a dead lion.

Prince Khurram attacking a lion
■ Painting from the *Padshahnama*,
by Balchand, circa 1640.
The famous incident which took place at
Bari in 1610, where courtier Anup Rai
saved the life of Emperor Jahangir.
Prince Khurram is about to strike the
lion which has pinned down Anup Rai;
the emperor is on the right.
*The Royal Collection ©2002 Her Majesty
Queen Elizabeth II.*

tackle it himself. At that very moment another lion did come out. Akbar shot it in
the eye with an arrow, but still the animal advanced and sat in such a position that
Akbar could not get a good shot even though he dismounted from his horse. In the
excitement of the moment a courtier shot an arrow which infuriated the lion who
mauled him. The animal had to be finished off by the other courtiers.[33]

In the *Ain-i-Akbari* Abul Fazl records two more instances of Akbar hunting lions.
One incident occurred in Bari where a man-eater attacked Akbar's elephant, and had
to be killed by his men. In another instance near Mathura, a lion came out to attack

THE GREAT MUGHALS GO HUNTING LIONS

THE GREAT MUGHALS GO HUNTING LIONS **99**

Shah Jahan hunting lions near Burhanpur
■ Painting from the *Padshahnama*, attributed to Daulat, circa 1635. Shah Jahan and his entourage hunt from elephantback harnessed with open howdahs which would increase manoeuvrability. The nets are used to confine the quarry, not to prevent them from jumping onto the elephant.
The Royal Collection ©2002 Her Majesty Queen Elizabeth II.

when one of Akbar's courtiers, Shujaat Khan, approached too close. But Akbar was able to subdue the lion with just a furious look: "The brute cowered down before that divine glance, and turned right about trembling all over. In a short time it was killed." [34]

There is only one painting of Akbar hunting a lion known to us. Preserved in the National Museum, Delhi, the painting titled "Akbar on a hunt" is by an unknown artist and may be dated circa 1598–1600.[35] The middle of the painting has Akbar on a chestnut charger. He has just shot an arrow which has pierced the lion's abdomen

Aurangzeb hunting lions

■ Mughal, circa 1670–1700.
The emperor sits on an open howdah.
The line of elephants bearing the imperial
party follows a phalanx of buffaloes
which would act as a buffer in case of a
lion attack. Here too the quarry is
confined by nets and a lion attacks an
elephant in the background. The use of
buffaloes to follow up wounded lions or
tigers was practised till the 20th century.
*Reproduced by kind permission of the Trustees
of the Chester Beatty Library, Dublin.*

Dead lioness

■ Mughal, circa 1600.
The quarry is carried home in the time-
tested manner that continued till the end
of shikar in the second half of the 20th
century.
*Reproduced by permission of the Trustees of
the Victoria & Albert Museum, London.*

A lion's court
■ By Miskin, 1596–97.
This painting from the *Anwar-i-Suhaili*
shows the lion as the king of the animal
world – a position rarely accorded to the
tiger.
Courtesy Bharat Kala Bhavan, Varanasi.

Study of a lion
■ This 18th-century Bikaner school painting is in sharp contrast to the painting attributed to Nanha, opposite. The animal is stylized and its mane appears to be in moult!
Courtesy Sudhir Kasliwal, Gem Palace, Jaipur.

and it is bleeding while it is in the act of killing a wild ass. On the lower left of the painting another wild ass is bolting from the scene of action. On the right-hand bottom of the painting are a group of courtiers that include Bairam Khan on a white horse, others carrying mace and gun, and a falconer with a falcon on his gauntlet. In front of Akbar's horse a male and a female blackbuck are leaping away along with other small animals which appear to be foxes and a hare. In the top right-hand corner are a group of men with hawks and a cheetah brought on horseback to the hunting grounds.

Though the painting has been dated circa 1598–1600, it pictures Akbar as a young man. From the foregoing passages we know that Akbar hunted lions with bow and arrow from horseback. The lion being killed while it is on its own kill of a wild ass is reminiscent of the painting of Bahram Gur hunting lions. While this may be a rendering of an actual occurrence, the presence of blackbuck, foxes, and a hare in such proximity to the lion suggests that the painting represents various events of a day's hunting or it is a collage of several hunts depicting Akbar's prowess in the field rather than a single event.

Akbar's bravery and fearlessness in the field have been recorded several times by his chroniclers. It is not at all surprising that he chose to hunt lions from horseback with bows and arrows and sometimes even on foot though guns were in common use

Lion drinking water after devouring its kill
■ Attributed to Nanha, circa 1618.
The lion is accurately portrayed and the jackal stealing from the remnants of the kill is a fine touch of realism.
Courtesy Maharaja Sawai Man Singh II Museum, Jaipur.

The Shah hunting
■ Late 17th century.
The king, probably Shah Sulaiman of Persia, is out hunting with tame lions. This is the only record in the public domain of such sport.
From the St Petersburg Muraqqa, after Kostioukovich, 1996.

in his time. His successors who inherited the grand empire, preferred the safer elephant and matchlocks for their lion hunts. (It is however interesting to note here that lions were speared from horseback by the British near Deesa in Gujarat in the 19th century.)

To Jahangir, the hunting grounds were a second home. His passion for the chase and his acute observations of flora and fauna from his memoirs have left us an incomparable record of this facet of his life and times. He could be as considerate as providing warm water for bathing the imperial elephants as they shivered in the cold or building a grand monument to his favourite blackbuck Mansraj at Shaikhupura near Lahore, and yet think nothing of ordering the execution of a servant for inadvertently interrupting his hunt. His records of game bagged show the variety of animals he shot, from the largest to the smallest. The lion hunt to him was special and it always featured at the top of his list. In February and March of 1610 he camped at Mandakar Garden near Rupbas. During his stay there of 56 days he accounted for 7 lions, 70 nilgai, 51 blackbuck, 82 other animals, 129 birds, and 1,023 fish![36] Again he records that over a period of three months at the beginning of 1611 he had accounted for twelve lions.[37] Here we get a clear glimpse of the lion's prey as well. Jahangir was hunting in open scrubland where he accounted for lions as well as their prey, nilgai and to a lesser extent blackbuck. It is interesting to note that he had hunted one lion per week in 1611, an indication of the abundance of these cats in the region. Of the several shikar events concerning lions recorded by him, some may be described here.

In February 1608 Jahangir was informed that lions were making a nuisance of themselves on the road between Panipat and Karnal in present-day Haryana. He went out to the spot, got onto a female elephant, and ordered the rest of the elephants to encircle the lions as in a Qamargha. Here was a quarry-specific variation of the large Qamarghas which used vast resources and in which all and sundry animals were taken. The method was successful and "by God's grace" the emperor was able to "eliminate the evil" of the pair of big cats that had harassed the people.[38] Elephants rather than any other animal were used for encirclement as they provided a perch from which the quarry could be seen, they were large enough to be respected by lions, and finally, they ensured a measure of safety to the imperial person.

Jahangir abstained from hunting with a gun on Sundays and Thursdays; yet when provoked he broke his own rule and it did not take much for him to do so. He records that on Sunday, March 2, 1617 while he was at Mandu, he was informed of the presence of a lion 3 *kos* away from the camp. He promptly rode out on an elephant and when he came to the spot he found the lion sitting under a tree. He fired from elephantback and killed it with one shot. The bullet entered its mouth leaving no external mark of injury. His retinue were baffled when they examined the animal's body, until Jahangir cleared up the mystery by pointing to its mouth.[39]

Jahangir also showed off his hunting skills to the young Mewar prince Karan who was at his court at Ajmer in 1615. On hearing of a lioness in the vicinity of his camp he went out to shoot it. He asked Karan where he should shoot the quarry. Karan indicated its eye. Jahangir obliged successfully, to the astonishment of all present. Jahangir knew that firing from elephantback which is not a steady perch, that too on a windy day and with a smooth bore musket, it was miraculous that the ball should find its predetermined minute target. He was honest enough to record in his

Ashrafi of Emperor Jahangir
■ One of the gold coins with zodiacal signs showing here the sign of Leo on the reverse, with calligraphy on the obverse.
Courtesy Bharat Kala Bhavan, Varanasi.

autobiography, "God almighty did not allow me to be ashamed before the prince, and as I had agreed, I shot her in the eye."[40]

Even for a Mughal emperor and for a keen marksman, things could and did go horribly wrong in a lion shoot. In 1610 when Jahangir was near Bari in Agra *suba*, one of his courtiers Anup Rai came across a half-devoured cow. Suddenly a lion came out of the thicket. It was promptly surrounded and the emperor was informed. Jahangir, Khurram, and others rushed to the spot. Jahangir set his musket on the stand and fired twice but missed as is not uncommon when it comes to judging the "elevation" of a bullet when firing from a height as Jahangir was doing. In the event, the lion charged, Jahangir's retinue bolted, and, according to him, some even trampled him in their flight! Anup Rai saved Jahangir's life by battling the lion almost with his bare hands, while Prince Khurram struck the animal with a sword. At the end of it the lion was dispatched and the emperor was saved. In recognition of his valour Jahangir gave Anup Rai the title of *Ani Rai Singhdalan* meaning commander of troops, lion crusher.[41] This incident shows the personal bonds between the Mughals and Rajputs which held the Mughal domains together until the early 1700s. The fact that Jahangir and Khurram were accompanied by a Rajput courtier in a hunt shows the trust and respect placed in him.

Hunting lions on foot was certainly not a recommended method for Mughal emperors and their family, unless of course the situation arose accidentally. There is an unpublished painting from the personal collection of Maharaja Sawai Bhavani Singh of Jaipur which has been examined by Dr Asok Kumar Das. He dates it circa 1600, it is by an unknown artist and it shows unmistakably a young Jahangir. It depicts a night scene where a remarkably accurately drawn male lion has attacked an attendant of Jahangir in the left hand side of the painting. Though the lion has pinned him down, the attendant is about to plunge a dagger into his tormentor. The night scene is lit by two torch bearers behind the lion while a third holds his torch down near the lion's body as if to illuminate it for Jahangir who stands slightly to the right of the lion. He is about to strike the lion – his arms are raised and he holds a sword. An attendant stands beside him with a mace-like staff in his hand. There is a hill in the background, and a few more torch bearers stand at the top right-hand corner of the painting. The incident is depicted in open country interspersed with tall grass. Hunting antelope, particularly blackbuck, at night with torches was known then. Was Jahangir out hunting antelope that night when his party surprised a lion? The painting has the moon partially covered by clouds – did Jahangir purposefully

Animals

■ Circa 1610.
An excellent study of the lion in the Jahangir period. On the top left-hand and right-hand corners the lion kills a nilgai and a chital respectively, both being part of the prey base of the lion.
From the St Petersburg Muraqqa, *after Kostioukovich, 1996.*

go after the lion on a moonlit night? Or is the painting entirely apocryphal? We do not know. What is certain, according to Dr Das, is that the painting is contemporaneous.[42]

On occasion there was even a romantic twist to a lion hunt. In April 1617 Jahangir went out lion hunting with his harem near Mandu. The party was on elephantback when four lions came out towards the elephants – presumably they were driven towards the hunters. Nurjahan asked permission of the emperor to shoot, which was readily granted. Two lions were dispatched with one shot each and the other two were accounted for by two bullets each, thus four lions were killed with six bullets. Considering that Nurjahan fired from a covered howdah with obviously restricted manoeuvrability, from a mobile, and therefore none too steady, elephant perch, and using a smooth bore musket, it was a truly remarkable feat of marksmanship. Jahangir was so pleased with the empress's hunting skill that he scattered a thousand *ashrafi*s over her head and gifted her a pair of pearls and a diamond worth a lakh of rupees.[43]

In his autobiography Jahangir referred to his father with the utmost reverence and yet if he had scored a point over him, he was quick to document it. For instance, he records that Akbar tried hard to get cheetahs to breed in captivity but failed though he had collected a thousand cheetahs. In the year 1613, however, a pair mated and three cubs were born at Jahangir's court. The emperor states that he has recorded the fact as it was strange.[44] In the same breath he goes on to record that in the benevolent reign of his times wildness had been eliminated, lions had become tame and were roaming in prides among people without the restraint of a chain, not harming them. This is farfetched and if such was indeed the case he would hardly have pursued them so vigorously in the field. However, the fact is that lions can be tamed easily and there is a painting by the artist Padarath depicting a young lion – it has a partially grown mane – being taken for a walk by a keeper, only lightly chained[45] in the manner of a not too aggressive canid. Jahangir notes further that he had heard from physicians that a lioness's milk was very good for the eyes. He tried to have a lioness who had given birth to three cubs milked, but did not succeed. He concluded that the milk could not be obtained owing to the irascible nature of the animal.[46]

As mentioned earlier, Jahangir had ordered a painting of the very large lion he had shot at Rahimabad, but the whereabouts of this painting, if it has survived, are not known. We may however look at another very remarkable work of his period. It is a painting entitled "Animals" in the *St Petersburg Muraqqa*.[47] It is a collage which Stuart Cary Welch calls a surrealistic *omnium gatherum.* The bottom of the painting has goats, sheep, and nilgai; in the lower centre portion a hound suckles one pup while the other two frolic about her. In the upper portion a cat suckles her three kittens. The artist is unknown but the cat with her kittens may have been painted by Abul Hasan according to Welch.[48] The painting has small figures of other animals, including an elephant attacked by a dragon-like creature. Of abiding interest is a couchant lion with the tip of the tail held high. The animal has been accurately rendered, its skin being the exact shade between dark yellow and brown, and its mane in darker brown with lighter hair around its face and sparse over its head as it should be – a characteristic of Indian lions. The tip of the tail is dark and the tuft prominent – another characteristic of the lion from India. Its mouth is slightly open, giving it a truly regal aspect. Of equal interest are the scenes at the top left and right corners of the painting. On the left a lion is in the process of strangulating a nilgai

*Maharao Umed Singh I of Kotah
hunting lions*
■ By Joshi Hathuwa, 1784.
The maharao, in *moongia* coloured shikar
dress, accompanied by his courtiers
hunts in a stockade in Alnia jungle unlike
the classic Mughal hunts of this type
which took place in open grasslands.
*Courtesy M. Brijraj Singh, Chairman, Board of
Trustees and other Trustees, Rao Madho Singh
Trust Museum, City Palace, Kotah.*

with his hold on its neck. On the right a lion is in the process of bringing down a
chital. These are both depictions of a lion's methods of killing its prey and in both
cases the animals are its usual prey. The artist was not only a master of his craft but
was also familiar with the hunting behaviour of the lion in the wild, which no doubt
would have been appreciated by Jahangir's discerning eye.

Though Jahangir's autobiography is replete with instances of lion hunts, only two
paintings can be identified with the incidents described there. One is the Anup Rai
incident which has been painted several times, the most famous rendering being the
one by Balchand circa 1640 in the *Padshahnama*. It shows Anup Rai under the lion,
while Prince Khurram is about to strike it. One member of the party strikes the lion
on its head with a stick, another has struck it with a sword on its hindquarters, yet
another courtier looks on as does Jahangir himself.[49] The other is the incident when
Jahangir shot a lioness in the presence of Prince Karan of Mewar.[50]

From these paintings we learn little of the techniques of hunting lions, since one
was a chance encounter while another tells us that the shikar took place from
elephantback. For this we turn to other sources. Bernier has left a firsthand account
of what he saw in Aurangzeb's time (1658–1707). When a lion was located,

> As a preliminary step, an ass is tied near the spot where the gamekeepers have
> ascertained the lion retires. The wretched animal is soon devoured, and after so
> ample a meal the lion never seeks for other prey, but without molesting either
> oxen, sheep or shepherds, goes in quest of water, and after quenching his thirst,
> returns to his former place of retirement. He sleeps until the next morning, when
> he finds and devours another ass, which the gamekeepers have brought to the same
> spot. In this way they contrive, during several days, to allure the lion and attach
> him to one place; and when information is received of the King's approach, they

Maharao Umed Singh I of Kotah hunting tigers
■ By Gumani, 1778.
Accompanied by Jhala Zalim Singh the maharao hunts in the Moti Paj jungle, Darah valley. Tigers and wild boar have been encircled in Qamargha fashion. The jungle here is much thicker than the one in the lion shikar painting.
Courtesy M. Brijraj Singh of Kotah.

fasten at the space an ass where so many have been sacrificed, down whose throat a large quantity of opium has been forced. This last meal is of course intended to produce a soporific effect on the lion.[51]

This time-honoured method, without the opium – Bernier himself states in the narrative that "it is a tale of the vulgar, and the lion is sufficiently disposed to sleep without it when he has eaten to satiety" – has been used in India by maharajas and nawabs for shikar and even in our own times when lions were "anchored" for census operations or for the "lion shows" which were staged until not so long ago for the benefit of tourists in the Gir forest. Bernier continues:

> The next operation is to spread by the means of the peasantry of the adjacent villages, large nets, made on purpose, which are gradually drawn closer in the manner practised in hunting the nil-ghaux. Every thing being in this state of preparation, the king appears on an elephant protected in places with thin plates of iron, and attended by the Grand Master of the Hunt, some *Omrahs* mounted on elephants, and great numbers both of *gourze-berdar* on horse back and of gamekeepers on foot, armed with half pikes. He immediately approaches the net on the outside, and fires at the lion with a large musketoon. The wounded animal makes a spring at the elephant, according to the invariable practice of lions, but is arrested by the net; and the king continues to discharge his musketoon until the lion is at length killed.[52]

A painting attributed to Daulat and dated circa 1635 in the *Padshahnama*, "Shah Jahan hunting lions near Burhanpur"[53] illustrates this technique. There are three elephants. Shah Jahan is seated on the middle one, the howdah is designed for the hunt as it is open on all sides to enable the hunter to manoeuvre the gun in all directions. Shah Jahan has rested his musket on the shoulder of the mahout; if he were shooting on the ground, it would have rested on a tripod or a bipod. A lion, a lioness, and two cubs have been encircled by nets though, unlike in Bernier's description, Shah Jahan and the lions are on the same side of the net.

In the incident of Jahangir showing his hunting skills to Prince Karan, there is no sign of the net or for that matter any obstruction between the lioness and the imperial elephant. Colonel Kesri Singh, head of the Shikar Khana of Gwalior state in the 1930s and a renowned tiger hunter of his time, describes a tiger hunt with nets. The occasion was staged for the Columbia Broadcasting Corporation in 1958. In this event the tiger was driven to the nets by a Land Rover whereupon the animal was speared by the people surrounding the net from the outside.[54] Bernier's observation therefore may not have been a common practice, as when the lion was hunted from elephantback with a musket it could be dispatched from a safe distance, whereas keeping the net between the hunter and the hunted would be necessary while using a bow and arrow or using a long spear from elephantback. There are paintings however, of lions being speared without the use of a net by imperial Mughal hunters, as we have noted earlier in the case of a painting of Akbar.

In the hunting field methods of hunting had to be adapted to the circumstances pertaining to the hunting grounds, the quarry, and naturally the wishes of the hunter. In a painting of circa 1660 by an unknown artist, Emperor Shah Jahan and his four sons are depicted. The painting may be titled "Shah Jahan hunting lions with the four princes" and is in the collection of Edmund de Unger. The whole hunting party involving Shah Jahan and all his direct and nearest in the line of succession illustrates the importance of the event. The location of the hunt is unknown but the painting is described by Robert Skelton as follows:

> ... Emperor Shah Jahan ... can be identified [on] the penultimate elephant in a line of five, advancing from the left. The emperor is shown preparing to aim his matchlock at a lion which is attacking the elephant. The howdahs of the three elephants to the right of Shah Jahan contain the figures of his sons Murad Baksh (next to his father), Dara Shikoh, and Shah Shuja. The figure on the elephant to the left of Shah Jahan is evidently one of the leading amirs. On the right hand side of the nullah are three elephants, two taking part in the beat and the central one bearing a prince who can probably be identified as Aurangzeb, about to throw [sic] at a lion which has leaped on to his elephant. On the left bank, three buffaloes ... are advancing on the nullah. A lion springs from a thicket and another lion mauls a fallen shikari. In the background is a line of nets supported by poles enclosing the hunting field. The perimeter is patrolled by elephants and a solitary horseman rides in the distance.[55]

While the net is a feature of the hunt, here the hunters and the hunted are again on the same side of it. Also the presence of buffaloes is not an accident. These animals are used as "stops" to confine the lions in a more or less predetermined area. The use of "stops" in driving game in or towards the desired ground or on the flanks of a beat has been known in India well into our own times. This method was not unique to lion hunts alone, it was used by the Mughals for other game as well such as confining nilgai on the hunting ground, as in the painting of "Dara Shikoh shooting nilgais".[56]

Bernier records that Aurangzeb put his son Sultan Muazzam to a strange test to check out his obedience and courage. He ordered him to attack and kill a lion which had been tracked down without the use of nets – that is without the help of

***Maharao Durjan Sal of Kotah
viewing a lion family***
■ By Shevdar Gangeyaji, circa 1750.
The maharao with Jhala Sheo Singh and
the royal party have come upon a lion
family at Joraki Beed. The lions are
highly stylized and even the cubs have
manes. The manes are much darker
coloured than those in Mughal paintings.
*Courtesy M. Brijraj Singh, Chairman, Board of
Trustees and other Trustees, Rao Madho Singh
Trust Museum, City Palace, Kotah.*

confining the dangerous prey in an area which would give the advantage to the
hunter. The prince obeyed, and in the event two or three men lost their lives, some
horses were mangled, and the wounded lion jumped on Prince Muazzam's elephant
before meeting its end.[57] Here was a peculiar Mughal variant of baptism by fire!

Bernier was also witness to a hunt in which a lion escaped Aurangzeb's gun. The
whole army was deployed to locate the escaped beast, it was "subjected to great
inconveniencies and thrown into a considerable degree of confusion" as a result and
the march had to be halted for three or four days. There were no bazaars pitched at
this place and many went hungry.[58] Bernier does not mention what happened to the
lion, but its escape was considered a bad omen, just as the king's success in killing it
would have been a favourable one. Was this a foreshadow of coming events?
Aurangzeb's policies left a fractured legacy and the end of his reign saw the
beginning of the decline of the Mughal empire.

Abul Fazl describes another method of hunting lions wherein a hunter rides a
male buffalo and makes it attack a lion, the buffalo tossing the lion with its horns
and killing it.[59] This is surely not a method recommended for the emperor or princes,

Lions in front of a cave
■ Mewar school, 18th century. The animals are somewhat stylized, the lion being the most accurate though its mane is light coloured and artistic in execution rather than real. Even the cubs sport manes.
Courtesy Bharat Kala Bhavan, Varanasi.

विजयंसर्वकार्येषु राजाप्रजासमागमं कार्यसिद्धिसर्वत्राया
घ्रैवविनिर्दिशेत् परउतसं

but a variation of it was certainly in vogue. A painting titled "Aurangzeb hunting lions" circa 1670–1700 by an unknown artist, preserved in the Chester Beatty Library,[60] shows Aurangzeb and his entourage on three male elephants on the right-hand side of the painting. The elephants are behind a phalanx of ten buffaloes in front of which are a lion and lioness. Towards the top left is an elephant which has been attacked by a lion from the back; another elephant is crushing a lion with its tusks. The emperor is aiming his gun at the lion while sitting on an open howdah, with the stock of the matchlock resting on its frame. Almost an exact reproduction of the picture is found in a painting from Bikaner by Rashid dated circa 1693. The crucial difference is that the hunters are Maharaja Anup Singh of Bikaner and his three brothers[61] instead of the Mughal party! In both these paintings the hunters and the hunted are both within the nets.

In many ways the Great Mughals were no different from their predecessors.

However, unlike the earlier sultans of Delhi, the lion to them was royal game. Though it was not spared in the hunting fields by them, no one else could meddle with it without their permission. It symbolized regal power and it sat proudly on their imperial standards. As was the case with everything they did, their shikar expeditions were larger than life. Their successors in the 18th century continued hunting but the pomp and circumstance progressively waned, until the last of the Mughals, Bahadur Shah Zafar, was exiled to Rangoon, Burma in 1858. The later Mughals were but a shadow of their fabulous predecessors, they could not be expected to add any new dimension to the courtly pursuit of hunting.

Jahangir did not describe a single lion in detail in his memoirs as he did, for example, the turkey, zebra, and barbary falcon. This is not surprising, as lions were plenty in his time, they were commonplace. It is estimated that the Agra *suba* at the heart of the Mughal empire had only 27.5 per cent land under cultivation in about 1600, and other *suba*s in the plains had even less.[62] The rest of the land was either uncultivable or cultivable wasteland. In other words the Mughal empire had large tracts which were suitable habitat for lions. They were numerous enough to be found almost everywhere the Mughal emperors went. They did not have to think of the Gir, the lion's present and only home in India. To them it was a far off corner in their domains and they estimated its area to be no more than 3 x 3 *kuroh*, that is just about 90 square kilometres![63]

But 200 years after Jahangir, lions had almost died out in India. The reasons for this are not far to seek. Unlike their Sultanate predecessors, the Great Mughals restricted the hunting of game animals and birds, and for the smaller creatures which could be snared they set aside large hunting grounds as well. With their eclipse, protection no longer remained effective. The lion was an easy target because of its gregarious nature and diurnal habits. The constant pursuit of this great cat in the field, along with steady encroachment into its habitat, took a heavy toll. The human population within the bounds of India had grown from an extrapolated/ estimated figure of 116 million in 1600 to 159 million in 1800.[64] Just before the last Mughal was to live out the final scene of the great drama, a single British officer is reported to have shot as many as 300 lions. Even if this figure was an exaggeration, which it probably was, we may recall that Emperor Jahangir with all his enthusiasm for the hunt and all the imperial resources at his command, had shot only 86 lions in a span of 39 years! What was left behind by the Mughals was about to be decimated by their successors.

CHAPTER 7

The British Come Calling

WITH THE DEATH OF Emperor Aurangzeb, the last of the Great Mughals in 1707, the fissures in the structure of empire became more than evident, they widened, and ultimately the edifice gave way. European traders had already established bases, and the successive wars among them and those with Indians saw much bloodshed, hardship, and suffering for the people in India. From these chaotic times the British came out winners with the Battle of Plassey in 1757 and the Battle of Buxar in 1764 which made the East India Company the dominant political power in the north. They had come a long way since they had set up their "factory", a trading outpost, at Surat in 1612 – when Emperor Jahangir was on the throne and the Mughal empire was at its zenith.

The British had met the Indian lion very early on. Ralph Fitch who visited Agra and Fatehpur Sikri during Emperor Akbar's reign had reported that the emperor's establishment at the two cities had "as they doe credibly report, one thousand Elephants, thirtie thousand Hourses, one thousand and four hundred tame Deer, eight hundred Concubines: such store of Ounces, Tygres, Buffles, Cockes and Hawkes, that it is very strange to see".[1] "Ounces" are cheetahs, of which there were a thousand at one point in the imperial collection. The word "tygres" was loosely used by European travellers to denote both lions and tigers and sometimes even smaller cats such as cheetahs.

The first "official" contact between India and England was made by Sir Thomas Roe, the ambassador of King James I to the Mughal court. Roe was in India between 1615 and 1619. He was presented to Emperor Jahangir at Ajmer in December 1615. The next year he saw a tame lion at the court and he describes the event thus:

> The King [Jahangir] commanded one of his brothers [Prince Daniyal's] sonnes ... to
> go strike a lyon on the head, which was brought before the king; but hee beeing
> afrayd refused yt. Soe the king bad his yongest sonne [Prince Sharyar] to go touch
> the lyon; who did so without any harme ... wheratt the king tooke occasion to send
> his nephew away to a prison where hee is never like to see day light![2]

Unlike his first encounter where he was only a spectator, the second one was more troublesome for Roe. The Mughal court with him in tow had moved to Mandu in 1617 where the ambassador had problems with marauders who were after his stocks of food:

> A lion and a woolfe used my house and nightly put us in alarume, fetching away
> sheeps and goats out of my court, and leaping a high wall with them. I sent to ask
> leave to kill it, for no man may meddle with lions but the king, and it was granted.
> I ranne out into the court upon the noyse and the beast, missing his prey, seized on
> a little Island dogge before me, that I had long kept. But the woolfe one of my
> servants killed, and I sent it the king.[3]

The lion escaped the English ambassador and thus began an uneasy relationship between the lion and the British, calamitous to the former. By 1947 just 200-odd lions survived.

Fifty years after the Battle of Plassey in 1757, as a result of which the East India Company was established as a temporal power, Captain Thomas Williamson's book on shikar made its appearance.[4] It was the first of its kind, extensively illustrated with forty coloured engravings. From tiger hunting to pig-sticking, the British took to "Oriental Field Sports" with great enthusiasm. Williamson's work being concerned with Bengal, lions do not feature in it. The pride of place among the hunted went to the tiger which came to be called the Royal Bengal tiger though there was nothing

The conquering British lion

■ (opposite) The Seringapatam Medal struck to commemorate the defeat of Tipu Sultan in 1799 has the "British" lion conquering Tipu's tiger.

The Trustees of The National Museums of Scotland.

■ (above) The Burma Medal struck to commemorate the victory of 1826 has the elephant of Ava properly deferential, crouching before the "British" lion.

Courtesy of the Director, National Army Museum, London.

■ (left) The Indian Mutiny Medal struck to commemorate the suppression of the revolt of 1857–58 has Britannia holding a wreath over the "British" lion signalling triumph.

Courtesy of the Director, National Army Museum, London.

The Reserve Bank of India's symbol, 1935

■ (below) The tiger for the Reserve Bank of India's symbol was taken from the gate of the residence of the Governor of Bengal, now the National Library, Kolkata.

■ (right) The "British" lion with its foot on a globe atop the gate of the residence of the Governor General of India, now the residence of the Governor of West Bengal, Kolkata, was not considered for the emblem of the Reserve Bank of India as it was a symbol of imperialism.

Author's collection.

the 16th century.[14] He records that these people were the finest trackers he had come across.[15] They had a superb knowledge of the terrain, they knew the territory of each lion, and they were sent out to track and locate the chosen animal to drive it out in a beat to the hunter's perch or machan. Alternatively a bait was tied to attract a lion or leopard so that the hunter could get a shot at it. Fenton enumerates two methods of shooting a tracked lion. One was to drive it in a beat towards the hunter, the other more dangerous one was "walking it up", that is going with trackers on foot to the lion and shooting it. He preferred the latter method as, according to him, it usually gave a good shot.[16]

The preferred object of shikar was the male lion. Its mane and larger size made it a good trophy either mounted whole or partly, or as a rug on the floor. C.A. Kincaid, Judicial Assistant at Rajkot went for a shoot to the Gir in 1905. He had permission from Junagadh state to shoot only one lion and he had hoped to shoot a maneater near Talala – a taluka town way out of the jungle today – but only a lioness offered him a shot. On returning to his camp he sent a letter to Nawab Rasulkhanji thanking him for the permission to shoot which he and his wife enjoyed. Quite unexpectedly he received a telegraphic reply stating "Take lioness for Madam Saheb, get lion for yourself". The maneater was tracked down and Kincaid sat in a machan on a tree to shoot it. The lion, he writes:

> ... was a wily old campaigner and had evidently sent out its younger ones [for two cubs came out earlier in the beat] to draw the fire of any lurking enemies. I took rather rashly a snapshot at it, as it galloped past. A lucky shot broke its spine and it collapsed. It was a noble beast but its canine teeth had been broken and it was that misfortune probably that had led it to take exclusively to human diet.[17]

The epitome of shikar for the British in India was a viceregal shoot. Viceroys and Governors of Bombay more often than not went to shoot in the Gir when on a visit to Junagadh state. The final such visitation for the lions was Lord Linlithgow's in 1942. As usual on such occasions the resources of the state were mobilized to the maximum extent possible. For months before the intended visit, baits of male buffalo calves were regularly fed to lions which were large and had good manes, and therefore marked for the event. Thus they were localized and "anchored" to use R.S. Dharmakumarsinhji's phrase, to their respective areas. On the appointed day the Viceroy and his party were installed in secure machans and the beat began. The result was predictable enough. A photograph of this last viceregal shoot shows the Viceroy and the Vicerine with their daughter and a daughter of Lord Irwin (a former Viceroy), standing in front of a dead lion carefully laid out to record the successful shoot.

Such shoots were a matter of prestige for the state and a failed shikar would be a major embarrassment. An amusing incident took place in 1890 when the Duke of Clarence visited the Gir to shoot a lion. Unfortunately for the administration of the state, the lion did not oblige. In desperation Haridas Viharidas, the Diwan of Junagadh, approached L.L. Fenton who was in charge of the royal party's shoot with a proposal that two lions brought out from the Junagadh zoo the previous night should be set free in the forest and then be driven out to be shot by the royal guest. Fenton notes that he had heard of such goings on in some states of north India – in these cases the quarry would have been the tiger – but he promptly refused. The Duke went home empty-handed[18] as did Prince Philip the Duke of Edinburgh almost a hundred years later in 1983 when he returned from Gir without seeing lions in the

The Reserve Bank of India's symbol, 1935
■ The tiger in front of a palm tree replaced the lion as the latter was thought to represent imperialism.
Courtesy RBI, Mumbai.

wild. Two large males had been "anchored" for him to see and photograph. However, the royal guest could not be taken there as the place had not been "sanitized" by the security personnel in time![19]

One of the perils of shikar is that sometimes things start going horribly wrong for the shikaris. General Godfrey Mundy noted that

> By *crack* sportsmen the lion is reputed to afford better sport than the tiger: his attack is more open and certain; a peculiarity arising either from the noble nature of the jungle king, or from the country which he haunts being less favourable for a retreat than the thick morasses frequented by the tiger.[20]

William Rice strikes a note of caution:

> Following up a wounded lion is considered most awkward work, for they have the credit of making their charge home good, and of not swerving on one side when fired at close enough to singe them almost, as I have known to be the case with tigers on more than one occasion....[21]

He goes on to add though, that he cannot say this from experience as he himself had been lucky enough to find all wounded lions dead.[22] But one British officer, Major H.G. Carnegie, Political Agent of Halar *prant* of Kathiawar at the time, was not so fortunate. He met his end in such circumstances in 1905 when Lord Lamington, Governor of Bombay was shooting in the Gir. Captain Foljambe, ADC to the Governor, fired at a male lion in a beat and missed. J.H. Du Boulay, Private Secretary to the Governor who was accompanying the Governor's party also fired two shots of which the second one struck the lion in the right shoulder. The animal retreated and they caught up with it in a nullah. Suddenly there was "a slight coughing roar", the lion's charge was swift. Carnegie fired a shot and grazed it. The lion went straight for him and struck "a blow on the left shoulder with his right paw, and then seized him and bore him to the ground". Several shots were fired which silenced the lion but Major Carnegie had had his last shoot.[23] Until recently a Carnegie Fountain erected in his memory stood at a major crossroads in Rajkot, a reminder of the sudden end of a popular British officer.

Up to the middle of the 19th century the lion was found all over north India but its frequent encounters with the British had disastrous consequences leading to its near total disappearance from India. This has been recounted by virtually every writer on the subject. A few instances illustrate the widespread devastation. William Fraser shot 84 lions, "being personally responsible for their extinction in the area [Haryana, Punjab]".[24] That was circa 1820. Central India in the 1850s was a stronghold of lions according to one authority. During the upheavals of 1857–58 Colonel George Acland Smith is supposed to have killed more than 300 of them of which fifty were from the Delhi region alone,[25] though this large number appears to be exaggerated. In Kathiawar William Rice shot fourteen lions in Gir in one shoot[26] and a Colonel D. killed as many as eighty lions around 1857.[27] This is only one side of the picture, for Indians were not far behind. Ten lions were shot in Kotah, Rajasthan in 1866.[28] Maharaja Ranjitsingh's lancers bayoneted these cats around Lahore in the 1830s.[29] A decade earlier Raja Bishen Singh of Bundi in Rajasthan

> would *bivouac* for days in the lion's lair, nor quit the scene until he had circumvented the forest king, the only prey he deemed worthy of his kill. He had slain upwards of one hundred lions with his own hand, besides tigers....[30]

In 1842 in Kathiawar peninsula itself "Lions ... [were] to be found in various parts of the country.... Panthers [leopards] cheetahs (or the hunting tigers) are very common" according to Captain George Le Grand Jacob, the Political Agent at Kathiawar.[31] Up to the 1870s rulers in Kathiawar were paying bounties to hunters for killing lions. In three years sixteen lions[32] were killed. From Kutch the lions had disappeared by then and only names such as *sinh khatlo* (lion hillock) and a *sinh jhar* (lion ravine) now remind people of their existence.[33] By 1891 there were only stray reports of lions around Mount Abu,[34] the animal had otherwise disappeared from the rest of India.

By the second half of the 19th century, it required an invitation to Junagadh to be able to shoot a lion. Thus it is not surprising at all that shikar literature of the British period barely mentions lion shikar. Lt. Col. R.W. Burton estimated in 1959 that there were 280 books on shikar and related subjects[35] whereas a more recent bibliography compiled by Kamal Prasad in 1965 lists some 400 books on these very subjects including ornithology and fishing.[36] It is significant to note that throughout the entire British period there were only three authors – William Rice, L.L. Fenton, and C.A. Kincaid – who had a chapter on lion shooting in their books, and all are of experiences in the Gir. Stanley Jepson's collection of *Big Game Encounters* by various hunters includes an encounter T.R. Lively had with three lions in the Gir forest.[37] There is not a single book devoted to lion shikar in the entire period. Two books by R.G. Burton who was the most prolific writer on the subject, have a chapter each on lions, but one has material on the African lion, whereas the other, on the lion in India, summarizes information from earlier sources.[38] In 1904 F.G. Aflalo's book on sporting opportunities in India was published, almost a hundred years after Williamson's work. This book does not mention any lion shooting, as the animal had all but gone from India by then.[39] This is a clear indication of the dramatic decline of the animal in the 19th century. Some of the instances of the number of lions shot by various hunters noted here represent the very last survivors of these animals in India outside of the Gir.

In fact, the game was almost up for the lions outside Kathiawar by the end of the 18th century. The four instances of the 1820s–60s we have noted here, i.e. those of Fraser, Smith, and in Bundi and Kotah, were of large figures and their total comes to 494 lions killed for sport. It is obvious that several hunters hunted in the areas, all details of which are not available. Their shikar bags may not have been so large. Even if one were to assume that 1,000 more lions were destroyed by other sportsmen and military officers during the same period whose records do not exist or are not in the public domain, we arrive at a figure of say 1,500 lions being killed during 1820–70 in India outside Kathiawar. Paul Joslin's compilation of lions shot between 1863 and 1888 outside Kathiawar gives a figure of only 37.[40] Compare this with the figures from a recent study: over 80,000 tigers, more than 150,000 leopards, and 200,000 wolves were slaughtered in the fifty years from 1875 to 1925.[41] Our figure of 1,500 lions and Joslin's 37 are both minuscule by comparison. A total of about 230 cheetahs were seen or shot between 1772 and 1967 on the Indian subcontinent.[42] Lions were probably more abundant during that period than cheetahs, but not as widespread or common as tigers. It is pertinent to note that there were no natural calamities in the 1850s and 1860s of a nature or magnitude that would take a sudden toll of lions during these two decades. Thus it was obviously British and other sportsmen who had delivered the coup de grace to the small pockets of lion populations by the end of the 1860s. The animals that survived thereafter were but a few stragglers that were mopped up.

Lion shikar and the British
■ Sir Charles D'Oyly's watercolours vividly illustrate the sport in the field. The last painting shows both a lion and a tiger brought home on elephantback, circa 1810. (See also page 115.)
By permission of The British Library, London, MS WD 4406/F28–34.

Lion and elephant
■ A sketch by General Godfrey Charles Mundy, which records an incident of 1828 when his friend was attacked near Hansi in Haryana. It was the elephant which ultimately killed the lion.
From Mundy 1858.

A comparison with the cheetah's disappearance is interesting. The last lion reported outside Kathiawar was in 1891 as noted earlier. The last cheetah seen in India was in 1967–68. Thus seventy years elapsed between the disappearance of the two.[43] The bigger, heavier cat which required bigger prey was the first one to depart from India except for the relict population of the Kathiawar peninsula.

The lion's preferred habitat is grassland and scrub jungle. Yet they were found on the periphery of thick jungles of Kotah and Bundi, and indeed they inhabit today the Gir, parts of which are thick jungle. The cheetah too inhabited the same type of habitat though its range extended further south beyond the Narmada river to the Deccan plateau and beyond. And its last reported sightings and shikar were near the edges of thick jungle in Madhya Pradesh, though jungles were their least preferred habitat. The other big cat, the tiger, also came under severe pressure in the 19th century. According to Valmik Thapar, as many as 20,000 tigers were shot for sport between 1860 and 1960.[44] Mahesh Rangarajan estimates that 80,000 tigers were destroyed between 1875 and 1925 as they were considered dangerous and bounties were paid for their destruction by the government.[45] In spite of such depredations a sizeable population survived, and the preferred habitat of the tiger was the last to be disturbed or substantially destroyed. In 1900 the tiger population was estimated between 25,000 and 40,000.[46]

The pressure on different habitats increased steadily over the centuries as a result of the human population growth between 1600 and 1800 from about 116 million to about 159 million as we have seen earlier,[47] and up to 254.51 million by 1880,[48] during which time most of north India was ruled by the Mughals followed by the British. By 1901 the human population had increased to 283.9 million.[49] The growth in human population implies also growth in cattle, sheep, and goat populations. The hundred years between 1757 and 1858 were a period of uncertainty and turmoil that were part of the consolidation process of the British Indian empire. It would be

Hunting in Gir
■ In this image titled "Lion shooting in the GHEER Kathiawar, Western India", a Britisher is shown hunting a lion with a gun, with "natives" following behind him. This incident is from *The Graphic*, October 4, 1873.
Author's collection.

difficult to assess the loss of grasslands and scrub jungle habitats of the lion as British settlement and other records for most of the region became available primarily in the second half of the 19th century, whereas regional records are beyond the scope of this work. But that their disappearance or reduction accelerated the process of extinction of the lion is a certainty.

Secondly, the depredations of shikar are an even greater certainty. Shikaris and "sportsmen" spared no animal that came their way. The slaughter was merciless and total. It was conducted without any impulse to protect the species. It was only towards the close of the 19th century when an alarmist belief took hold that there were only a dozen lions left in the Gir that the British administration turned its attention to preservation. Lord Curzon's subsequent decision not to go for lion shikar in the Gir during his state visit to Junagadh in 1900 was the high watermark.[50] His subsequent letter to the Burma Game Preservation Association is the first call in modern times for preserving Nature for its own sake from the highest in the empire.[51] The letter's mastery over the broad range of the subject is a delight, and it is a beacon worthy of the lion itself. The issues Lord Curzon addressed are still with us a century later. It is regrettable that his own viceregal successors, other high-ranking British officers, and Indian princes and potentates honoured his call more in its breach.

There was a curious debate during the British period, which continued after independence, about which of the two great cats, the lion or the tiger, was stronger and whether the tiger "drove out" the lion[52] and reduced it to its present minuscule domain. It is not clear how the debate started but it was for decades the subject of many a fireside chat, with even serious shikaris labouring over it.

From the evidence we have it is clear that the tiger was noticed by humans in the Indian subcontinent earlier than the lion. If this is a reflection of the commonness of a species at a particular period of history, then the inescapable conclusion is that the

Lion shikar from a machan
■ An illustration by William Rice of an incident in the 1850s from the Gir forest which shows the lion bolting after being fired on. The bait used for the shikar is the traditional buffalo.
From Rice, 1884.

Trophy brought home
■ This scene is from the Gir. Before motorized transport and in the absence of elephants an animal the size of the lion could only be brought on a camel through a roadless jungle.
From Leipziger, 1888.

Sasan ness, circa 1880
■ This was a Maldhari outpost in the 19th century – visitors had to "camp" there. A thriving township has sprung up around the nawab's hunting lodge, now the forest resthouse.
From Leipziger, 1888.

lion arrived and increased in numbers just before and in the early centuries of the common era. Whether it did so at the cost of tiger habitat and therefore tigers is moot, though such would appear to be the case. Equally importantly there are no records of any natural conflict between the two species. It would be strange if humans failed to record it if it did happen.

The fact is that the two cats lived in different habitats. Even Kotah paintings show lions in thinner jungle than tigers. There is of course a possibility of an overlap in the range of the two species, the most preferred habitat of the one being the least preferred of the other. Skirmishes if any between the two would be rare and peripheral to the issue of one "driving out" the other.

While both cats are of near equal size and weight, lions are gregarious and they live in prides of varying sizes. To expect that a single tiger which is essentially a solitary animal, could succeed in annihilating a pair of lions, leave alone a pride of them, would be in the realm of imagination.

We have seen that one could extrapolate a figure of say 1,500 lions living in India outside of Kathiawar in the early part of the 19th century as against a minimalist figure of 25,000 tigers around 1900. Tigers were reduced to less than 2,000 within the succeeding seventy years, a tiger's fate similar to that of the lion or the cheetah though later in coming. The causes of its decimation, as in the case of the lion or cheetah, were human interference with its life and its habitat. The large swathes of dense jungles where it lived were the last to be attacked by humans.

That having been said, we may turn to the representation of the two cats as symbols of political power. As discussed in earlier chapters, Ashoka propagated *dhamma* in the far-flung Mauryan empire through his edicts on rocks, caves, and pillars – some of the last of which were surmounted by lions. The Mughals had the lion couchant and the rising sun as the symbol on their pennant.[53] The British were no different. They too had their symbols where the lion played a prominent part. Their long journey from trade to empire, though unplanned, had been as bloody as the foundation of any previous paramount power in India, and with their victory the

CHAPTER 8

Soruth Sarkar Saves Lions

Armorial bearings of Junagadh
■ A banner with these armorial bearings was presented by Queen Victoria to Nawab Mahbatkhanji II. The supporters are naturally lions.
Author's collection.

THE SAURASHTRA OR KATHIAWAR PENINSULA under the British was divided into four sub-cultural and sub-linguistic units – Jhalawar, Halar, Gohilwar, and Sorath or Soruth the central and coastal portion over which the nawabs of Junagadh ruled. The state of Junagadh often used the title Soruth Sarkar for its government. Sorath was of immense historical significance. To the Mauryas the peninsula was important as the Saurashtra *vana* was one of the eight elephant forests, though not the best, that provided them with this indispensable war machine.[1] Emperor Ashoka caused fourteen of his edicts to be engraved on a granite rock at the foot of Girnar mountain on the outskirts of Junagadh, the first edict being an injunction against slaughter of animals and birds for sacrifices and feasts.[2] On the same rock Rudradaman the Western Kshatrapa king of the 2nd century CE engraved his deeds of repairing a dam built by the Mauryas, and Skanda Gupta who once again repaired the same dam added his inscription in the 5th century.[3]

Sorath's fortunes changed with the march of history. It came to be ruled by the Raizada (Chudasama) Rajputs until they were defeated by Sultan Mahmud Begda of Ahmedabad in 1472–73. During Emperor Akbar's consolidation of his empire, the region came under Mughal rule. However by 1735 the Mughal empire had weakened and from its debris arose Sher Khan Babi who threw out the Mughal governor of the region to establish his dynasty around 1735[4] which ruled Junagadh for nine generations until 1947.

The Babis themselves claimed descent from one Abdul Rashid who had been in the service of Paigambar Muhammad himself. Their principality located as it was at such a historically important place, was the premier state of Kathiawar, a fact that was emphasized throughout the dynasty's rule. By the beginning of the 19th century however, the dynasty had to be content under the authority of the new imperial power, the British. The chaos of Kathiawar had to be settled and the British did so with persistence.[5] By 1821 external relations of states of the region were taken over by them under the settlement made by Colonel Walker to the extent that the *zortalbi* tribute collected by Junagadh from 134 states and talukas of Kathiawar would henceforth be collected by the British on the state's behalf,[6] of which naturally the British kept a percentage for themselves by way of a fee. While Junagadh and other large states were more or less free to conduct their own internal affairs, warfare and external relations went out of their hands. Even in the internal affairs of states, the British empire from their paramount position henceforth would ensure restraint.

The first half of the 19th century was a period of considerable turmoil in Kathiawar. There were claims and counter-claims of territories by various states particularly between Junagadh and Baroda[7] and Junagadh and Gondal. The Gir forest itself had become a haven for outlaws – *baharvatia*s who had taken it upon themselves to avenge wrongs done to them by the state.[8] The tract was notorious for being malarious and there were hardly any maps to assist the administration. Matters came to a head when a British officer was taken prisoner by the outlaws. A military expedition by Junagadh and other state forces led by a British colonel had to be mounted to pacify the area. In course of time territorial disputes between states were settled, though Junagadh considered itself the successor to the Mughal empire in the region. Peace was finally attained with a British garrison permanently stationed at Rajkot.

As was to be expected, the relationship with the imperial authority would deepen. During the time of the sixth nawab, Sir Mahbatkhanji II who ruled from 1851 to

1882, a Governor of Bombay Presidency visited the state for the first time. Sir Bartle Frere (who had earlier hunted lions in western India and had killed four lions in a day's shoot)[9] came to Veraval by sea in 1867. He was followed by Sir Seymour Fitzgerald who came to Rajkot to inaugurate Rajkumar College, the princes' college, on December 16, 1870.[10] After this landmark event he proceeded to Junagadh and Gir for shikar. He "bagged" five lions there,[11] thus starting a dubious tradition which was to continue on and off for more than sixty years.

Though stray lions were reported outside Kathiawar up to 1891,[12] in the peninsula itself they were already disappearing, apart from the environs of the Gir forest which spread outside of Junagadh state into Amreli district of Baroda state and the Mytiala area of Bhavnagar state. Good lion habitat extended into the Alech and Barda hills and their environs which came under Porbandar and Navanagar states. Jam Ranmalji who ruled Navanagar from 1820 to 1852[13] is reputed to have hunted one large male lion in 1833, another male in 1842, five lions in 1850, and three more in 1851, in his domains.[14] There is a fresco of Jam Ranmalji hunting lions from horseback with his nobles in the Barda hills in the "Lakhota" bastion in Jamnagar, the capital of Navanagar state. Ranmalji's successor Jam Vibhaji who ruled Jamnagar from 1852 to 1895 had hunted lions in his youth in the same area. According to L.L. Fenton, lions had last been reported in Barda and Alech hills, areas of Chotila and Dhrangadhra, but had all gone by the middle of the 19th century. A lion, a lioness, and a cub were reported circa 1884 in a part of Porbandar state neighbouring Navanagar state, but were killed by Rabaris and Navanagar police stationed there.[15] The upshot of the near total disappearance of lions from the rest of Kathiawar was that Junagadh state which had the largest portion of the Gir forest (though as we have noted some areas of the Gir ecosystem were part of Baroda, Bhavnagar, and other states and talukas where lions were found from time to time) would have to bear the brunt of sportsmen both British and Indian, who were important enough to get a permit from the state. If the imperial government required to obtain a specimen even for its zoological gardens or a museum, it had to ask Junagadh state. Thus in 1867 the political agent in Kathiawar Colonel W.W. Anderson addressed a letter to Junagadh making a request for procurement of a live lion, a lion skin, or a lion's skeleton. Gokulji Sampatram Jhala, Chief Diwan of the state notified the request in the State Gazette and offered rewards as follows:

	Rs
Sawaj (lion) a large live specimen	150/-
A small live cub	50/-
A dead lion's body with skin, bones, and claws intact	50/-
A complete skeleton	35/-
A complete skin	25/-[16]

These rewards were very generous for those times. But it will be noticed that the state did not have the administrative machinery for forest or wildlife management and had to offer a reward to its own subjects to procure lions! It has not been possible to ascertain the outcome of this gazette notification, but a lion reported to be of Asian origin was exhibited at the Alipore Zoo, Calcutta for ten years in the 1870s and a pair was obtained by them though it is not clear from where, in 1884, which was doing fine eight years later.[17]

The first salvo for the protection of lions was fired as early as 1879. Junagadh state had been exercised for some time about the number of lions left. In that year, the sixth nawab, Mahbatkhanji II had ordered strict protection of lions in his domains. He had been encouraged in this endeavour by Lord Sandhurst, Governor of Bombay. The nawab soon asked the Political Agent of Kathiawar Colonel L.C. Barton to help in his effort as a result of which the Agency published the following notification in its gazette:

> At the request of His Highness the Nawab of Junagadh, it is notified for public information that an interdict has been issued by His Highness against the destruction of lions in the Gir forest.
>
> As this order has emanated from a request preferred by His Excellency the Governor of Bombay who fears that this race of free nature [i.e. lions] may become extinct unless means are taken for their preservation, it is hoped by the undersigned that it will be respected by the European sportsmen.[18]

In April 1880, Junagadh state notified rules regarding shikar, which were considered important enough for the notification to be issued over the signature of the Principal Diwan, Khan Bahadur Saleh Hindi himself in the Junagadh state gazette. The notification stated that keeping in mind the Political Agency's notification of February 1880, Junagadh was promulgating the following rules. Firstly, no person within the state boundary would be allowed to do shikar of any type of animal, or trap it, without the permission of the state government. Secondly, the latter would permit such activities solely at its discretion on an application by the interested person. Finally, Junagadh state would allow subjects of neighbouring states to do shikar within its borders only if the state concerned would honour it reciprocally for Junagadh subjects with such permits. The subjects of other states would have to apply to Junagadh for permission on the strength of their state's permit. Anyone violating these rules would be liable to have his weapons confiscated and face other punishment according to the rules.[19] Here is a clear legal expression of monopoly over shikar. It is noteworthy that in British India, while the elephant received protection from 1879 onwards, the 1870s saw a systematic destruction of wild animals. According to one estimate 20,000 animals, including large carnivores, were being killed annually and Kotah state paid Rs 25 for a lion and Rs 10 for a tiger shot.[20] Junagadh state was way ahead of its times in protecting the lion.

These rules were superseded by new rules of the state introduced by a notification issued in 1896 under the signature of the then acting diwan, Behchardas Viharidas. The rules were made more stringent. A person caught poaching would face a jail term of one month and a fine of 200 koris (the Junagadh state currency – 1 imperial rupee = 3½ koris) and anyone found poaching a lion would face a jail term of six months and a fine of 1,000 koris. Permits for shikar would be issued on application to the diwan. A permit would be issued for a specific location, species, and period of time. It would not be granted for the shikar of a peacock or a peahen whereas, for a lion, special permission would have to be sought which would be granted for special reasons and circumstances only. It may be noted though that it was further notified that these rules would not apply for fishing and for snaring of small birds such as parakeets, sparrows, and pigeons.[21]

All these developments meant that henceforth lions were to receive protection and that permits would be granted in rare cases only for special reasons which included naturally raison d'etat. It also meant that permission had to be taken at the highest level. It may be noted as an aside that the nawab was extremely sensitive of his Hindu subjects' religious sentiments and banned the shikar of peafowl throughout his state thus anticipating the Republic of India by 75 years. The Political Agency's notification meant three things. First, Europeans, mainly the British, were to respect Junagadh state's efforts. Secondly, it meant that they could not any longer shoot or spear lions at will even in territories under direct British control, though by this time there were no lions left outside the Gir forest and its environs and in any case there was very little British territory in the Kathiawar peninsula, as it consisted almost entirely of princely states and talukas. However, British officers of stature could and did get permits to shoot in Junagadh state, which it appears were given liberally enough.[22] Finally, it meant that the imperial government fully supported the efforts of Junagadh state. Actually, however, the nawab and his administration were merely giving a "modern" legal form to the age-old custom of shikar where lions were considered royal game and their shikar was permitted only with the nawab's approval. At any rate, these rules and their practices were the basis of lion protection in the state. The dispensation of lion protection that came into being after 1879 remained in force till 1947 with only a few minor modifications.

But there was a major loophole in these arrangements. While Baroda and Bhavnagar states had strong administrations, and lion shikar being the prerogative of the ruler there was a considerable measure of control, there was to be friction between these states and Junagadh from time to time. The more troublesome problem however was of smaller principalities surrounding the Gir forest and Junagadh state, such as those of Jetpur, Mendarda, Bilkha, and other primarily Kathi states, and talukas whose darbars were free to do what they liked in their territories over whose activities neither the nawab nor the British administration had much control. This was the bane of Junagadh and its nawabs.

Junagadh state had an area of 8,499 square kilometres and a human population of 3,95,428 of which 80 per cent were Hindus, according to the 1901 census. The Gir forest extended from the sea coast to Girnar and Datar hills – the latter being a part of the Girnar massif – covering half the area of the state in the middle of the 19th century. When the great trigonometrical survey was done in 1875–76, the Gir was found to be 96 kilometres in length and 48 in width with an area of 3,109 square kilometres. Many parts consisted of thick jungle. Though the state had made some effort at protecting the forest, it was being continuously exploited. In 1879, Colonel Barton, Political Agent of Kathiawar (1878–83), suggested a survey of the jungle to prepare a plan for its protection. This was done by a Mr Bar in 1880, however the effort was found wanting, no action was taken, and almost two-thirds of the jungle was lost in the following twenty years.[23]

In 1892 Nawab Bahadurkhanji III died without leaving a direct heir. His brother Rasulkhanji had no training in statecraft and spoke little English. He was a devout Muslim, and having led the life of an ascetic had no interest in taking over the reins of state. However, he was persuaded by Haridas Viharidas the then diwan to answer the call of duty. He finally agreed to take on the challenge and after various representations to the British authorities he became nawab in 1892 at the age of forty. With the imperial government's acceptance of his accession began his benevolent reign of two decades.

Rasulkhanji had to learn on the job. He was shrewd enough to select able diwans. Haridas having performed his duties retired in 1895, and he was succeeded by several Hindu diwans who were Nagar brahmans, to be followed by Mirza Abbas Ali Beg and Abdullahmian A. Kureishi. During Rasulkhanji's reign, the state had

Nawab Rasulkhanji
■ In robes of state, he stands beside a ceremonial chair with lion armrests. He gave protection to lions which ultimately saved them.
Author's collection.

enlightened administrative policies and it made steady progress on all fronts with religious harmony among its subjects. It went through the disastrous *chappanyo kal* of 1899–1900 (the famine of Vikram Samvat 1956), when 157 relief works were implemented to sustain the poor subjects of the state.[24] Rasulkhanji in his youth was a remarkable marksman, who could toss a coin in the air and take it out with one shot. He had hunted several leopards earlier, but he had never shot a lion and had no desire to do so. With this background the nawab, his state, and the lions entered the 20th century and lived through its first decade. Rasulkhanji died in 1911.[25]

Rasulkhanji's administration had to take steps to protect the Gir which became a priority as the situation had become worrisome. The *Kathiawar Gazetteer* had declared in 1884 that there were only about a dozen lions left.[26] This was alarming enough, and a few years after Rasulkhanji came to the throne, the state as indeed all of Kathiawar, faced unprecedented famine which brought further travails to the lions and the administration of the state. Some measures of protection were taken early in his reign, but by 1906–07 only 883 square kilometres of forest remained with the Forest Department. The nawab decided to add 45,550 acres (18,448 hectares) to this area by transferring land from the revenue department. In the same year F.R. Desai who had been trained in forestry practice at the National Forest School, Nancy, France was appointed the first Conservator of Forests. He toured the entire area of the forest and put up a detailed proposal for its management so that the vandalization of this precious resource would stop and a steady income from its produce would accrue to the state. In 1906–07 the average income of the state on the basis of the previous five years was Rs 34.5 lakhs of which Rs 95,000 was earned from the forest with a net surplus of Rs 69,000.[27] In fact, the state showed a surplus from its forest income right up to 1945.[28] That apart, F.R. Desai had laid down boundaries of the forest, measured the area, divided it into blocks, and produced the first working plan. When Lord Lamington, Governor of Bombay, visited Junagadh in 1906 he publicly acknowledged Nawab Rasulkhanji for agreeing to create a sanctuary for lions in the Gir.[29] The land was earmarked by F.R. Desai and by 1908–09 the area of the Gir forest with the Forest Department had increased to 1,530 square kilometres, which included a sanctuary for lions of 326 square kilometres, a fraction of the area but a beginning nonetheless.[30]

Nawab Mahbatkhanji III

■ The last nawab in full military regalia, a rare picture. He continued the state policy of protecting lions started by his father, taking on the establishment of empire to do so.
Author's collection.

Though the Gir continued to be ravaged by grazing, forest fires, and the like, it came under the systematic control of the administration. It had been terra incognita to most Europeans at the close of the 19th century. In places the jungle was so dense that it was impossible to find a trail or move about without a good guide.[31] To compound the general inhospitable nature of the forest, "a very bad type of malarial fever prevails in the forest and its outskirts especially during the latter end of the rains and cold weather".[32] Which meant that the British would suffer the depredations of mosquitoes the most as they usually travelled in the cool six months between October and March. To top it all, the jungle was still reverberating with the exploits of the outlaws who had made it their home in the 19th century.

C.A. Kincaid, the Judicial Assistant to the Agent to the Governor of Bombay in 1902, sang the praises of the Gir in his poem "Kathiland":

Would you know the joys of waking
ere the earliest dawn is breaking,
Lest the cheetal at the pool should drink his fill?
Would you know the joys of sitting
till the night birds are a flitting,
That the panther may return to his kill?
You shall know them at Tellala
where the Hirun rushes foaming,
As it strives in vain to batter down its weir;
Where the sambhur bells the night through
to the hinds that may be roaming,
And the lions wake the echoes of the Gir.[33]

There were few takers for this sentiment and unfortunately those few were usually after the lion's skin, literally, which led to the alarming drop in lion numbers. Lord Curzon having heard of the lions' plight cancelled his visit to the Gir during his proposed state visit to Junagadh in November 1900. Lieutenant Colonel

Hunting party of Jam Ranmalji in Barda hills

■ Frescos from the Lakhota palace, Jamnagar, depict a noble hunter about to strike a charging lion with a sword, and (opposite) a dead lion about to be carried away.

Courtesy Jaydev Nansy C.E.

Darbar was always very liberal in giving both local officers and others permission to shoot one.[40]

It may be noted that this description of the situation was less than a decade into Nawab Rasulkhanji's reign. The nawab quickly followed with a letter to Lord Curzon the viceroy himself, on August 8, 1901:

Your Excellency's kind and considerate suggestion of preserving the Gir Lion – a noble but a very rare animal – from extinction, is most scrupulously attended to, but the task has become specially hard and difficult because the natural strength and ferocity of the animals has generally been impaired to some extent owing to the scarcity of animals of prey in the Gir Jungle, consequent on the last famine, and one or two have been reported to have died of starvation, some of them have left their lairs in the forest and gone over to the plain country on the borders of the Gir, belonging to my territory, as well as over that under His Highness the Gaekwar and other minor states and Talukas in search of prey.

It is apprehended that their truancy from their ordinary haunts, and falling upon domestic animals such as cattle belonging to the subjects of this state as well as of others in the vicinity and precincts of villages may induce the persons suffering to shoot them.

Orders prohibiting the killing of lions are strictly enforced in the state and as regards other states and Talukas in the neighbourhood, I am trying my best, through the Political Agent, to induce them as to arrange that neither their subjects nor their officers might kill the truants, but drive them back to the jungles by frightening as usual. It is however to be seen how far these endeavours will prove effective.

I have ventured to trouble Your Excellency with this narration as I deem it a pleasant duty to do everything to carry out Your Excellency's suggestion to preserve this rare animal. But in spite of our strenuous efforts in this direction, I am afraid that this noble race will be extinguished by the hands of common people, unless the prohibition of destroying it is strictly enforced in all surrounding places alike.[41]

The problem of Junagadh state is clearly set out here. While protection was enforced within its boundaries, i.e. lions were only allowed to be shot if permission was granted by the state, there was a problem once the lions crossed the state boundary. For the lions of course a state or administrative boundary had no meaning. The British government could only coax, advise, or threaten the neighbouring states and talukas, and there were limits beyond which they could not go. Such actions were not effective enough to preserve the lions, as the rulers of these small principalities were free to do what they chose in their territories. They considered Junagadh's lions "fair game" in their areas.

The silver lining was that, on Junagadh state's prompting, Baroda state amended its law of 1876 to protect lions effectively, though the Gaekwad reserved the right to give permission for killing a lion under certain circumstances.[42] In Bhavnagar state as well, there was a similar ban. But in both states the maharajas kept the right to hunt lions and every once in a while this caused some friction with Junagadh as many a lion was decoyed out of Junagadh to be shot. Fenton records:

> Moreover, although there are no lions in the adjoining district of Amreli under
> Baroda, the country being unsuitable, one of the best jungles on the Junagadh side,
> abuts on the boundary between the two states, and I should be sorry to say how
> many *lions have been decoyed across this line and killed by unscrupulous
> sportsmen* [emphasis added].[43]

The end of the famine period also saw what Wynter-Blyth describes as a "profound" change in the behaviour of lions. They were never again heard of as being a menace to humans, which was probably owing to conditions returning to normal in the Gir, the cattle moving out, and the prey base recovering.[44]

Though lion shikar was regulated and controlled by the nawab throughout his reign, he did allow them to be shot off and on. In March 1905 Lord Lamington, Governor of Bombay, went to the Gir. His party shot four lions, Lord Curzon's example notwithstanding. It was in this shoot that Major H.C. Carnegie, Political Agent of Halar, was charged and killed by a wounded lion as we have seen earlier.[45]

Protectors of lions
Gir forest straddled three major principalities – Junagadh, Baroda, and
Bhavnagar. The rulers of these states
jealously guarded the lion as it was
considered royal game. Strangely for this
reason the lion survived until the
independence of India and beyond.
■ The last Nawab of Junagadh with his
trophy. Unlike other princes he was not
an avid shikari and shot very rarely.
Author's collection.

services of W.A. Wallinger of the Forest Department of Bombay Presidency were
sought in 1913 and his working plan became the basis of resource management and
protection of the forest.

On the question of protection of lions, H.D. Rendall took up the matter where the
nawab's administration had left it. W.A. Wallinger painted a very gloomy picture of
the number of lions left[54] and making that the cause, he dashed off a letter on May
13, 1913 to the Agent to the Governor asking the latter to ensure cooperation from
neighbouring states and talukas. In June of the same year, he issued a notification of
Junagadh state wherein he referred to the 1909 notification of Nawab Rasulkhanji,
stating that the number of lions was now "seriously diminished" and all steps would
be taken for the preservation of lions and directed that all "Junagadh subjects should
cooperate in this purpose". The same notification was published in the *Kathiawar
Gazetteer* under the authority of W.P. Cowie, Personal Assistant to the Agent to the
Governor, with the addition that it requested the neighbouring states and talukas to
endeavour to cooperate in the effort.[55]

Three princes wanted to shoot lions about this time and approached the
administrator L. Robertson. Kumar Shri Vijayrajji of Kutch was informed that two
lions had already been promised to other sportsmen and he, therefore, could not be

Protectors of lions

■ Maharaja Sayaji Rao Gaekwad of
Baroda shot this lion in Amreli district in
1900, the trophy was among the largest
lions recorded in India.
Author's collection.

■ Maharaja Krishnakumarsinhji of
Bhavnagar (right) stands beside Yuvraj
Pratapsinhji of Wankaner with a lion shot
by the latter in Mytiala forest in
Bhavnagar state, 1932.
Courtesy Y. Digvijaysinh of Wankaner.

accommodated. Maharaja Jam Saheb Ranjitsinhji of Navanagar whose depredations were to exasperate Junagadh was somewhat sternly informed that he could not be granted permission to shoot in the Gir because, as Robertson put it:

> I say roundly that my jungle [Junagadh's Gir] will be quite enough shot by my own friends....
>
> I hear today that you have gone to shoot at Mendarda, of course the Mendarda jungle has nothing to do with me ... and I am sending orders that my men are not to prevent animals [leopards] from the Junagadh Gir crossing the boundary should they be attracted by your kills [baits].
>
> I have done so on the understanding that your party will not shoot a lion, should a lion appear in any of your beats or at any of your kills.

Navanagar state had extended financial assistance to Jetpur state which had a small enclave of Gir forest. Ranjitsinhji often camped at Andhaniya in Jetpur territory and shot lions to the chagrin of Junagadh's nawabs and administrators.

The third applicant Maharaja Ganga Singh of Bikaner was informed through his private secretary that the request for his visit to the Gir in 1913 could not be accommodated. Citing Wallinger's findings on how few lions were left in the Gir, Robertson wrote, surely the Maharaja would take a "sportsman's view and understand the difficulties of our position", though before Wallinger's report was received, he had agreed in February to the visit. A few years later in 1917 the Raja of Poonch, a feudatory of the state of Jammu and Kashmir, was informed that his request for a lion shoot could not be met as such permissions were given only in exceptional circumstances and "moreover many applications [were] already upon our waiting list"![56] After all the ruler of Poonch was not in the same league as the Maharaja of Bikaner.

Another ticklish problem developed during the British administration of Junagadh. H.D. Rendall received a letter in 1914 from L. Robertson who by this time had become Secretary, Political Department of the Government of Bombay Presidency, that the Secretary of State for India had received a request from the British Museum, London, for an Indian lion – which meant that a skin and complete skeleton were required. It may be noted that Nawab Rasulkhanji had sent a live lion in 1902 to the Alipore Zoo, Calcutta which arrived there much the worse for wear, and the skin of a lion had been procured for the Bombay Natural History Society. The administrator was therefore in a delicate position. He replied that the request should be postponed for at least a year or two because he

> ... had during the last year to refuse requests of several Chiefs for a shoot in the Gir. It is extremely difficult to secure cooperation in this direction, and you are aware that there have been one or two unpleasant incidents in this connection. We might therefore be liable to misconstruction of an undesirable kind if we transgressed our own pact, even in the interest of science, and I am particularly anxious to avoid any such impression.[57]

In the event, the matter rested there.

It appears that at the turn of the 20th century it was a common practice to send all captured cubs from the jungle to Junagadh to be kept there in one or another garden of the town.[58] In 1919 this practice was banned by a state circular addressed to the officers of the Gir:

> ... a havaldar of a block caught cubs of a vaghan [tigress] and gave them to the block officer who in turn sent them to us. In this manner innocent cubs have been

harassed which has not been liked by us at all. Similarly Namdar Hazur Shree
[Nawab Saheb] has also not liked it, therefore in future cubs of vaghan [tigress] or
singhan [lioness] are not to be caught or harassed....[59]

There were no tigers in the Gir and the cubs could have been those of a leopard.
Considering that the circular is signed by K.G. Trivedi, Chief Range Officer of the
Gir, it is an inexplicable error.

The British administration also faced other problems of cattle killed by lions in
Junagadh and beyond, lions shot in Baroda and elsewhere, and so on. But they
remained steadfast in their resolve to enforce protection for these animals. They
built on the foundation laid by Nawab Rasulkhanji and his diwans which in itself
was supported by the British government.

Many princes had hunting grounds in India and larger states such as Gwalior,
Mysore, Cooch Behar, and others had exceptionally good ones. They protected them
as state properties, animals were monopolies regulated by the rulers themselves,
particularly the large carnivores which were usually tigers. Many of these princes
hunted extensively, the epitome of them all being the well known case of the
Maharaja of Sarguja who accounted for over 1,100 tigers. And yet state monopoly
gave breathing space and time to the animals because their habitat was strictly
protected and the number of persons hunting them was limited to the maharaja, his
family, and perhaps a favoured guest. Two species, the hangul and the sangai,
survived because of the protection they received from the administrations of the
states of Jammu and Kashmir and Manipur.

While the case of the lion is similar to that of the hangul and sangai it is unique
in its own way. Nawab Rasulkhanji had never shot a lion. He was not interested in
shooting lions, and their protection he considered to be his responsibility. As he
himself has recorded, the lion was to be found only in the Gir in India and its
disappearance from there would spell doom for the species.

His bid to give protection to a large carnivore was the earliest anywhere in the
world. Though lions were hunted in his state, the numbers of such hunts were very
few and permissions were hard to come by. He began the effort that pulled the lion
back from the precipice of annihilation.

There is another important fallout from his policy. His demise saw a British
administration take charge of Junagadh followed by the effete administration of the
last nawab. However, Rasulkhanji had built a tradition which was easy to follow and
difficult to ignore. This was his noble legacy.

CHAPTER 9

The Last Nawab Battles On

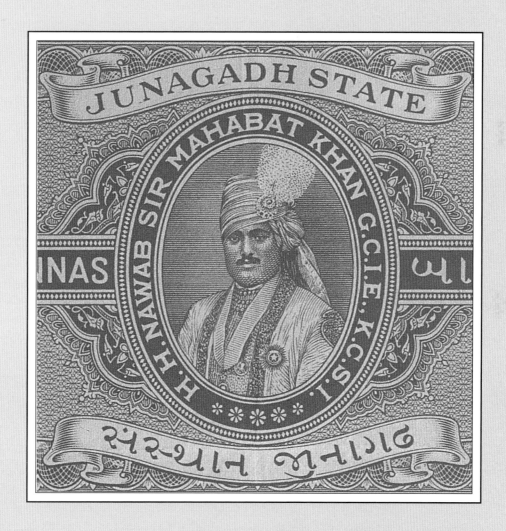

Tipu Sultan on his throne
■ Unlike other princes and kings in India Tipu was obsessed by tigers, his throne naturally was a "tiger throne".
The Trustees of The National Museums of Scotland.

Honorary Colonel His Highness Sir Mahbatkhanji III, G.C.I.E., K.C.S.I.* Nawab Saheb of Junagadh[1] as he would become by 1947, was invested with full powers in 1920 by the British government on his attaining majority. On ascending the throne he issued a proclamation saying:

> With complete confidence I command my beloved subjects to obey my orders; to be loyal to me as you have been to my dynasty hitherto, to give respect to my duly authorized officers, and to live with each other with understanding, peace and harmony for that is how happiness and development are attained....[2]

With these lofty words began the reign of the ninth and last nawab of the Babi dynasty. In general, in spite of the economic crash of 1929, the second world war of 1939–45, and the turbulent waves of the independence movement beating the shores of princely India, it was a time of peace and progress in the state. The administrative machinery set up over the previous two decades held fast and served the nawab well, with a few hiccups now and then, until everything came apart in the fateful year of 1947. But there were foreshadows of coming events. As early as 1911, the British Administrator had some misgivings about the child who would be nawab, for the state's administration report for that year declares:

> The Minor Chief [Mahbatkhanji] is somewhat backward, but under the care of his tutor and guardian Mr. Turkhad, he has already advanced both in physical and mental attainments....[3]

As mentioned earlier, the teenage prince was sent to England and after that to Mayo College, Ajmer, under the guardianship of English tutors and with his companion Mahamad Bhai. Even after assuming the title of nawab, he remained for the most part, a nominal head of state. It is said that though he took interest in the administration of the state, he preferred to let his diwans have a free hand. Between 1920 and 1924 three Hindu diwans who were Nagar brahmans held office, until his childhood companion Amir Sheikh Mahamad Bhai Saheb, as he was now styled, was elevated to that office in 1924 and held sway till February 1932. He was given the honorific title of vazir in 1931, but came under a cloud soon thereafter and had to suddenly leave his post. The nawab had to fall back on the imperial government's resources and Sir Patrick Cadell took over as diwan. He was followed by J. Monteath in 1935[4] who revamped the entire state machinery. Three Indian Muslim diwans came after this, two of whom served the state faultlessly. The last one presided over the final fateful days of the state.

Today Mahbatkhanji is all but forgotten in India, his one monumental act of political folly having consigned him to oblivion. If remembered at all, it is for his fondness for dogs and his excesses, real or imagined. The redoubtable V.P. Menon, Secretary to the Ministry of States, Government of India, who was one of the architects of the integration of Indian states into the Dominion of India, wrote that the nawab had "hundreds" of dogs and he had organized a wedding for two of his pets on which a huge sum of money was spent, the wedding day being declared a state holiday![5] According to another source, the nawab's favourite golden retriever bitch was "married" to "Bobby" of the Nawab of Mangrol. The groom rode on an elephant and was accompanied by a wedding party of 250 dogs. A three-day holiday was declared in the state to mark the event.[6] While it is true that the nawab was fond

---

* Extra Knight Grand Commander of the Indian Empire and Honorary Knight Commander of the Star of India. The Order of the Star of India was instituted in 1861 and the Order of the Indian Empire was instituted in 1877 by Queen Victoria to honour, among others, Indian princes and British subjects who had served the Indian Empire.

Junagadh throne and chairs of state with lion handles
■ These are preserved in the Darbar Hall at Junagadh. The throne is surmounted by a *chhattra*, the traditional Indian symbol of royalty. It is like the throne of any Hindu ruler.
Photograph: Bhushan Pandya.

of dogs and had many of them, enquiries with the late Shambhuprasad Desai, IAS, who was on the nawab's personal staff, with Jaisukhlal P. Sodha the author of the only biography of the nawab and others in Kathiawar reveal that such reports were often exaggerated.[7] All those who knew the nawab talk of his benign and gentle nature. His love of the Kathi horse (the Kathiawari breed) was legion. He maintained a fine stud farm and preserved the breed from extinction. These horses, used as mounts by the Gujarat police today, are a part of his legacy. He was equally fond of cows and particularly the Gir breed which he protected. Sodha records that the nawab's two favourite cows were named Kapila and Janaki. The nawab's administration banned slaughter of draught and milch cattle and forbade selling of cattle for slaughter in 1944–45.[8] According to Shambhuprasad Desai, the nawab's favourite cow was called Kaveri and she went wherever the nawab went in his state. He had to see Kaveri's face first thing in the morning. Once while returning from Veraval to Junagadh on his special train, he suddenly found that Kaveri had been left behind. He stopped the train for her to be brought on to it, and when she was, he went to her, embraced her, and said "Mother, did I forget you? Do forgive me."[9]

As for the lions, he considered them to be his own. They were royal game and he shot them as per the custom of his time though he exercised self-imposed limits. However, his impulse was always to protect rather than shoot. Often the nawab would go for shikar to the Gir. He would sit on the machan and wait. The Forest Department staff would have worked tirelessly to produce the largest lion with the darkest mane for the Master of Junagadh. The beat would begin, the lion would come through the path in front of the machan but the nawab would not shoot. He would come down and say "*Mian, kala nahin hai, agle jumme aunga*" (The lion's mane is not black, I'll come next Friday). He thus made sure that he knew what was happening in the jungle and generally kept his staff on their toes.[10]

One way of gauging the number of lions shot by sportsmen is to look at the records of taxidermists who specialize in making trophies. Of the several establishments that came up, two stand out – Cuthertson & Harper of Calcutta and own modern postal system. In 1928 a decision was made by the state to issue postage stamps which were to be printed at the Security Press at Nasik. Four symbols were chosen: a likeness of the nawab, Junagadh city, a Kathi horse, and a Gir lion. When the samples of the stamps arrived in Junagadh, the likeness of the lion did not satisfy Diwan Amir Sheikh Mahamad Bhai. He remarked, in a letter to Colonel G.H. Willis, Master of Security Printing, Nasik, India, that it was "… a poor effort, but I think you can perhaps arrange a lion for us. The Gir lion and the African lion are identical as you will see from the picture"![18]

The final result was satisfactory enough and postage stamps were issued with the denomination of ½ anna and 4 annas with the Gir lion and denominations of 2 and 8 annas for the Kathi horse.[19] The mane of the lion and its general aspect are realistic enough to identify it as a specimen from the Gir. This was the first time that any animal had featured on a postage stamp anywhere in the Indian Empire. On an enquiry from one Mr McDonald from Jabalpur, the diwan's office replied on February 28, 1931 explaining the symbolism of the two animals:

> … "Gir lion" symbolizes the survival of the Indian lion in the Gir forest of this state alone throughout India. The Gir lion, accordingly, is also one of the symbols in the Armorial bearings of this state.
>
> …"Kathi Horse" signifies *Zortalbi* or tribute formally collected by the Junagadh State Cavalry mounted on Kathi horses (though it is collected since 1821 through the British Government) from no less than 134 out of 193 states and Talukas of Kathiawar.[20]

The lion had to wait another 34 years to again grace a postage stamp in India,[21] while the Kathi horse, once an indispensable war machine, still awaits its turn. It is strange that the lion did not make an appearance on the British period postage stamps as it had done on East India Company gold mohurs very much earlier. Actually, as early as 1853, the East India Company prepared essays (a contemplated design drawn and laid out) for postage stamps with the lion on them. Proofs from steel engraved dies in vermilion, black, and blue were printed. Pulls from copper plates were taken as late as in 1922 as well, but that is where things remained.[22] For whatever reason, these postage stamps were not issued.

The reign of Rasulkhanji and the British administration had set the stage for Mahbatkhanji's battles. He had inherited both the problem and the response to it. It is to his credit that he continued on the path of preservation in spite of all odds. He may have had other faults, but lions for him held a special place as we shall see. Within one year of Mahabatkhanji ascending the throne, he was faced with a full-blown lion crisis. He received a letter from Maharaja Jam Saheb Ranjitsinhji of Navanagar informing him that he and Maharaja Ganga Singh of Bikaner were invited by Darbar Muluwala of Pithadia, Jetpur (a Kathi taluka enclave in Junagadh state) to shoot in the Mendarda portion of the Gir. He was writing to Mahbatkhanji at the request of Maharaja Ganga Singh for permission to shoot a lion. The nawab replied by telegram to say that he could not allow a lion to be shot from Mendarda territory and followed it up with a letter to Jam Saheb Ranjitsinhji to say that twelve lions had been shot that year already and the matter of such depredations in neighbouring territories had already become a subject of correspondence with the British government. He was sure, he added, Maharaja Ganga Singh would not think of shooting "my lions" in the territories of neighbouring principalities. On receiving this letter Jam Saheb Ranjitsinhji sent a letter to Mahbatkhanji asking if he and

Maharaja Ganga Singh could call on him at Junagadh. The same request was made by Maharaja Ganga Singh as well. The nawab sent a polite reply but regretted that he was unable to meet them as he was busy with the approaching Ramazan Id and subsequent engagements in the state![23]

Relations between Jam Saheb Ranjitsinhji and Junagadh state thus reached a nadir. It is interesting to note that in 1907 when Ranjitsinhji had become the Jam Saheb of Navanagar, it was Junagadh state which had been his benefactor. The latter had even provided him with Arab bodyguards, a large retinue of servants and even cooks to accompany him to Jamnagar to ensure his safety when he went there to take charge of his principality.[24] Now in 1920, barely thirteen years later, the son of his benefactor had had enough. Incidentally, Junagadh was not the only state which suffered Jam Saheb Ranjitsinhji's shikar forays; he regularly tied baits for leopards along the Navanagar Porbandar border to lure them into his territory for shikar.[25] Out of exasperation the nawab addressed a letter to E. Maconochie, Agent to the Governor in Kathiawar, along with the correspondence he had had with Jam Saheb Ranjitsinhji and Maharaja Ganga Singh. The letter bears quoting at some length as it hits at the nub of the problem as seen by Mahbatkhanji. He wrote:

> As a matter of fact the real point at issue is the ownership of lions and the political right of inviting distinguished visitors to Kathiawad for lion shikar. The occasional shooting of lions which stray from the forest to surrounding territories is of no particular importance. The race can never be wiped out thereby. But what I complain of is that lions are tempted to stray outside by tying up buffaloes just over my borders ... organized shikar parties go out and shoot lions under cover of the pretext that they are doing damage outside the forest. This is nothing more or less than poaching from which I think I have a right to be protected by [the Imperial] Government. If I were to take the law into my own hands as my forefathers would have done, the result would be a constant series of border affrays which would endanger the peace of this part of Kathiawad.
>
> It is an unquestionable fact that the house of the lion is the Gir forest and equally unquestioned that the forest is my ancestral property. The preservation of the forest which covers about 500 sq. miles [1,295 square kilometres] of my territory is supposed to be of value to the province as a whole, not only as a constant source of grass and fire wood, but also because of its effect on rainfall. But what has undoubtedly weighed with the Nawabs of Junagadh in the past and carries weight also with me is that the forest is the last sanctuary of Indian Lions. If the lion were eliminated, I should certainly adopt a policy of disafforestation which would add to my revenues and simplify the difficulties of administration. The sacrifice which the neighbouring jurisdictional holders are called upon to bear by reason of the existence of the lions is small. The brunt of it is borne by Junagadh and ownership with all that it implies rightly appertains to Junagadh.
>
> I would therefore ask that the [Imperial] Government may fully consider the matter and use their influence to see that my rights are respected and especially the scandal of tying up buffaloes within sight of my borders is stopped.[26]

Apart from the nawab claiming ownership of lions, for the first time he points out that the lion is what we would call today a flagship species for the forest which has wider direct and indirect benefits to humans.

E. Maconochie referred the matter to A. Montgomery, Secretary to the Government, Political Department, Bombay with a covering letter which pointed out:

Postage stamps of Junagadh 1929 issue

■ Four types of stamps were issued: one had the likeness of Nawab Mahbatkhanji III wearing a *safa,* he looks like any one of his brother Hindu princes. One had a scene of Junagadh town and Girnar mountain, and the other two types had the Gir lion and the Kathi horse. These were the earliest representations of animals on postage stamps in the Indian empire.

Author's collection.

explicitly states that the situation was alarming and therefore, all shikar was being banned until further orders and permission henceforth would be given by the nawab himself only in exceptional cases.[37] This declaration too was during the tenure of an Indian diwan, Darbar Viravala Muluvala of Bagasra.

Thus in effect only very limited shikar would take place within the state and more often than not only Indian princes and British officers were given permission for it. For example, Maharaja Ganga Singh of Bikaner shot four lions between 1940 and 1941[38] in spite of all the previous problems he had earlier with Mahbatkhanji. Khan Saheb Gulammoinuddinkhanji of Manavadar sent seven lion skins – three in 1940 alone – to van Ingen & van Ingen.[39] It is likely however, that most of his trophies were obtained outside Junagadh territory.

While there was a method in the control of shikar within Junagadh, the neighbouring states and talukas remained a problem. For instance, in 1934 M.K. Chandrabhanusinhji of Wankaner went to Mendarda for lion shikar on the invitation

of Darbar Mansurwala of Anida, one of the talukadars of the Mendarda enclave within Junagadh state. He shot one lion and three lionesses, though Junagadh had advance information of this shikar and according to Chandrabhanusinhji's diary "The Junagadh people gave us a lot of trouble by firing shots in the air, they used to frighten animals [refers mainly to lions] all day and night."[40]

M.K. Natwarsinhji of Gondal wounded a lion in 1938 near the village of Dadar in the Gondal state enclave within Junagadh. He followed up the animal on foot. According to one source he was carrying his rifle in *dang* (shepherd's staff) fashion across the back of his neck, supporting his hands on it, when he was charged and mauled by the wounded lion. Another source says his shikari who was carrying his rifle ran away on being charged.[41] He was hospitalized in Junagadh but succumbed to his injuries. The internal report of the Forest Officer, Sasan Division which went up to the diwan of Junagadh wryly states that on November 26, 1938 the Gondal prince had wounded a lion or lioness which in turn mauled him and two other men and "it is not clear whether it [the animal] is dead or still alive",[42] but there is no mention of the condition of the prince or any members of his party!

Among the unusual incidents of princely sport was that of Thakore Dharmendra Sinhji of Rajkot who died of a heart attack while drinking coffee after having shot a lion in 1940 at Dalkhania in Baroda Gir.[43] During the early decades of the 20th century one prince took great delight in poaching lions and paying a fine in Baroda territory. When Baroda state wrote to tell him that the next time he wanted to do lion shikar the state would readily make the necessary arrangements, the erring prince lost interest and stopped shooting lions! Another prince is reputed to have brought his son-in-law for a lion shoot. He had an understanding with the Junagadh *pagi*s whom he was to pay a truly "princely sum" of Rs 5,000 to drive out a lion from Junagadh into a neighbouring state. Finally, the sum was not paid and the shikar party returned empty-handed. Bilkha, another neighbouring state was ruled by Darbar Rawatvala who was Nawab Mahbatkhanji's contemporary and a close friend. He shot about ten lions between 1937 and 1950. The nawab invited him to Sasan Gir in 1941 and gave him a healthy male lion in the hope that he would stop shooting lions, now that he had his own. It did not have the desired effect.[44]

Among the prominent British personages who went to the Gir for a shoot were Sir George Ambrose Lloyd, Governor of Bombay in 1922, General Lord Rawlinson, Commander-in-Chief of the Indian Army in 1923, and the highest of them all – Lord Linlithgow, Viceroy who shot a lion in 1940.[45] Lord Curzon's plea was conveniently forgotten if his successors were at all aware of it.

It appears that the Junagadh state gave permission to shoot about three lions every year according to one authority, while another mentions a figure of four or five lions per year. Thus about five lions annually were being shot legally within the state.[46] The administration reports of Junagadh started mentioning that steps were being taken to protect lions in the state from 1914–15 onwards right up to 1942–43. The reports for the same years also gave information about lions, which the state had claimed as theirs, that were being shot outside the Junagadh territories without control. The reports give the following figures:

YEAR	NO. OF LIONS SHOT	NO. OF LEOPARDS SHOT
1920–21	12: large and small	
1935–36	12: 5 lions, 2 lionesses, 5 cubs	3: 2 leopards, 1 leopardess
1936–37	4: 1 lion, 3 lionesses	4: 3 leopards, 1 leopardess
1937–38	11: 9 lions, 2 lionesses	
1938–39	6: 4 lions, 2 lionesses	10
1939–40	9: 4 lions, 5 lionesses	4
1940–41	16: 12 lions, 4 lionesses	
1941–42	12: 8 lions, 4 lionesses	
1942–43	7: 2 lions, 5 lionesses[47]	

On an average therefore the neighbouring princes shot 9.6, say ten, lions a year during the eight-year period between 1935–36 and 1942–43 based on the information reaching Junagadh officials. It must be noted however that the information could not have been complete and the actual number may have been higher. Thus, while Junagadh was shooting a maximum of five lions a year, the neighbouring states and talukadars accounted for twice that number in spite of all the efforts of the nawab. Protection of the lion remained the latter's problem till the end. In fact the 1934–35 report mentions that a census had been ordered to see how far poaching from outside the state had diminished the numbers of Gir lions. The next year gives the result of the census and declares that only about 150 lions were left in Junagadh territory.[48]

Effectively, this meant that on an average more than fifteen lions were shot annually. This was after all the efforts the nawab made to protect them and particularly to stop or reduce the number of lions being shot outside Junagadh. What would have happened without his efforts can easily be imagined. It is evident that the nawab's policy was a resounding success, in spite of lions being shot at this level and the chaos of 1947 caused by the nawab's accession to Pakistan, when several more lions were shot. The lion population not only survived but actually increased impressively between 1936 and 1950. M.A. Wynter-Blyth's census figures of 1950 threw up a conservative number of 217 to 227 lions and a maximum number of 243 to 251 lions surviving in that year.

The protection of lions in Junagadh was a result of the traditions and beliefs of the time. Traditionally, the largest predator was reserved for royal game, and in Junagadh this was the lion. The rulers of the state considered the lion their property as indeed were the forests in which it lived. The last nawab of Junagadh laid claim to lions everywhere in Kathiawar on the grounds that his lions were wandering about and the princes of neighbouring states and talukas were poaching his lions when they entered their territories. Though the nawab never propagated a complete ban on shooting lions, he was concerned that the total loss of the lion would be a loss to zoology and though unstated, it would cause the disappearance of a unique source of state pride and patronage as well. Whatever the nawab's other faults, on the matter of protecting lions, he was steadfast in his pursuit. It was the efforts of Junagadh state under the last two nawabs, with some encouragement from the British administration, that we have to thank for the survival of over 200 lions and their habitat, the Gir forest, in 1947.

CHAPTER 10

The Dominion of India Inherits Lions

Princely shikar in independent India
The control of lion shikar passed on to the Rajpramukh of Saurashtra state, Jam Digvijaysinhji of Navanagar, who permitted shikar to favoured princes.
■ Maharaja Sawai Man Singh II of Jaipur, Rajpramukh of Rajasthan, with his lion trophy during this period.
■ Maharaja Hari Singh of Jammu and Kashmir with the Rajpramukh and his shikar party.
Author's collection.

The change of guard

■ Dr Rajendra Prasad, the first President of India, on a visit to Gir in 1952. After a decade a head of state had come calling on lions. Unlike his predecessor Linlithgow, he had come only to see them and visit the Somnath temple nearby.

Author's collection.

The events of 1947 were an unexpected disaster for the Gir and its inhabitants. At the time of independence, 1,720 square kilometres of the forest were under the Forest Department of Junagadh state. Gaekwad's Baroda state had 300, Bhavnagar 37, and Jetpur 51 – that is a total of 2,111 square kilometres.[7] In addition, the jungle extended to smaller principalities in the neighbourhood such as Bilkha and Mendarda. While peripheral areas of the Gir forest became a part of the Dominion of India without a hitch, its heart arrived after much confusion, uncertainty, and vandalization over a period of four months, from August to November 1947. The administration of Junagadh state which had been well organized and strong hitherto, became lame. At its head the nawab, his diwan, and the Executive Council had been engulfed by the larger-than-life events which led to the state itself being snuffed out. The protection of Gir and its inhabitants took a backseat during these tumultuous times. Minor princes from neighbouring principalities and other shikaris who would normally not have a hope of shooting a lion were now emboldened. Most of the principalities surrounding Junagadh had always considered lions fair game if they had strayed out of Junagadh territory. With the central authority of Junagadh weakened and preoccupied, here was a chance not to be missed. It appears that several lions were shot, of which no record exists other than those of fading memories.[8] E.P. Gee recorded that a "wholesale killing of wildlife" took place, "particularly of herbivores".[9] This is not surprising, for venison is a delicacy for a Rajput or Muslim shikari though traditionally minded Kathi shikaris would not kill chinkara or blackbuck. M.A. Wynter-Blyth, Principal of Rajkumar College (the former princes' college at Rajkot which had opened to the public in the early 1940s),

a renowned lepidopterist whose work is standard reference today half a century after its appearance, and an expert on the Gir and its lions, was far more forthcoming about these goings on. Writing barely 1½ years after these events, he records that "at least 5 lions and 2 lionesses ... [were] shot there [in Jetpur state territory alone, the time honoured recipient of vagrant lions of the Junagadh Gir] in 1947.... The slaughter in this year, however, was exceptional."[10]

Several states provided their police force for security duties in Junagadh state after the administration collapsed. One such state was Lunawada whose ruler Maharana Virbhadrasinhji requested Shyamaldas Gandhi for, and was granted, a lion in recognition of his state's services. He shot a male lion in Savarkundla.[11] I have it on good authority that at least three more lions were shot in the same locality about that time and there were similar reports from other areas on the borders of former Junagadh state territory.

What if anything the nawab thought of this, if he knew about it, is unknown. He had spent his entire reign trying to protect lions, but this destruction was the direct consequence of his own actions, something which he seems to have realized moments after he left his palace for Karachi. But there was yet more to come. Three events took place in quick succession. In January 1948 the princes of Kathiawar signed a covenant "to unite and integrate their respective states to form The United State of Kathiawar". A supplementary covenant appointed Jam Saheb Digvijaysinhji of Navanagar Rajpramukh of this state for his lifetime. And finally, yet another supplementary covenant was signed to integrate the states and principalities of Junagadh, Manavadar, Mangrol, Bantwa, Sardargarh, and Babariawad into the "United State of Saurashtra" as it had now come to be known.[12] Thus, Junagadh's political identity was totally merged into the new dispensation while the nawab was in self-imposed exile in Karachi. It will be recalled that Nawab Mahbatkhanji and his administration had consistently taken exception to Jam Saheb Ranjitsinhji's shikar activities on the borders of Gir in years gone by. Now Ranjitsinhji's successor by adoption, Digvijaysinhji had become the Rajpramukh for life. He was quick to take unto himself the nawab's lost prerogative of protecting and permitting lion shikar! This surely was the unkindest cut of all for the nawab.

It is tempting to speculate about what would have happened if the nawab had acceded to India. As head of the premier state of Kathiawar, he would have ended up being the Rajpramukh. This would have given him direct control over the protection of lions including over his troublesome neighbours for the decade 1947–56, for which he had strived all along. It would also have meant that the virtually free-for-all lion shikar would not have taken place in 1947–48.

However, the administration of the new state quickly recovered and started taking corrective action. Wynter-Blyth observed that the new administration of Junagadh stepped in to enforce protection "even more strictly than before" and the Saurashtra government took steps to "prevent the shooting of lions in its territories adjoining the Gir, they are in no danger of extinction, and, an increase in numbers may well occur. Their only enemy seems to be man, and if left alone by him, I believe them well able to look after themselves."[13] He went on to record that between November 1947 and March 1949 lion shikar was stopped completely and only a "negligible" number of lions was poached. By March the situation was considered stable and encouraging enough to allow trophy shikar of four male lions per year,[14] now the Rajpramukh's prerogative, as had been the practice during the nawab's time, though *his* administration had restricted the numbers usually to three per year. The real achievement would have been to stop the shooting of lions in the territories of the principalities bordering Junagadh, but that would take some time. According to Wynter-Blyth, ten to twelve lions were shot in such encounters annually before the integration and merger of princely states in 1947 and 1948,[15] and this continued for a couple of years more. But there was another downside too. He feared that, with the propensity of lions to multiply fast, if such strict protection was continued the population would increase in a short span of time and lions would wander out far away from Gir, which in turn would increase lion-human conflicts. He therefore saw "no reason to suggest any modification in the quota of permits to shoot lions that are being granted at the moment".[16] It should be noted that he was talking of a time when the administration of the state was far more effective and abuse of the system, particularly for such a visible activity, was hardly possible.

In faraway New Delhi the lion was receiving attention in symbolism of the highest order. The Constituent Assembly had come into being to draft the Constitution of India. It laboured from December 1946 to November 1949 when it completed its task. Its own emblem was an outline of India with a tusker superimposed on it encircled by a double circle with the words "CONSTITUENT

On postage stamps again

■ More than thirty years after its first appearance the lion adorns a postage stamp in 1963. It is the well known "Tilyo".

■ Thirteen years later in 1976 another lion appears on a postage stamp.

■ (opposite) Twenty-three years later another encore, this time four stamps on a first-day cover.

Author's collection.

ASSEMBLY INDIA" in the Latin script. One of its objectives was to decide on the national flag and the national emblem.

At my instance, my son Udaybhanusinh, an advocate of the High Court, Bombay undertook research to ascertain how both the flag and the emblem of the Republic came about (see Appendix 5).

An ad hoc committee chaired by Rajendra Prasad and which included among other luminaries Maulana Abul Kalam Azad, C. Rajagopalachari, K.M. Munshi, and B.R. Ambedkar was constituted to make recommendations to the Constituent Assembly regarding the national flag and the national emblem. The committee met on July 10, 1947 and decided that the flag should be the flag of the Indian National Congress with modifications. The tricolour was to have saffron (kesari) on top, white in the middle, and dark green at the bottom. The emblem on the flag would be the "wheel on the capital of Ashoka's Sarnath pillar" in dark blue colour placed at the centre of the middle white band.

The committee also took a tentative decision regarding the emblem and the seal of the republic-to-be which was that

(1) The emblem and the seal should be of the same design.

(2) The design should be an exact reproduction of the whole of the Sarnath Ashoka capital till it joins the stem of the pillar (*sthambha*).

(3) The words "Republic of India" should be superscribed around the emblem and "seal of the Republic of India" around the seal.

The committee decided to meet again to finalize these decisions. They met on July 18, and decided to go ahead with their decision regarding the national flag, but as far as the state seal and emblem were concerned, the committee felt that the matter "was not of immediate urgency, and [the decision] should be postponed until more designs were prepared"![17]

The Constituent Assembly took up the matter of the national flag on July 22. The resolution for its adoption was moved by Jawaharlal Nehru himself and several prominent members spoke in favour of the proposed flag. The resolution was passed unanimously with the whole Assembly standing.[18] The matter of the emblem and the seal however took a curious turn. The Constituent Assembly never approved it and the deliberations were wound up leaving the matter undecided – Udaybhanusinh's research did not throw up any gazette notification and therefore the reasons for and views about the selection of the Ashokan capital remain a matter of speculation.[19] Upon my request Ashok H. Desai, Senior Advocate, Supreme Court of India and former Attorney-General of India, looked into the matter. He came up with a copy of a Press Communiqué dated December 29, 1947 issued by the Ministry of Home Affairs which records the decision on the state emblem and seal.[20] It reads as follows:

> The Government of India have now approved a design of their State Emblem and Seal. It has been decided that the State Emblem and Seal should consist of the Sarnath Lion Capital of Ashoka as it exists at present, looked at from the side which shows the lions standing on an abacus which has a Dharma Chakra in the centre, a bull on the right and a horse on the left, and the outlines of the Dharma Chakras on the extreme right and left. The bell shaped lotus at the bottom of the capital has been omitted as the capital would become too long for effective use as a State Emblem or Seal. The reproduction of the capital should be enclosed in a plain double line (the inner line being thin and the outer thick) rectangular frame.

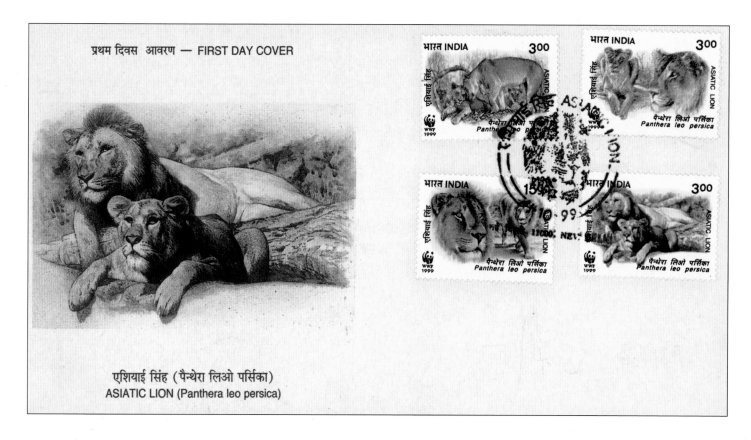

एशियाई सिंह (पैन्थेरा लिओ पर्सिका)
ASIATIC LION (Panthera leo persica)

A suitable motto will be included in due course as soon as one has been decided upon.[21]

But the emblem had an early critic. M. Krishnan, the conservationist and arguably the most prolific popular writer on nature, was not amused. He wrote:

> Have we no animal more representative of the nation, more nobly rendered in our stone, that could have taken the place of Ashoka's lions, which are not Indian in their art and which are third rate as lions?[22]

He made a plea for the elephant, the "king of our forests" which was "entirely Indian" and was most "brilliantly rendered of all our beasts in our art".[23] Krishnan was from Madras and therefore more familiar with the elephant in art, culture, and in nature. His advocacy of the elephant was natural enough. However, the Constituent Assembly had adjourned, and the elephant was not to be the symbol of the Indian Republic.

Thus, deprived of their lotus base and without the motto of *satyameva jayate* which was to follow, Ashoka's lions replaced the British signet as the emblem of the Dominion of India, its most palpably visible bequest. That such a momentous decision was taken by an executive fiat and not by the Constituent Assembly is a fact which has passed into history unnoticed. We have inherited the epitome of a monarchical symbol – of Ashoka who was known as *chakravartin*, universal king – for a republican dispensation.

CHAPTER 11

The Great Numbers Game

THE NEED TO PREPARE an inventory of an asset arises because of its perceived value. Such is the case with animals as well. In India the Asian one-horned or Javan rhinoceros barely survived the 19th century while the Asian two-horned or Sumatran rhinoceros was last reported half a century ago – though there was an unconfirmed report of its sighting from Mizoram in 1972.[1] At any rate, both animals became extinct in India without ever having been counted. The Great Indian one-horned rhinoceros on the other hand did get counted or, rather, estimated. It is believed that there were only twelve animals left in the special reserve created for it at Kaziranga in Assam in 1908.[2] The cheetah on the other hand became extinct in India, with its numbers being estimated more than three decades *after* the event.[3] The tiger population was believed to be about 40,000 in India at the turn of the 20th century according to an estimate by E.P. Gee, whereas M.K. Ranjitsinhji and K. Sankhala felt there were between 25,000 and 30,000 of them left at that time.[4] But when the Government of India and various state governments got down to enumerating tigers as a result of the alarming news of their swift decline, they came up with a figure of 1,827 in 1972,[5] which led to a special programme for their protection.

The case of the lion was no different from the general trend though the particulars were unique to itself. The earliest attempt to guess or estimate lion numbers is reported by Major General William Rice of the Indian Army, who knew Bombay Presidency and Kathiawar and had hunted lions in the Gir around the 1850s. According to him "A native Officer, Jemadar J.K., of Joonaghur State, has shot an immense number of lions in the vast 'Gheer Forest', their chief abode." He computed that there were not above 300 lions left in that country.[6] Though lions were encountered and shot outside the Saurashtra peninsula up to 1891,[7] Gir was their last stronghold. Hence the estimate of their numbers would represent almost their entire surviving population at that time. How accurate was this figure is a moot point.

More than thirty years after General Rice's attempt, the *Kathiawar Gazetteer* of 1884 stated that "there are probably no more than ten or a dozen lions and lionesses left in the whole Gir forest".[8] The statement appears to cover the entire jungle in the states of Junagadh, Baroda, and Bhavnagar, including various other principalities which had some part of the jungle in their territory. The basis of this estimate is not known. But in the same year Colonel J.W. Watson's statistical account of Junagadh was published. Under the heading "wild animals", the lion is described as "the most famous of wild animals" and details are given as to its size, habits, the propensity of males to live in pairs, hunting methods, and so on. Watson, however, does not mention any imminent danger of lions becoming extinct or that their numbers were so low. In fact he does not give any numbers at all.[9] Junagadh state appears to have prepared an estimate in 1893, giving a figure of about 31.[10] Colonel L.L. Fenton, who was in Kathiawar during the great famine of 1899 and hunted lions in the Gir, does not express any alarm about the falling lion population, but merely states that these animals are now found only in the Gir. On the contrary, in his opinion, "The Gir [in 1886] was then at its best in the matter of game of all kinds and a terra incognita to all except a few local Europeans" and Junagadh state officials.[11] There is no doubt that the alarming figure of 12 or even 31 was inaccurate. In fact Edwardes and Fraser, the authors of the "authorized" work on Junagadh state, assert that the *Kathiawar Gazetteer*'s reports were "very misleading".[12]

On hearing that very few lions were left in the Gir, Lord Curzon decided not to pursue his earlier goal of shooting one on his forthcoming visit to Junagadh on

November 3, 1900. When the Political Agent, Rajkot, sent a telegram to that effect on October 10, 1900, it evoked an illuminating reply from Nawab Rasulkhan on November 27, after the viceregal visit to Junagadh. In a semi-official letter the nawab wrote:

> I cannot but observe here that though I fully appreciated and admired your noble consideration in abandoning the lion shooting Your Excellency's giving up the idea has greatly disappointed me.
>
> The cry raised on this side of India that the lions were almost extinct in the Gir forest and that the shooting would help in the final extermination of the animal was far from correct. But as Your Excellency's decision had been published, I did not think it proper to request you to alter it immediately.
>
> I propose however to approach Your Excellency later on with the request to favour me with a shooting excursion in the Gir before Your Excellency's departure from India.[13]

Lord Curzon never came back but the numbers game continued unabated. In 1905 Major H.G. Carnegie the then Political Agent at Halar who was soon to meet his end in the Gir, "was at great pains to investigate the matter during his two years' residency in Junagadh...." He said that in one particular week he had so many cases notified to him that he calculated he had heard of 25 separate lions in that week alone. He gave it as his firm opinion, after considering all the information he had collected, that "there were *in 1905 between sixty and seventy* lions in the Gir. The Junagadh authorities basing their belief on the reports of trackers and jungle villagers, hold that the lions at that time numbered *at least one hundred* [emphases added]".[14] It is not out of place to note here that Jam Saheb Digvijaysinhji of Navanagar told E.P. Gee in 1956 that his estimate was that there were a hundred lions in the Gir circa 1900, though Nawab Rasulkhan let it be known that "only a few" were left.[15]

By 1913 there was another scare about a decrease in the number of lions caused ostensibly by the depredations of Junagadh's neighbours who were shooting them beyond the state's control. H.D. Rendall, the Administrator of Junagadh, thought it fit to address a letter to J. Sladen, Agent to the Governor, Kathiawar, asking him for a notification in the *Agency Gazette* for the protection of lions. He stated in the letter that W.A. Wallinger, F.R.Z.S., the temporary Conservator of Forests, Junagadh, had toured the Gir extensively along with Brook Fox the Chief Engineer of the state, who was knowledgeable in his own right. Their estimate was that only six or seven male lions were left![16] In his report on the Gir forest Wallinger goes on to state that during his visit to Gir of two months in 1913, he had heard of four or five kills. He had seen very few pug marks and made his estimation on that basis. He goes on to add:

> I do not feel justified after so short an experience however, to give a very definite opinion on a subject which is of such great importance to India from a Natural History point of view. The total number of lions in the Gir could not be put down, in my opinion, at over 20 with any degree of safety and my advice is to exercise even greater strictness in the matter of granting permits to shoot them than hitherto. Unless this is done, it may be confidently asserted that lions stand in considerable danger of being exterminated altogether, especially in view of the inter breeding that will occur.[17]

Two more estimates were made in 1920, one by P.R. Cadell and another by

CHAPTER 12

A Second Home

Kuno, Madhya Pradesh
■ The proposed site of the second home awaits lions from Gujarat state which is in no mood to part with them.
Photograph: Brigadier Ranjit Talwar.

The second attempt at translocation took place in Nepal in 1938–39. An African lion and lioness from the Nepal zoo were released in the terai region of Chitwan. There was however some apprehension about zoo-bred animals being able to fend for themselves and also survive with the tigers which were in abundance in the region. As matters turned out, the pair took to cattle lifting causing an outcry among the local population. A decision was taken to shoot them as it was thought too dangerous to leave them alone. They were both shot in February 1939 and the villagers were compensated for the livestock they had lost. It may be noted that this area was teeming with tigers – six tigers and two leopards were shot in one day. A total bag of 120 tigers, 38 rhinos, 27 leopards, and 15 bears was recorded between December 1938 and March 1939 in the same locality for the shooting party of Maharaja Joodha Shumsher Jung Bahadur Rana, Prime Minister and Supreme Commander-in-Chief of Nepal. There appears to have been no conflict between the lions and tigers, in any case the lions had been in the wild for only a month[13] before they were shot. It is also interesting to note that though these lions were zoo-bred, they took to killing prey, albeit domestic cattle, on release.

In the post-independence era, the Indian Board for Wildlife sponsored the translocation of lions from the Gir to the Chakia forest near Varanasi, UP,[14] in 1957. However, there was a lone voice raised against the proposed translocation. K.S. Lavkumar of Jasdan, a renowned ornithologist and nature educationist, had severe reservations. He observed that lions are essentially animals of the open country and they were found more in the surrounding cultivations than in the forests of Gir except in the eastern part of the reserve. He went on to write:

> That they [lions] are found in the Gir is no doubt owing to the broken nature of the
> terrain which allowed the last of the animals shelter from the shikaris who wiped
> them out over the rest of the country, and possibly also due to the great numbers of
> cattle grazed in the forest, providing them with plentitude of food. In former times
> the lions ranging across the north-west of India must have fed on nilgai and [black]
> buck which were found in plenty in the areas frequented by the lions. Now where is

there a place where these antelopes can be found in the concentrated numbers, sufficient to support a pride of lions.... Bearing this in mind, would it be fair to impose economic loss on people living around the proposed new lion sanctuary [Chandraprabha] and has the danger to these people who are not familiar with the lion and his ways been considered. Finally, what will prevent the lions from wandering away as they apparently did when some were introduced by the Maharaja of Gwalior....

... Lions have existed in the Gir for centuries and even if in the past epidemics might have reduced the race, they have always managed to multiply again to their former numbers, so it has never been claimed that the present reduction of the once widely spread lion to its limited habitat has resulted from causes other than their destruction by man and by depopulating of the game that comprised their food. Since the killing of lions has been completely banned, the Gir lions have kept on increasing most vigorously, and there is every possibility that if the animals are given continued protection, they will slowly spread out into the country around their present range. This natural increase will create a need to keep their numbers down by judicious shooting. It is therefore apparent that there need be no anxiety about possible extinction of the lion in the Gir and consequently this scheme [of translocating lions to Chandraprabha] is quite uncalled for, unless of course it is intended to give another state the pride of being the possessor of Asiatic lions. This privilege however is fraught with much danger and is not worth the effort.[15]

These words were written nearly half a century ago. In the event however, these prophetic warnings fell on unheeding ears and the experiment went ahead. Two possible host sites were initially considered: one was near Tikamgarh in what was then Vindhya Pradesh and the other was Chakia which was finally chosen. The question naturally came up regarding the number of lions that should be translocated for which purpose several authorities were consulted. Keith Caldwell of the Kenya and Uganda Game Department felt that a whole family of lions i.e. a pride should be moved so that it would over time split into two and spread. Ideally, he felt, two families should be moved. C.R.S. Pitman, the Game Warden of Uganda, suggested two young lions and four lionesses from different family groups. R.A. Critchley, President of the Game Preservation and Hunting Association of Northern Rhodesia, agreed with the suggestion. M.H. Cowie, Director of Royal National Parks of Kenya, also agreed but suggested an alternative of a lion and lioness with female cubs. Once the cubs grew and moved on, he suggested, a male lion preferably "more virile" than the first should be introduced who would be willingly accepted by the cubs which would have grown to become adult lionesses. E.P. Gee concluded from all this that just one adult male, preferably a good maned specimen, would do the job with two lionesses and cubs. Once the cubs grew up, a "more virile" lion could be introduced at a later date.[16] The information was considered by the relevant government departments – demonstrating a more healthy eclectic approach than one would expect from the insular park managers commonly met with today.

The executive committee of the Indian Board for Wildlife met at Sasan Gir in 1956 and accepted the offer of the Uttar Pradesh government to introduce lions in the Chakia forests. An area of 96 square kilometres was set aside as the Chandraprabha Sanctuary, named after the river which flows through it. The sanctuary is in the Vindhya Range with similar flora to Gir, and having what was believed to be an adequate prey base of nilgai, chital, chinkara, sambar, and wild

Iran in exchange for cheetahs from there which could be reintroduced in India.[23]

In Iran the proposed area was converted into the Arzan National Park. But the project came under severe criticism for it involved buying land from local farmers and resettling them elsewhere. On the other hand, scientists questioned the efficacy of the project on the grounds that the environment of the area may not prove suitable for the lions though it had been their haunt in the past.[24] Two years later the Shah had gone the way of the lion in Iran and the country became an Islamic Republic with a different set of priorities which did not include the restoration of a royal symbol. The idea was soon forgotten in India.

It is heartening to record that the quest for a second home in India for Asiatic lions has never really been given up in spite of all the odds and past experience. A population and habitat viability assessment workshop was held in Baroda in October 1993. The state governments of Rajasthan, Madhya Pradesh, and Gujarat were requested to submit proposals for potential sites. Three sites – Darrah-Jawaharsagar Wildlife Sanctuary and Sitamata Sanctuary both in Rajasthan, and Kuno Wildlife Sanctuary in Madhya Pradesh – were selected for an intensive survey which was done by a team from the Wildlife Institute of India. They recommended the Kuno Wildlife Sanctuary and its environs as the most suitable host site of the three.[25]

This study has made specific recommendations for preparing the host site which briefly include the following: The primary requirement is protection and enhancement of the existing prey base. In the study's model, a biomass of 480,000 kilograms would be required to sustain a growing population of initially eight lions. This chital and nilgai based prey population requirement would take thirteen years to be achieved at the host site. The time period could be shortened to say seven years if 500 chital and 800 nilgai are introduced from elsewhere either from captive or wild populations. This time span is based on the assumption of ideal conditions with a high order of commitment from government agencies and the local human population.

Secondly, the study recommends that an area of 700 square kilometres be declared as a national park. The existing wildlife sanctuary of 344.68 square kilometres which had a human population of 7,400 persons in nineteen villages, would form part of the national park and the villagers and their livestock would have to be resettled outside. The total area of the proposed conservation unit is 3,700 square kilometres – roughly double the total Gir forest area, of which 3,300 square kilometres is forest land.

According to the study, five to eight lions consisting of two or three males and three to five females from a "free-ranging stable social unit" should be captured from Gir and translocated. Since the lions would be from a single pride they would adjust to the new area without internecine aggression. They should be released in a holding pen of 1 square kilometre for a period of ten days to acclimatize them before being freed into their new home. All animals must be radio-collared to check and monitor their activities. Once the initial population has settled down, fresh stock must be brought in to supplement the population by capturing lions from the fringes of the Gir Sanctuary. This is a requirement of population management. The study concludes that it would be possible to establish a population of thirty to fifty free-ranging lions in ten years' time. Though the conclusions of the study are very cautious, e.g. (a) expectations of thirty to fifty lions in ten years and (b) a requirement of forest area twice the size of Gir, it is a viable starting point and a

Kuno river and habitat
■ A second home for the lions of Asia is a necessity to ensure their survival in case of a natural disaster.
Photograph: Brigadier Ranjit Talwar.

guiding beacon for the managers of the effort. With the participation of the Indian government, it is to the credit of the Madhya Pradesh government that it has taken on this difficult but rewarding task.

On the ground, however, the situation has progressed slowly. The work in the last five years has resulted in shifting 23 out of 24 villages from the sanctuary, consisting of 1,650 families with a population of 7,000 persons. Twenty villages have been resettled in Agra on the periphery of the sanctuary. They have been given housing, agricultural land, drinking water, and fair weather roads, while they await electricity and irrigation. Three villages have been shifted to Karahal subdivision and are in an early stage of resettlement. Apart from adding field staff for protection, which has shown results in reduction of illegal grazing, the state government has also notified 1,268 square kilometres as the Kuno Wildlife Division and this area includes the present sanctuary area of 344.68 square kilometres. In addition 923 square kilometres have been transferred from Sheopur division to the new Kuno division thus making unity of management possible and more efficient.[26]

However, there are several problems which need to be addressed urgently. The Wildlife Institute study had recommended that a national park be created with a sanctuary and a buffer zone, as has been noted earlier. So far this has not transpired. The study also envisaged translocation of prey species to shorten the time frame of getting the habitat ready to receive lions. Only three nilgai were translocated in 2001, which is nothing more than symbolic. Further, there is no ecological research

CHAPTER 13

Life in the Republic:
The Lion in Winter

A Gir lion in the Berlin Deer Park

■ This Asian lion photographed in 1998 in the zoo in eastern Berlin, came to it from Zurich which had acquired it from India. The lion has over the years developed a luxuriant black mane which covers the lower part of its chest and abdomen similar to the lions found on Assyrian friezes of Ashurnasirpal and Ashurbanipal.
Photograph: Lothar Schlawe.

A crouching lion

■ All attention, it looks past the photographer at a herd of chital.
Photograph: Divyabhanusinh.

more than 20,000 cattle grazed in it which caused a loss of food for the prey base of the lion. Further, most of the fertile valleys of the sanctuary had come under cultivation. In the absence of their natural prey, lions fed almost exclusively on domestic cattle of which 23 per cent could not be eaten by them as the dead animals were taken away by tanners for removing and curing the skins. In addition, about twenty per cent of the lion population was getting tethered baits. These were warning bells which could not be ignored. Guy Mountfort, International Trustee of the World Wildlife Fund wrote to Prime Minister Indira Gandhi soon thereafter, enclosing a report prepared by experts from India, Britain, and the USA who had visited the sanctuary in December 1970. He pointed out that unless the threats to the lion were tackled swiftly, India's national symbol would become extinct.[18]

The Expert Committee of the Indian Board for Wildlife too had visited the Gir a few months earlier in April 1970 and had expressed its own concerns. Since Gujarat was under President's Rule, Governor Sriman Narayan turned his attention to the establishment of a stable ecosystem wherein lions and other animals could roam freely, as also to the socio-economic upliftment of the Maldharis of Gir. The Council for Ecology was set up in November 1970 by the Government of Gujarat under the chairmanship of Y. Digvijaysinhji of Wankaner, which approved a set of objectives prepared by Amrita H. Patel on behalf of the Ecological Research Centre (a body set up by the Smithsonian Institution, Yale University, Government of Gujarat, and Bombay Natural History Society). These objectives were all-encompassing in their reach. They included, inter alia: to conserve the Gir habitat and if possible improve it; to encourage wildlife for its own sake, especially the lion; to exclude all exotic species; to reverse or minimize human conflict; to protect the habitat from overgrazing and lopping; and to improve the lot of the Maldharis and phase their resettlement outside the sanctuary. Pursuant to these recommendations, the state government issued formal orders on January 17, 1972 to the effect that (a) the sanctuary area was to be permanently closed to grazing by livestock from outside, (b) the area should have a physical barrier to make the closure effective, and (c) Maldharis staying inside the Gir should be shifted along with their cattle in a phased manner and settled in villages around the sanctuary by allotting them land for cultivation as well as common grazing ground for their cattle.[19]

Soon there was a change at Government House. The new Governor, K.T. Satarawala, took a keen interest in the progress of the project. Though the drought of 1972 created problems of grazing as some 70,000 cattle entered the Gir, effective steps were soon taken. A rubble wall over 209 kilometres along the sanctuary's boundary was built by 1975, which was later increased to a length of about 380 kilometres. In 1974, 147 square kilometres of adjoining forest areas of Amreli were added to the Gir Sanctuary. An area of 140 square kilometres of the Jamwala and Chodavdi ranges was constituted as a sanctum sanctorum, which became a National Park under the recently enacted all-India law, *The Wildlife (Protection) Act, 1972*. Its total area was increased to 258 square kilometres in 1978. Further, the government declared its intention to create the entire sanctuary area as a National Park.[20] The relocation of Maldharis was a crucial part of the project. In 1971 there were 129 nesses with 845 families owning about 17,000 domestic cattle according to one government source[21] while another gave a figure of 714 families with a livestock population of about 13,000.[22] The resettlement programme continued till the year 1986–87 and a total of 592 families were relocated.[23] By the year 1995–96, 54 nesses

At a waterhole

■ Lions will avoid getting wet almost at all costs. This lion is about to drink water but has bent his front left leg to avoid getting his paw wet.

Photograph: Divyabhanusinh.

out of the original 129 were left within the protected area, with 361 households, a human population of 2,540 and a livestock population of about 10,000.[24]

Protection yielded visible results. The combined herbivore population of chital, sambar, nilgai, chowsingha, chinkara, and wild boar which was estimated at 5,500 in 1969, went up to 10,000 in 1974, and to 15, 000 by 1979. During the same period the lion population went up to 180 in 1974, and 205 in 1979.[25] S.P. Sinha's research on the lion showed that in the years 1982–84 when he collected and analysed lion scats, 48 per cent contained livestock hair as against Paul Joslin's findings of 75 per cent in 1968–71.[26] By 1990, the combined herbivore population had gone up to nearly 33,000 and the lions had increased to 284.[27] Ravi Chellam found remains of cattle and buffalo only in 25 per cent of scats analysed by him in the year 1989.[28]

At the national level the 1970s saw a more widely known wildlife crisis. The realization finally dawned on the powers that were, that they had a near disaster on their hands. A 1972 nationwide census revealed that the total tiger population in the country had collapsed to 1,827 animals which was an indication of the alarming condition of the protection of the forest cover in the country. Project Tiger was quickly put in place and the tiger was "lionized", as R.S. Dharmakumarsinhji put it,[29] as it was anointed the national animal in place of the lion. While Ashoka's lions continued as the national symbol, the wild variety of the species had to be content with becoming the state animal of Gujarat, an indication of its reduced pocket-size range. In the lion's case the state government would have to largely take upon itself the job of protection, unlike the tiger the preservation of which became a national movement of sorts as it caught the attention of the urban middle class as no animal had before.

A battle royal
■ Two free-ranging lions charge an inmate across the fence of the Devalia Safari Park which occupies prime lion habitat in Gir. Here tourists are shown lions at close quarters. This kind of confrontation among lions can lead to injuries.
Photograph: Prerna Kumari Singh.

The mid 1970s were a watershed in Indian politics. The imposition of emergency rule between June 1975 and January 1977 by Indira Gandhi was the dividing line. Subsequent to it, for the first time in India's history, a non-Congress government took office. The Central government was never to exercise the extent of power it had done for the thirty years so far. It is a curious fact that by the Forty-Second Amendment to the Constitution of India which came into effect on January 3, 1977, the two subjects *Forests* and *Protection of Wild Animals and Birds* were taken from the State List and brought to the Concurrent List, giving the Central government the opportunity to legislate concurrently with states on these subjects. This, at a time when the states had become more powerful with local aspirations. It was by the same amendment that a new Directive Principle of State Policy was inserted, by which the state was required to "endeavour to protect and improve the environment and to safeguard the forests and wildlife of the country".[30]

The foregoing narration gives the impression that the lion is more or less secure in its habitat, and the template for strict preservation of the species and its habitat is in place. But the problems both lions and their habitat face are serious and their solutions are in the realm of human action or the lack of it at the local level. The lion population has increased steadily over the years. At the last count in 2001 it stood at 327 and the total of the six herbivores had reached about 55,000, increasing at the rate of 14 per cent annually during the preceding three decades.[31] The forest within the National Park and Sanctuary limits was preserved and the lion had gone back in large measure to predating on its natural prey. Any way one looks at it, here is a success story, and those involved in making it happen deserve the nation's appreciation. Having said that, it must not be forgotten that success brings in its

Marking territory

■ A lion demarcates his territory by spraying. A male can traverse territories of more than one lioness or pride.

Photograph: Divyabhanusinh.

wake a new set of problems which need to be addressed at the earliest, in addition to the existing unfinished agenda.

The Gir forest has never carried more than 300 animals – 267 in 1990, 262 in 1995, and 271 in 2001. The eastern Gir portion of the protected area which had very few lions earlier showed a remarkable change. By 2001 it had 106 lions in an area which was half that of the western portion. Also, the lions had started moving away and establishing themselves outside the protected area.[32]

In 1995 as many as 42 lions lived outside the Gir protected area, whereas by 2001 the number had increased to 59. It was natural that they would move within their earlier haunts. The Girnar mountain, at the foot of which is the city of Junagadh, was originally part of the Gir forest but now it is 22 kilometres away from the nearest boundary of the Gir Sanctuary with an area of 279 square kilometres of deciduous and dry scrub patches. It was always home to lions with a relict population up to 1963. However, dispersal of lions started after the drought year of 1987 and the censuses of 1995 and 2001 recorded 13 of them there. In the Mytiala forest of the old Bhavnagar state, there were three lions in 1995, but their number had increased to sixteen in 2001. It lies due east at a distance of 6 kilometres from the boundary of the sanctuary with an area of just 19 square kilometres. In the Hapavadli zone beyond Mytiala in the eastern part of Bhavnagar district, eleven cubs were reported in the 2001 census. The coastal forests of Una-Rajula-Jafrabad and of the Kodinar-Sutrapada belts had 26 lions in 1995 and the animals were breeding there. In 2001, however, the number had reduced to 20. This forest is dominated by *Prosopis chilensis* and the planted *Casuarina equisetifolia*, and harbours nilgai and wild boar, both of which are a nuisance to the farmers. But they form a part of the lion's diet, though livestock has remained the major food source for them here. Seven lions were also reported from villages near the Gir protected area.[33]

By the roadside
■ Lions often sit on the road or in clearings nearby. Still, they merge beautifully with their surroundings and are often missed from a moving vehicle.
Photographs: Divyabhanusinh.

A lioness and two cubs were found on the island of Diu, having crossed the creek presumably by the bridge, in 1996. A lion and a lioness pair were found near Porbandar, which killed and ate five domestic cattle in February 2003. These lions died in mysterious circumstances after they were captured and brought back to the Gir Sanctuary.[34] A lioness was reported from Kotda Sangani almost on the outskirts of Gondal.[35] All these instances are of lions found several kilometres away from the nearest forest boundary. Lions had lived so close to human populations in ancient Palestine that the Hebrew Bible could record "The slothful saith, a lion is in the street",[36] and one wonders if it is about to happen again, in Saurashtra this time. It is not fanciful to imagine a sizeable stable lion population living near human settlements surviving on wild boar and nilgai, which are also found in increasing numbers outside protected areas, and on cattle.

The immediate action that is required is the upgradation of the forests, thickets, and grasslands now occupied by lions, and their protection by making sanctuaries of these areas. Equally important is the preservation of the "corridors" used by lions to migrate out. In these, particularly between Gir forest and Girnar – the largest forest patch chosen by lions, the distance is large and their passage is of necessity through open and cultivated lands. It is estimated that the home range of the lion was spread over 8,500 square kilometres in the year 2000,[37] whereas its range has increased to about 10,000 square kilometres by 2004.[38] There is relentless and increasing human pressure on such areas which would make it difficult to leave them in the present state of development. A detailed study would advise if acquisition of some of these lands is at all possible. Hitherto land is acquired by government through fixed rates which are way below market rates. A method must be found to make such transactions voluntary which may be done through offering market rates. Here is a role for non-government organizations to bring in funds and expertise. A plan already exists for the "ecorestoration" of Girnar and an overall strategy for regional planning across the lion's home range has been prepared.[39] The Girnar forests have an additional problem as the mountain harbours Hindu and Jain shrines of antiquity which results in large-scale influx of pilgrims several times a year. And there is a large and increasing human population all around. The prey base is very low as there are few sambar and chital. There is even talk of a ropeway to cart pilgrims to the shrines on the mountain, which will bring in its wake its own problems. The task is enormous, but it has to be attempted to make a success of the lions' own survival plan, for it is they who have spread out without help from us. If urgent steps are not taken to secure the habitat, the increase in their population may spark another lion migration elsewhere. There was a recent newspaper report that a lion and a lioness which had made the *Prosopis chilensis* thickets of Savarkundla taluka their home were reduced to drinking water from cattle water troughs in villages and sometimes ended up drinking the water overflow from such troughs.[40] Such occurrences may increase in time which would have their own implications for lion-human conflict.

The one locality which the government of Gujarat has often talked of as a possible area for lion reintroduction is the Barda Wildlife Sanctuary. It is near the coastal city of Porbandar with an area of 192 square kilometres. Its major problem is that today it has 68 nesses with 750 families of Maldharis, a total population of 4,000.[41] The lions themselves have shunned the area so far and, if the matter is left to them to decide, it appears to be out of the running for their reintroduction for the time being.

The mating game
A lion and lioness come together to mate when the female is in oestrus. Over a period of four or five days they mate repeatedly for a few minutes each time, and then go their own way.
■ Ready to mate.
■ The lion mounts and licks the lioness.
■ The lion bites the lioness and dismounts.
■ Time to rest again.
Photographs: Divyabhanusinh.

While the lion population is definitely on the increase, the question must be asked – just how many lions can their present home range sustain? According to H.S. Singh's estimation, up to 400 lions is a possibility but not the magical figure of 500,[42] unless they spread farther afield along the coast and also occupy outlying forest patches around the hills of Alech, Dalasa, Barda, and Shetrunjay. While absolute numbers need not detain us here, it is evident that the increasing population by itself is reason to remove some lions to a second home large enough to sustain and further increase the population there. None of the areas where the lions have moved within Saurashtra is large enough to sustain a healthy breeding population on a long-term basis. On the other hand, if the lion population goes up in such pockets, they could become potential flashpoints of human-lion conflicts. It is in the interest of the species to have a viable home such as Kuno-Palpur or elsewhere for their long-term survival.

The other Damoclean sword over the lion is the ever-present threat of a natural calamity such as drought, fire, or an epidemic. Serengeti in Tanzania lost over 1,000 lions in 1993 to a canine distemper. This disease is prevalent in India as is *Ehrlichiosis*, the Nairobi bleeding disease, which is fatal if not treated in time. It is endemic in Mumbai's canine and feline populations. The disease has spread to tigers

On the prowl
■ A solitary lion walks beside a road, patrolling its territory.
Photograph: Divyabhanusinh.

in the Safari Park at Borivli and recently to leopards in a zoo in Lonavla. Such diseases could assume epidemic form and strike a small felid population in a restricted area such as the Gir. Serengeti could sustain the loss and recover. Such an occurrence would be calamitous to Gir and its lions. This is yet another reason for the government of Gujarat to agree to the transfer of a few lions to Kuno-Palpur to establish a second home, and to support this satellite population on a continuing basis to ensure its health.

With the dense human and cattle population around the Gir protected area, there is constant and relentless pressure on it for fuel, grazing, and other forest produce. There are 79 villages located within a periphery of 6 kilometres all around the Gir Sanctuary with a human population of 1,36,000 and domestic livestock population of 1,00,000. Since 1995–96 the government has embarked on an ambitious Eco-Development Project from the funds made available from the Global Environment Fund and the World Bank. This is a unique experiment insofar as the government is trying to implement the project with local support through village level Eco-Development Councils where their participation is sought in providing liquid propane gas units in villages for cooking, land levelling, barbed-wire fencing, supplying agricultural implements, and so on. While the target of this project includes peripheral villages and the Maldharis' nesses inside the protected area, it also targets improvement of the protected area and its management such as preventing soil erosion, removal of the menace of the "mad babul" – *Prosopis chilensis*, and *Lantana camara*, training of the Forest Department staff, improvement of their living conditions, and other such activities. Between 1995–96 and 1999–2000 a sum of Rs 472 lakhs was spent on the project.[43] It has also initiated ten studies including man-animal conflict, study of satellite lion populations, impact of tourism, studies of lesser known fauna, and so on.[44] The results of these studies are now in the process of becoming available to the managers in the field. The human population in India is likely to keep growing at an average of around 1.5 per cent per annum till 2016.[45] A continuous audit by independent experts is essential, to assess the direct impact of the project on the Gir forest, such as reduction in livestock grazing through increased stall-feeding, reduction in amount of fuel wood being removed from it through greater use of gas for cooking purposes, reduction in damage to fauna and flora, etc. These would be the true indicators of the project's success or otherwise, and would help to identify what mid-course corrections are required. Any project targeted at the human population must therefore continue over a long term with increased resources.

In the final analysis, the success of the project depends on how speedily and honestly it is carried out by the administration of the state government. Delays and leakages have caused the failure of so many schemes of socio-economic benefit that there is a real danger of this project going the same way.

In the meantime threats to the lions from various quarters still exist. Lions on the periphery of the forest continue to predate heavily on livestock. In 1998–99 alone 1,902 cattle were killed by them, of which 1,329 were compensated for at a total cost of approximately Rs 1.15 crores.[46] The government's procedures and false claims denied compensation for 573 claims of cattle kills. This is a source of constant friction.

Lion-human conflicts are another continuous occurrence in the Gir. A study of the problem revealed that there were totally 193 attacks by lions between 1977 and

1991 with 28 human mortalities, i.e. an average of 2.2 per year. The year 1987–88 was witness to the severest drought since 1918, which profoundly altered the conflict ratio: in that year alone, forty attacks were recorded,[47] reminiscent of lion attacks causing 66 people to lose their lives during the years 1901–04 that followed the great Chappanyo Kal of 1899–1900.[48] Between 1991–92 and 1994–95, 54 persons were injured by lions, of whom six lost their lives.[49] There is no simple solution for such conflicts which can only be reduced substantially if humans and lions do not need to interact as much as they do, and this does not seem likely to happen in a hurry, if at all.

The relocation of Maldharis which started under the Gir Lion Project in 1973–74 continued till 1986–87. The impact on the forest was visible for all to see and the lion's food content changed dramatically as we have noted earlier. This in itself is sufficient proof of the benefits of the effort. However, the matter is now at a standstill and 54 nesses with 2,500 people and about 13,000 livestock remain according to the 2004 figures. In 1971 there were 714 Maldhari families and about 13,000 cattle in the Gir protected area, of which 592 families were relocated.[50] In other words around 10,700 livestock moved out of the protected area (if we are to take an average of eighteen heads of livestock per person) leaving behind some 3,000. Given the 2004 figure of about 13,000, the growth in livestock population has negated the process of relocation. This tendency, if not checked, is a potential threat to the sanctuary.

It is a matter of record that the resettlement of Maldharis was fraught with problems. Of the 592 families resettled, only 323 families remained in their new homes by 1992–93,[51] the others having moved on or returned to the Gir to one of the existing nesses. The relocation of Maldharis needs to be done in a phased manner and it can succeed only if the scheme is implemented sensitively, giving them facilities which are attractive enough to persuade them to move. The first effort in the 1970s fell short of success; the next one does not have room for error. If the Maldharis continue to remain within the sanctuary, their numbers and their livestock numbers must be limited. In a study of the impact of management practices on lion and ungulate habitat of Gir, Diwakar Sharma recommends a minimum distance of 8 kilometres between two nesses to leave disturbance-free forest of sufficient size between them for sambar. This would involve relocation of some thirty nesses and their livestock.[52] Popular government and local resistance has ensured the virtual abandonment of any relocation and that is why the conversion of the entire sanctuary into a National Park remains unfulfilled.

Apart from the Maldharis, there are fourteen forest settlement villages in the sanctuary with a human population of about 4,500 and a livestock population of about 4,200[53] which pose a similar problem. In the past, man had a niche in nature. When one propagates traditional rights in protected areas one forgets that human and cattle populations were naturally controlled before the advent of Western medicine and veterinary services. Besides, even fifty years ago the forest cover was larger and the human population far smaller. Today if such populations grow in protected areas – as they will surely do – their existence and prosperity will be at the cost of their immediate environment.

There are three places of worship which are in the Gir, namely Tulsishyam, Banej, and Kankai shrines. The last mentioned is the most frequented of the three. Situated in the heart of the sanctuary, it has expanded into a complex of 24

A solitary lion emerges from thick jungle
■ Lions adapt to different types of habitat easily, though their preference is for scrub jungle or grassland.
Photograph: Divyabhanusinh.

The lion at ease
■ Sitting in the open, it enjoys the evening breeze as can be seen from its wind-blown mane.
Photograph: Divyabhanusinh.

permanent structures covering an area of 9,516 square metres. I remember the shrine as a small, charming, and peaceful spot in the mid-1950s, which is long gone. In 1987–88 it was visited by over 8,000 pilgrims in 1,049 vehicles. In 1997–98, nearly 50,000 pilgrims visited it in 4,700 vehicles! The demands of the temple are manifold and ever-increasing, and it is a source of major problems to the preservation of the sanctuary.

The number of tourists visiting the Gir has increased exponentially. In 1977–78 there were 14,000; this figure increased to over 57,000 in 1994–95 which brought a revenue of nearly Rs 13 lakhs.[54] While the state government has still not found a way to divert such income entirely or substantially to the Gir, there is also a need to monitor and regulate this activity. Many of the tourists visit the Lion Safari Park at Devalia which no doubt brings down the pressure on the rest of the sanctuary. However, this park built over an area of 400 hectares in prime lion habitat, should never have come up in the first place at this location. It should have been built on revenue land abutting the sanctuary, not inside it. It certainly would be worthwhile to consider this option and convert the existing enclosure into a non-invasive research centre for conservation or better still, remove the structures and restore the natural vegetation. The lions within it brought from Sakkarbag Zoo, Junagadh, often attract their wild counterparts from the surrounding sanctuary area, causing them to make futile attacks on the chain-link fence of the Safari Park which could cause them grave physical harm.

The railway line running through the forest and the 89 kilometres of Public Works Department roads (including 29 kilometres of State Highway between Jamwala and Sapnes) are a constant threat to the lions. As many as eleven lions were killed on the railway tracks between 1983–84 and 1995–96.[55] It is a metre gauge line and it should be discontinued. Ideally, the roads too need to be permanently closed, which has not happened because of heavy pressure from the users. In fact there are constant demands for their improvement. The recent decision of the local administration to restrict vehicular movement on the 16-kilometre-long Visavadar to Sasan road has led to strong protest,[56] and it remains to be seen if the government will be able to weather the storm.

Lions are also being poached or killed. In all, fourteen lions were done away with between 1985–86 and 1994–95. Of these, three were killed inside the protected area.[57] The reason for such killings appears to be either accidental or it is sometimes the result of poisoning. As of now there is no reason to believe that any of these animals were killed for "sport" though in May and June of 1996 there were several reports in *Phulchchab*, a popular Gujarati daily published from Rajkot, of the arrest of a gang of poachers who were killing lions to sell body parts. Claws fetched a sum of Rs 500 locally,[58] as these are believed to be "charms" which protect humans from diseases and the evil eye.

The problems of the Gir forest are well known and the more prominent ones have been briefly stated here. The forest and its flora and fauna, including the lion itself, have been subjects of intense study and reports in the last half century by princes, naturalists, and lately by scientists from India and abroad. There is no dearth of technical information or analyses, there are proposed solutions to the issues facing the lion and the Gir forest. The Indian government and particularly the government of Gujarat have managed to preserve a viable ecosystem so far; lions and other animals in the Gir forest have increased under their stewardship for which kudos to them. But the relentless increase in human population with the attendant livestock population reminds one of an increasing number of mice gnawing away at the same small piece of cheese. Our administrative dispensation and conservation efforts are largely continuations of the British imperial and Indian princely traditions. More and more local aspirations are at variance with them and the republican top itself is not as strongly or personally interested in conservation as was the case in days gone by. Preservation of forests and their non-human inhabitants usually goes against the vote-giving estates of our law-makers. Lions and tigers have no votes, so the politicians do not need them to survive in the short term – and they are interested only in the short term. On the other hand, successful local community movements for conservation are few and far between despite all the fanfare that often attends them. They would have an impact only if they can replicate their smaller local successes on a large enough scale and on a continuing basis. Under these circumstances, the efforts of the government of Gujarat to take local communities into their programme of eco-development are a step in the right direction. The success or failure of the programmes will be known only in the years ahead. In the meantime an honest, committed administration backed by a strong political will is the need of the hour.

The crux of the problem of preserving the Gir forest is the same as elsewhere: the exploding human population is likely to negate most efforts. In 1951 still 361 million in strength, by 2001 we are 1,027 million strong[59] and we are growing. We have put ourselves above the environment and we are cutting the very branch of the tree on which we are sitting, like Kalidasa of ancient times. He at least got enlightened in the process of the fall. No such spark has yet become apparent in our case. Surely, Reginald Heber, Lord Bishop of Calcutta (1823–26) was right when he lamented, albeit in a different context:

Though every prospect pleases
And only man is vile:
In vain with lavish kindness
The Gifts of God are strewn....

references

CHAPTER 1

ASIA'S LIONS TODAY

1 Wynter-Blyth, c. 1961. Though dated, this little essay is by far the most instructive on the subject.

2 Singh, 2001, pp. 67–74.

3 Sunquist and Sunquist, 2002, p. 238.

4 Mr Bharat J. Pathak, pers. comm., 2004.

5 Chellam, 1993.

6 O'Brien, 2003, p. 47.

7 See Appendix 2.

8 Dr M.A. Mehendale, pers. comm., 1999.

9 Anon, 1833; Pocock, 1930.

10 Patterson, 1907, frontispiece, pp. 92–93, 103.

11 Caputo, 2002, p. 146.

12 Freer Gallery of Art, Washington D.C., Acc. No. 48.8 in Welch, 1978, pp. 56–57.

13 The British Library, London, Acc. No. 1920, 9.17.05 in Pal, 1991, p. 29.

14 Bharat Kala Bhavan, Varanasi, Acc. No. 9069/6 in Krishnadasa, 1999, p. 70, plate B. See also p. 101.

15 Kostioukovitch, 1996, pp. 97–98, plate 146/folio 72 recto. See p. 106.

16 Falk and Digby, 1983, p. 22, plate 10.

17 Maharaja Sawai Man Singh II Museum, Jaipur, Acc. No. Ag. 863 in Rashid and David, 1992, plate 5. See p. 103.

18 Soustiel, 1973, pp. 20–21.

19 Beach and Koch, 1997, pp. 77–78, plate 30. See p. 98.

20 Ibid., pp. 110–11, plate 46. See p. 99.

21 The Chester Beatty Library, Dublin, Acc. No. In. 11A.28. See p. 100.

22 Falk, Smart, and Skelton, 1978, p. 60, plate 69.

23 Stuart Carey Welch Collection, Arthur M. Sackler Museum, Harvard University Arts Museum, Cambridge, Mass., in Kossak, 1997, pp. 62–63.

24 Rao Madho Singh Trust Museum, in Singh, 1985, p. 26, plate I. See p. 108.

25 Jerdon, 1867; pp. 90–91.

26 Prater, 1948, p. 67.

27 Pocock, 1930.

28 See Appendix 3.

29 Dollman and Burlace, 1935, pp. 365–67.

30 Smith, Mcbee, and Mathews, 1989, pp. 752–58.

31 See Chapter 11.

32 Wynter-Blyth, c. 1961, p. 2.

33 Wildt, et al., 1987.

34 O'Brien, 2003, p. 51.

35 Fenton, c. 1924, p. 6.

36 Rangarajan, 2001.

37 Ranjitsinh, 1997, p. 50.

38 Ibid., p. 51.

39 Watson, 1884, p. 6.

40 Apte, 1965, p. 934.

41 Monier-Williams, 1899, p. 1105.

42 Gida, 1999.

43 Meghani, 1997, pp. 538–40.

44 Meghani, 1997A.

45 Sursinh, 1893, pp. 73–74.

46 Desai, 1983, p. 125.

CHAPTER 2

AN ORIENTAL PATRIMONY

1 Macdonald, 1992, p. 62; Turner, 1997, pp. 72–73.

2 Hemmer, 1974, pp. 229–34, 271–72.

3 Houlihan, 1996, p. 2.

4 Ibid., pp. 94–95.

5 Guggisberg, 1962, pp. 244–45.

6 Houlihan, 1996, p. 93.

7 Ibid., pp. 41, 70–73; Guggisberg, 1962, p. 156.

8 Houlihan, 1996, p. 71.

9 Saunders, 1991, p. 83.

10 Reade, 1983, p. 72.

11 Moscati, 1960, pp. 62–63.

12 Reade, 1983, p. 39.

13 Van Buren, 1939, p. 3.

14 Luckenbill, 1927, p. 363.

15 Weissert, 1997.

16 Reade, 1983, p. 74.

17 Weissert, 1997.

18 Reade, 1983, p. 73.

19 Mukherjee, 1969, pp. 11–12.

20 Ibid., pp. 9–10.

21 Ibid., p. 90.

22 Albenda, 1974.

23 Reade, 1983, pp. 72–79.

24 I am grateful to Dr Julian Reade for pointing out the unsculpted outlines of the tails on the exhibits at the British Museum.

25 Pocock, 1930; Hemmer, 1974.

26 Reade, 1983, p. 72.

27 Layard, 1853, p. 487.

28 Bodenheimer, 1960, p. 134.

29 Toynbee, 1973, p. 19.

30 Judges 14:6; Daniel 6:2.

31 Ezekiel 20: 3–9.

32 See Chapter 6, pp. 109–10.

33 Modi, 1932.

34 Hartner and Ettinghausen, 1964.

35 Godrej and Mistree, 2002, p. 670; Humphreys and Kahrom, 1995, p. 80.

36 Godrej and Mistree, 2002, p. 670.

37 Titley, 1983, pp. 14, 87. See p. 50.

38 Graves and Ali-Shah, 1967, p. 53, verse 18.

39 Hassan, 1937, pp. 4–5.

40 Ibid.

41 Ibid.; Layard, 1853, pp. 556–57.

42 Harting, 1883, pp. 364–65.

43 Rawlinson, 1898, pp. 149–50.

44 Layard, 1853, p. 487.

45 Kostioukovitch, 1996, pp. 95–96, plate 136, folio 100, recto. See p. 103.

46 Dr A.H. Morton, pers. comm., 2002.

47 Ibid.

48 Heptner and Sludskii, 1971, p. 82.

49 Balfour, 1885, pp. 719–20.

50 Pocock, 1936A.

51 Heaney, 1944.

52 M.K. Ranjitsinhji, pers. comm., 2003.

53 Harrington, 1977, pp. 72–73.

54 Ms Daphne M. Hills, pers. comm., 1999; Pocock, 1930. See p. 22.

55 Joslin, 1973; Kinnear, 1920.

56 Guggisberg, 1962, p. 42; Kinnear, 1920.

CHAPTER 3

A SEARCH THROUGH ANTIQUITY

1 Chattopadhyaya, 2002.
2 Thomas and Joglekar, 1994.
3 Ibid.
4 Dutta, 1976, quotes Pilgrim, 1910, 1938.
5 Kinnear, 1920.
6 Sunquist and Sunquist, 2002, p. 286.
7 Mahadevan, 1977, pp. 793–94.
8 Jarrige and Hassan, 1989.
9 See Chapter 2. I am grateful to Dr Julian Reade for specifically drawing my attention to this anatomical aberration while showing me the black obelisk at the British Museum.
10 Jarrige and Hassan, 1989.
11 Schwartzberg 1978, p. 11, plate II-5.
12 Iyer, 1977, p. 14.
13 Possehl, 1999, pp. 198–99.
14 Parpola, 1994, pp. 246–47.
15 Mahadevan, 1977, p. 793.
16 Misra, 2000.
17 Irwin, 1973, 1974, 1975, 1976, 1983, 1985. These articles must be read as one whole. The conclusions which are summarized in this chapter are culled from them.
18 Thapar, 1961, p. 269.
19 Prof. Romila Thapar, pers. comm., 2003.
20 Prof. Helmut Hemmer, pers. comm., 1999. For a description of the "flehmen" expression see Schaller, 1972, p. 95; Allaby, 1985, p. 252.
21 Prof. Helmut Hemmer, pers. comm., 1999.
22 Ibid.
23 Irwin, 1976.
24 Ibid.
25 Thapar, 1961, p. 261.
26 Irwin, 1973.
27 Bopearachhi, 1998, plates 13–14.
28 Zeuner, 1963, p. 419.
29 Allan, 1936, pp. 223–27, plates XXXII–XXXIII.
30 Jha and Rajgor, 1994.
31 Rapson, 1908, pp. 2, 10–13, plates I, III.
32 McCrindle, 1877, Fragm. XII, pp. 56–57.
33 Ibid.
34 Ibid., pp. 10–12.
35 Ibid., pp. 220–21.
36 Ibid., pp. 280–81.

37 Basham, 1954, p. 196.
38 Pathan, 1921, pp. 31, 33, 41, 42.
39 Mr Shantanu Kumar, pers. comm., 2003.
40 McCrindle, 1901, pp. 74–75; Jones, 1966, 122.
41 Pathan, 1921, plates 44–51.
42 Mr Shantanu Kumar, pers. comm., 2003.
43 McCrindle, 1901, p. 144; Scholfield, 1959, p. 235, Vol. III.
44 McCrindle, 1901, p. 149.
45 See pp. 48–49, 103.

CHAPTER 4

MRIGARAJA: KING OF THE BEASTS

1 Thapar, 1966, pp. 29–31.
2 *RV*, I 64.8, 95.5, 174.3; Banerjee, 1980, p. 153.
3 Through exchanges of letters between September 1998 and January 2000, Dr M.A. Mehendale of the Bhandarkar Oriental Research Institute, Pune, very kindly guided me with literary sources. This portion of the chapter is based on the information he so generously gave on the lion in early literature.
4 Prof. Romila Thapar, pers. comm., 2003.
5 *RV*, 9.97.28.
6 Ibid., 1.64.8.
7 Ibid., 5.83.3.
8 Ibid., 5.15.3.
9 Ibid., 10.28.10.
10 *Śat. Br.*, 5.5.4.18.
11 Zimmermann, 1987, pp. 100–05.
12 McCrindle, 1901, pp. 14, 31.
13 *Life and Times of Apollonius*, Book ii, 28, pp. 53–54 quoted in Modi, 1932.
14 Rangarajan, 2001.
15 *Śat. Br.*, 5.5.4.10.
16 Dr M.A. Mehendale, pers. comm., 1998–2000; *Śat. Br.*, 12.7.1.1 and 8.
17 Dr M.A. Mehendale, pers. comm., 1998–2000.
18 Ibid.
19 *Ait. Br.*, 8.2.1; *Śat. Br.* 12.8.3.4.
20 *Ait. Br.*, 8.5.6.
21 *Śat. Br.*, 5.2.1.22–23; 5.4.4.1; Bole and Vaghani, 1986, pp. 49, 33.
22 Dr M.A. Mehendale, pers. comm., 1998–2000.
23 Ibid.
24 Zimmermann, 1987, p. 215.
25 Dr M.A. Mehendale, pers. comm.,

1998–2000; *Raghuvaṁśa*, IV.72.
26 *Mbh.*, 2.53.19.
27 Ibid., 5.135.23.
28 Ibid., 5.154.18; 6.93.22; 12.1.119; 6.22.12.
29 Kangle, 1963, 2.20.3, p. 59.
30 Thapar, 1961, p. 260.
31 Ibid., p. 264.
32 Misra, 1966, pp. 393–404; Shrigondekar, 1939, 1715–24, Vol. II, pp. 303–04.
33 Kangle, 1963, 8.3.46, p. 395.
34 See Chapter 2, p. 42.
35 Mukherjee and Raychaudhuri, 1990, p. 14.
36 Ibid.
37 Iyer, 1977, p. 63.
38 Sivaramamurti, 1974, p. 14, fig. 20b.
39 Iyer, 1977, p. 63.
40 Mukherjee and Raychaudhuri, 1990, p. 15; Sivaramamurti, 1974, p. 14, fig. 20a.
41 Mukherjee and Raychaudhuri, 1990, p. 15, plates IVA, IVB.
42 Shastri, 1910, pp. 79–93.
43 Bole and Vaghani, 1986, p. 15.
44 Shastri, 1910, p. 85, III 41; p. 89, III 58, 59.
45 Dadhimatha, 1915, p. 183.
46 Sharma, c. 1970, p. 105; Monier-Williams, 1851, p. 457.
47 Kosambi and Gokhale, 1957, p. xcvii; Ingalls, 1965, Sec. 33, No. 1091, p. 315.
48 Kosambi and Gokhale, 1957, p. lxx; Ingalls, 1965, Sec. 33, No. 1071, p. 312.
49 Ingalls, 1965, Sec. 33, No. 1034, p. 306.
50 Suryakanta, 1962, 1.6.
51 Sarma, 1991.
52 *Subh.*, 38, p. 623; tr. by Dr M.A. Mehendale, pers. comm., 1998–2000.
53 Dr M.A. Mehendale, pers. comm., 1998–2000.
54 *Subh.*, 7, pp. 621–22; tr. by Dr M.A. Mehendale, pers. comm., 1998–2002.
55 *Subh.*, 5, p. 358; tr. by Dr M.A. Mehendale, pers. comm., 1998–2002.
56 See Chapter 6, p. 99.
57 Iyer, 1977, pp. 62–69.
58 Ibid., pl. 91.
59 Campbell, 1974, Vol. II, pp. 118–27; Liebert, 1976, p. 138.
60 Deekshitar, 2004.
61 Thapar, 2002. This work is a brief but

wide-ranging survey of the various tiger cults in India and elsewhere in Asia. It has surveyed several instances of tiger worship.

CHAPTER 5

UNDER THE DELHI SULTANATE

1 Rizvi, 1987, pp. 8–9.
2 Hussain, 1967, 1017–1025, Vol. I, p. 108.
3 Ibid., 2006–2007, Vol. I., p. 214.
4 Nizami, 1997, p. 73.
5 Ibid.
6 Hussain, 1976, 6939–6940, 6947–6950, Vol. II, pp. 563–64.
7 Ibid., 1977, 11276–11298, Vol. III, pp. 880–81.
8 Nizami, 1997, pp. 73–74.
9 Hussain, 1891, pp. 316–17; 326–27; Dr A.H. Morton, pers. comm., 1993.
10 Nizami, 1997, p. 74.
11 Hussain, 1976, 2529–2535, Vol. II, p. 252.
12 Ibid., 4876–4894, Vol. II, pp. 428–29.
13 Ibid., 5221–5225, Vol. II, p. 449.
14 Ibid., 5131–5135, Vol. II, pp. 443–44.
15 Ibid., 1977, 11079–11082, Vol. III, p. 866.
16 Ibid., 1977, 10566–10583, 10585–10588, 10589–10594, Vol. III, pp. 832–33.
17 Rangarajan, 1996, p. 141.

CHAPTER 6

THE GREAT MUGHALS GO HUNTING LIONS

1 Beveridge, 1922, pp. 384–85; Thackston, 1996, p. 279.
2 Beveridge, 1922, p. 393; Thackston, 1996, p. 285.
3 Foster, 1926, p. 297.
4 Ibid., p. 324.
5 Rogers and Beveridge, 1909–14, Vol. II, p. 233.
6 Habib, 1982, plates 4B, 6B, 7B, and 8B.
7 Constable, 1934, p. 374.
8 Beveridge, 1904, Vol. II, pp. 422–24; Sen, 1984, pp. 39–40.
9 See Chapter 7, p. 116.
10 Constable, 1934, p. 378.
11 Welch, 1986.
12 Beach and Koch, 1997, p. 18.
13 Ibid., pl. 34.
14 Constable, 1934, p. 379.

15 Thackston, 1999, p. 216; Rogers and Beveridge, 1909–14, Vol. I, p. 369 gives the same figure but identifies the animal as a tiger. We shall come to this matter presently.
16 I am grateful to Dr Asok Kumar Das for bringing this painting from the Maharaja Sawai Man Singh II Museum, Jaipur, Acc. No. 863, to my attention and dating it.
17 Constable, 1934, p. 379.
18 Thackston, 1999, pp. 411, 473.
19 Habib, 1963, p. 368.
20 Thackston, 1999, p. 473.
21 Sunquist and Sunquist, 2002, p. 288.
22 See Appendix 3.
23 Humphreys and Kahrom, 1995, pp. 75, 77.
24 I am grateful to Professor Muzaffar Alam who checked the Sayeed Ahmud text of *Tuzuk-i-Jahangiri* and found the word *shir* in all relevant cases on pp. 65, 78, 80, 89, 92, 117, 140, 175, 179, 182, 185, 221, 366, and 375; Ahmud, 1864.
25 Sunquist and Sunquist, 2002, pp. V–VI.
26 Sen, 1984, plate 20; Divyabhanusinh, 1986 and 1999 for a detailed analysis of the event.
27 Dr Asok Kumar Das, pers. comm., 2003.
28 Thapar, 2004, p. 250.
29 Dr Asok Kumar Das, pers. comm., 2004.
30 Rogers and Beveridge, 1909–14, Vol. I, p. 351.
31 Ibid.; Thackston, 1999, p. 207; Rogers and Beveridge, 1909–14, Vol. I, p. 351.
32 Beveridge, 1904, Vol. II, pp. 294, 482–83. Professor Muzaffar Alam checked the *Akbarnama* text edited by Maulvi Abdul Rahim and found the word to be *shir* in both cases on pp. 189 and 238.
33 Ibid., pp. 482–83.
34 Blochman, 1873, Vol. I, p. 294. Prof. Muzaffar Alam checked the *Ain-i-Akbari* text edited by Saiyad Ahmad Khan and found that the word is *shir* on p. 145.
35 Daljeet, 1999, p. 41.
36 Thackston, 1999, p. 108.
37 Ibid., p. 120.
38 Ibid., p. 91.
39 Ibid., p. 213.
40 Rogers and Beveridge 1909–14, Vol. I, p. 286; Divyabhanusinh, 1999 for a detailed analysis of the incident.

41 Thackston, 1999, pp. 117–18.
42 The description of the painting is based on my discussions with Dr Asok Kumar Das.
43 Thackston, 1999, p. 219.
44 Divyabhanusinh, 1987 for a detailed analysis of the event.
45 Alvi and Rahman, 1968, plate VII.
46 Thackston, 1999, p. 144.
47 Kostioukovitch, 1996, plate 146/folio 72 recto, text pp. 97–98.
48 Ibid., pp. 97–98.
49 Beach and Koch, 1997, plate 30.
50 Das, 1978, frontispiece; Divyabhanusinh, 1999.
51 Constable, 1934, p. 378.
52 Ibid.
53 Beach and Koch, 1997, plate 46.
54 Singh, 1959, plate opp. p. 161; Singh, 1965, pp. 116–19.
55 Robinson, 1976, plates 130–31, p. 264.
56 Koch, 1998, p. 23.
57 Constable, 1934, pp. 182–83.
58 Ibid., p. 379.
59 Blochman, 1873, p. 294, the translated word for *shir* is tiger here.
60 Acc. No. CBL IN 11A.28.
61 Goetz, 1950, plate 77, p. 170.
62 Trivedi, 1998.
63 Habib, 1982, Sheet 7A, p. 25.
64 Guha, 2001, pp. 34, 58. Earlier estimates by Irfan Habib (1982A), which have now been pared down, were a population of 145 million in 1600 and less than 200 million by 1800.

CHAPTER 7

THE BRITISH COME CALLING

1 Kaul, 1979, pp. 424–25.
2 Foster, 1926, p. 176.
3 Ibid., p. 365.
4 Williamson, 1807.
5 Archer, 1969, Vol. I, pp. 162–63.
6 D'Oyly, 1810–15.
7 Dr J.P. Losty, pers. comm., 2002.
8 Ibid.
9 Jerdon, 1867, p. 238.
10 Mundy, 1858, p. 159.
11 Elgood, 1995, p. 157.
12 Anon., 1873, Vol. I, pp. 137–39.

13 Rice, 1884, p. 137.

14 Mehta, 2001, pp. 66–69.

15 Fenton, c. 1924, pp. 6–13.

16 Ibid., p. 13.

17 Kincaid, 1935, pp. 10–11.

18 Fenton, c. 1924, pp. 21–22.

19 M.K. Ranjitsinhji, pers. comm., 2003.

20 Mundy, 1858, p. 159.

21 Rice, 1884, p. 140.

22 Ibid.

23 Edwardes and Fraser, 1907, pp. 179–80.

24 Elgood, 1995, p. 157.

25 Kinnear, 1920.

26 Rice, 1884, p. 138.

27 Newall, 1882–87, Vol. II, p. 445.

28 Rangarajan, 2001.

29 Ibid.

30 Tod, 1832, p. 407.

31 Jacob, 1842, p. 19.

32 Rangarajan, 2001.

33 M.K. Himmatsinhji of Kutch, pers. comm., 1997.

34 Joslin, 1973.

35 Burton, 1959.

36 Prasad, c. 1965.

37 Jepson, 1936, pp. 131–35.

38 Burton, 1931; Burton, 1933.

39 Aflalo, 1904.

40 Joslin, 1973.

41 Rangarajan, 2000, p. 32.

42 Divyabhanusinh, 1995, pp. 196–97, 215–23.

43 Ibid., pp. 222–23.

44 Thapar, 1992, p. 42.

45 Rangarajan, 2000, p. 32.

46 See Chapter 11, p. 178.

47 See Chapter 6, p. 113.

48 Guha, 2001, p. 58.

49 Visaria and Visaria, 1982.

50 See Chapter 8, pp. 141–42.

51 See Appendix 4.

52 Sankhala, 1978, pp. 117–79.

53 See Chapter 6, p. 94.

54 Fox-Davies, 1909, p. 172.

55 Archer, 1962, p. ii.

56 Archer, 1959, pp. 4, 20.

57 Forbes, 1813, Vol. 4, p. 200.

58 Ibid.

59 Archer, 1959, p. 5.

60 Gould, 1971.

61 Joslin et al., 1988, entry no. 38.

62 Ibid., entry no. 75.

63 Ibid., entry no. 96.

64 Nott, 1886, p. 59.

65 Pocock, 1930.

66 Bhavnagar, 1911, opp. p. XIV.

67 Mukherjee, 1990, pp. 87–88, plate IXB.

68 Balachandran, 1998.

69 K.D. Kaur Singh, 2003, pp. 55, 101, 105.

CHAPTER 8

SORUTH SARKAR SAVES LIONS

1 Trautman, 1982.

2 Rajan, 1985, p. 16.

3 Ibid., p. 29.

4 Anon., 1939, pp. 320–21.

5 Shaikh, 1936, p. 1. For general background see Anon., 1903.

6 Wood and Meher, 1998, p. 98.

7 Rangarajan, 2001.

8 Ibid.; Kincaid, 1905 for a detailed account of the outlaws.

9 Rangarajan, 2000.

10 Edwardes and Fraser, 1907, p. 104; Bhavnagar, 1911, Vol. I, p. 385.

11 Shaikh, 1936, p. 8.

12 Joslin, 1973.

13 Wilberforce-Bell, 1916, p. 277.

14 Ratnu, 1934, p. 310.

15 Fenton, c. 1924, pp. 1–2.

16 *DUSJ*, Vol. I, No. 4, January 27, 1868.

17 Sanyal, 1892, p. 40.

18 GA, File No. nil, Political Agency Notification No. 22 of May 10, 1879.

19 *DUSJ*, Vol. 13, No. 9, April 1880.

20 Rangarajan, 2001, p. 28.

21 *JRM*, Vol. 3, pp. 1907–08, Notification No. 1683, Resolution No. 1877.

22 Fenton, c. 1924, p. 7.

23 *JAR*, 1907, pp. 1, 21–22.

24 Srivastava and Srivastava, 1999, p. 46.

25 Shri Shambhuprasad Desai, pers. comm., 1996; Edwardes and Fraser, 1907, pp. 92–102; Shaikh, 1936, pp. 11–14.

26 See Chapter 11, p. 178.

27 *JAR*, 1907, pp. 1, 21–22.

28 *JAR*, 1945, p. 112.

29 *JAR*, 1907, pp. 2, 21.

30 *JAR*, 1908–09, pp. 32–33; 1909–10, p. 31.

31 Edwardes and Fraser, 1907, p. 171.

32 Fenton, c. 1924, p. 5.

33 Kincaid, 1905, p. 151.

34 GA, File No. 1, 1900–21.

35 Mosse, 1957.

36 GA, File No. 1, 1900–21.

37 NAI, Home Public, August 1904, No. 15; see Appendix 4.

38 Wynter-Blyth, 1950, pp. 3–5.

39 GA, File No. 1, 1900–21.

40 Fenton, c. 1924, p. 7.

41 GA, File No. 1, 1900–21.

42 Wynter-Blyth, 1950, p. 5.

43 Fenton, c. 1924, p. 7.

44 Wynter-Blyth, 1950, p. 5.

45 Edwardes and Fraser, 1907, pp. 173, 180–82; see Chapter 7, p. 122.

46 Taparia, 1979, p. 220.

47 GA, File No. 1, 1900–21. Junagadh Notification No. 696 of April 29, 1909; Agency Notification No. 25 of June 24, 1909.

48 Shaikh, 1936, pp. 14–15.

49 Sodha, 2002, p. 171.

50 Cadell, 1933.

51 Srivastava and Srivastava, 1999, p. 46.

52 *JAR*, 1911–12, p. 30.

53 Ibid., p. 32.

54 See Chapter 11, p. 179.

55 GA, File No. 37, 1913, Junagadh Notification No. 9 of June 3, 1913; Kathiawar Notification No. 28 of 1913.

56 GA, File No. 60, 1912, letter to Kutch of February 18, 1912; File No. nil of 1912, Letter to Jamnagar of March 22, 1912; File No. 17, 1913, Letters to Bikaner of February 16 and April 10, 1913; File No. 15, 1917, Letter to Poonch of February 23, 1917.

57 GA, File No. 15, 1914 and 1940, letter of December 1914, Rendall's reply of December 9, 1914; Hony. Sec. Zoological Garden, Calcutta's letter of April 5, 1902 and Hony. Sec. BNHS's letter of March 11, 1909.

58 Fenton, c. 1924, p. 7.

59 *JRM*, 1930, p. 1911, Circular no. 118, July 5, 1919.

CHAPTER 9

THE LAST NAWAB BATTLES ON

1 Low, 1947, p. 1342.

2 *JRM*, Vol. III, 1930, p. 1719.

3 *JAR*, 1910–11, p. 3.

4 Shaikh, 1936, pp. 20–22.

5 Menon, 1956, p. 125.

6 Paul and Kapoor, 2003, p. 252.

7 Shri Jaisukhlal P. Sodha, pers. comm., 2002.

8 Sodha, 2002, pp. 32, 82.

9 Shri Shambhuprasad Desai, pers. comm., 1995.

10 This account of the nawab's love of animals is based on several conversations with the late Shri Shambhuprasad Harprasad Desai, as indeed conversations with several members of the princely order and other persons in Junagadh and Kathiawar.

11 Mr E. Joubert van Ingen, pers. comm., 1997.

12 Ibid.

13 Ibid.

14 Cadell, 1933.

15 Shaikh, 1936.

16 Watson, 1884, frontispiece.

17 Gee, 1964, p. 87.

18 Wood and Meher, 1998, p. 95.

19 Anon., 1959, p. 842.

20 Wood and Meher, 1998, p. 98.

21 Anon., 1980, p. 768.

22 Jain, 1999, p. 3.

23 GA, 1922, File No. nil, Letter No. 2713 of September 30, 1922. GA, Shikar Daftar, 1921, File No. nil, Letter from Navanagar to Junagadh of May 31, 1921; Letter from Junagadh to Navanagar of June 1, 1921; Letter of Navanagar to Junagadh of June 5, 1921; Letter of Bikaner to Junagadh of June 5, 1921; Letter of Junagadh to Bikaner of June 6, 1921.

24 Rodrigues, 2003, p. 54.

25 M.K. Ranjitsinhji, pers. comm., 2003.

26 MA, 1921, File No. 1438 Pol. Dept., Junagadh's letter to A.G. of June 29, 1921.

27 MA, File No. 1438, Pol. Dept., June 29, 1921. AG's letter to Sec. to Govt. of July ..., 1921.

28 MA, File No. 1438, Pol. Dept., Sec. to Govt's letter to A.G. Kathiawar of September 8, 1921.

29 Cadell, 1933.

30 GA, File No. 5, 1917–25, letter dated September 30, 1922.

31 GA, File No. 10.8 circular no. 22 of V.S. 1984 (1928).

32 GA, File no. 6, 1914–18; *JRM* Vol. 3, p. 1312, Memo No. 1675/77 from M.J. Vasavda, Revenue Commissioner.

33 GA, File No. 17, 1921. Letter from Junagadh to Agent to Governor, Kathiawar, February 1921.

34 GA, File No. 60, 1913, letter of Administrator to Diwan of Manavadar.

35 GA, File No. 13, 1935, letter of Junagadh to Manavadar of February 5, 1935.

36 M.K. Ranjitsinhji, pers. comm., 2003; Rangarajan, 2001, p. 32.

37 *JRM*, Vol. 3, pp. 1910–11, Firman no. 62 of September 29, 1925.

38 Dalip Singh, pers. comm., March 28, 1997.

39 Mr E. Joubert van Ingen, pers. comm., May 14, 1997.

40 Wankaner, 1952.

41 M.K. Ranjitsinhji, pers. comm., 1997; Darbar Saheb Jaswantsinhji of Bilkha, pers. comm., 1997.

42 GA, File No. 76, Note dated November 4, 1937.

43 Darbar Saheb Jaswantsinhji of Bilkha, pers. comm., 1997.

44 Ibid.

45 Shaikh, 1936, p. 17; photographic record of Viceroy's shoot with Joshi Studio, Rajkot.

46 Wynter-Blyth, 1949; Caldwell, 1938.

47 *JAR*, 1914–15, p. 57; 1915–16, p. 69; 1916–17, p. 56; 1918–19, p. 45; 1920–21, p. 39; 1921–22, p. 50; 1922–23, p. 62; 1923–24, p. 53; 1924–25, p. 59; 1925–26, p. 48; 1926–27, p. 54; 1927–28, p. 66; 1928–29, p. 51; 1929–30, p. 82; 1930–31, p. 70; 1931–32, p. 67; 1932–33, pp. 73–74; 1933–34, p. 63; 1934–35, p. 75; 1935–36, p. 79; 1936–37, p. 78; 1937–38, p. 76; 1938–39, p. 80; 1939–40, p. 82; 1940–41, p. 76; and 1942–43, p. 85.

48 See Chapter 11, p. 182.

CHAPTER 10

THE DOMINION OF INDIA INHERITS LIONS

1 Mohan, 1990, p. 1.

2 Menon, 1956, p. 177; Low, 1947, p. 1342.

3 *JAR*, 1936–37 to 1944–45; Low, 1947, p. 1342.

4 Wolpert, 1984, p. 347; Wolpert, 1993, pp. 25–26. The description in the chapter of the event in 1947 is based on Menon, 1956, pp. 125–50, as also the stories heard by the author while at school at Rajkot in the early 1950s.

5 Maharana Raj Saheb Pratapsinhji of Wankaner, pers. comm., 2002.

6 Ibid.

7 Shri Mahesh Singh, D.F.O. Sasan, pers. comm., 1999.

8 Shri Shambhuprasad Desai, pers. comm., 1996; Darbar Saheb Jaswantsinhji of Bilkha, pers. comm., 1997; stories heard by the author in the early 1950s.

9 Gee, 1964, p. 94.

10 Wynter-Blyth, 1949.

11 M.K. Pushpendrasinhji Lunawada, pers. comm., 1997.

12 Anon., 1948, p. 20; Anon., 1950, pp. 49–50, 239–51.

13 Wynter-Blyth, 1949.

14 Wynter-Blyth, 1950.

15 Ibid.

16 Ibid.

17 Rao, et al., 1966, pp. 496–97.

18 *CAD*, Vol. IV, 1947, pp. 761–93.

19 See Appendix 5.

20 Mr Ashok H. Desai, pers. comm., April 14, 2001.

21 Ibid.

22 Guha, 2000, p. 42.

23 Ibid., p. 43.

CHAPTER 11

THE GREAT NUMBERS GAME

1 Ranjitsinh, 1997, pp. 97–99.

2 Ibid., p. 97; Gee, 1964, p. 153.

3 Divyabhanusinh, 1995.

4 Gee, 1964, p. 87; Ranjitsinh, 1997, p. 22; Sankhala, 1978, p. 176.

5 Ranjitsinh, 1997, p. 25; Sankhala, 1978, p. 177.

6 Rice, 1884, p. 144.

7 Joslin, 1973.

8 Edwardes and Fraser, 1907, p. 172.

9   Watson, 1884, pp. 6–7.

10 Rashid and David, 1992, p. 94; Singh and Kamboj, 1996, p. 64; Singh, 2001, p. 160.

11 Fenton, c. 1924, p. 13.

12 Edwardes and Fraser, 1907, p. 173.

13 GA, File No. 49, 1901.

14 Edwardes and Fraser, 1907, pp. 172–73.

15 Gee, 1964, p. 85.

16 GA, File No. 6, 1913, Letter of May 13, 1913.

17 Wallinger, 1913.

18 Rashid and David, 1992, p. 94; Singh and Kamboj, Vol. I, 1996, p. 64; Singh, 2001, p. 160.

19 Nicholson, 1935.

20 GA, File No. 10/8, 1937.

21 Wynter-Blyth, 1949.

22 Watson, 1884, p. 4.

23 Srivastava and Srivastava, 1999, p. 46.

24 Wynter-Blyth, 1949; Wynter-Blyth and Dharmakumarsinhji, 1950.

25 Wynter-Blyth, 1956.

26 Ibid.; Dharmakumarsinhji, 1969.

27 Ibid.

28 Ibid.

29 Dharmakumarsinhji, 1959, pp. 7–13.

30 Dharmakumarsinhji, 1969; Dalvi, 1969.

31 Singh, 2001.

32 Jain, 2001, p. 191.

33 Jhala, et al., 2002.

CHAPTER 12

A SECOND HOME

1   Singh and Kamboj, 1996, p. 20.

2   Seshadri, 1969, p. 117.

3   Kinnear, 1920.

4   GA, File No. 49, 1901.

5   Dr Mahesh Rangarajan, pers. comm., 2003.

6   Bull and Haksar, 1926, p. 242.

7   Singh, 1965, p. 87; Srivastava, 1969.

8   Singh, 1965, p. 88. He records that another lion was shot near Jhansi. This appears to be questionable as no such record has been found.

9   Stracey, 1963, p. 97.

10 Maharao Brijraj Singh of Kotah, pers. comm., 1977.

11 Minshull, 1937.

12 Thompson, 1999.

13 Smythies, 1942, pp. 108, 115, and 165.

14 Stracey, 1963, p. 97.

15 Lavkumar, 1956.

16 Gee, 1956.

17 Gee, 1962; Negi, 1966 and 1969; Srivastava, 1969; Bachkheti, 1995.

18 Dharmakumarsinhji, et al., 1970.

19 Oza, 1973.

20 Negi, 1969.

21 Ibid.; Joslin, 1985.

22 Humphreys and Kahrom, 1995, p. 77.

23 M.K. Ranjitsinhji, pers. comm., 2003.

24 Humphreys and Kahrom, 1995, pp. 77–78.

25 Ashraf, et al., 1995; Chellam, et al., 1994.

26 Sharma, et al., 2002.

27 Ibid.; Mr P.K. Sen, pers. comm., 2002.

28 *PH,* January 24 and February 15, 1995.

29 *PH,* April 14, 1994; April 20, 1997.

30 *PH,* July 30, 2002.

31 *The Times of India,* Jaipur, August 3, 2002.

32 Ranjitsinh, 2001.

CHAPTER 13

LIFE IN THE REPUBLIC: THE LION IN WINTER

1   *COI,* 2003, Seventh Schedule, State List Nos. 18 and 19, p. 226.

2   Rangarajan, 2001.

3   Ibid.

4   Vaidya, 1958, pp. 125, 130; Ylla, 1958, pp. 32–33.

5   Gee, 1964, p. 90.

6   M.K. Ranjitsinhji, pers. comm., 2003.

7   For a detailed description of tracking lions see Dharmakumarsinhji, 1992, pp. 74–75.

8   Jamkhandikar, 2000, p. 48.

9   Ranjitsinh, 1997, p. 51.

10 Dharmakumarsinhji, et al., 1970, pp. 37–38.

11 Ghorpade, 1983, pp. 88–98.

12 Ranjitsinh, 1997, p. 52.

13 Stracey, 1963, p. 98.

14 Joslin, 1973; Rangarajan, 2001.

15 Rangarajan, 2001.

16 Singh, 2001, p. 69.

17 Anon., 1972, p. 14.

18 Ibid., p. 11.

19 Ibid., pp. 12–14.

20 Ibid., pp. 22–24; Singh, 2001A, p. 69.

21 Anon., 1972, p. 16.

22 Singh and Kamboj, 1996, Vol. II, pp. 54–56.

23 Ibid., p. 57.

24 Ibid., pp. 60–61. More recently the number of livestock has been put at approximately 13,000 heads (Mr Bharat J. Pathak, pers. comm., 2004).

25 Singh and Kamboj, 1996, Vol. I, p. 54.

26 Sinha, 1987.

27 Singh and Kamboj, 1996, Vol. I, p. 54.

28 Chellam, 1993.

29 Dharmakumarsinhji, 1979.

30 *COI,* 2003, Seventh Schedule, Concurrent List No. 17A and 17B, p. 229; Directive Principles of State Policy Article 48A, p. 29.

31 Singh, 2001A.

32 Singh, 1997; 1998; 2001A; Lal, 2000.

33 Singh, 2001A.

34 *PH,* January 5 and 7, and February 1, 2003.

35 Maharana Raj Saheb Pratapsinhji of Wankaner, pers. comm., 2001.

36 Proverbs 26:13.

37 Singh, 2001A.

38 Mr Bharat Pathak, pers. comm., 2004.

39 Lal, 2000; Singh, 2001A.

40 *PH,* April 21, 2003.

41 Singh, 2001, p. 77.

42 Singh, 2001A.

43 Anon., 2000.

44 Ibid.

45 Mukhopadhyaya and Aiyar, 2002, p. 32.

46 Mahesh Singh to Nagendra Singh Hada, pers. comm., 1999.

47 Saberwal, et. al., 1994.

48 Wynter-Blyth and Dharmakumarsinhji, 1950.

49 Singh and Kamboj, 1996, Vol. I, p. 88.

50 Ibid, Vol. II, pp. 56–61.

51 Ibid., p. 59.

52 Sharma and Johnsingh, 1996, pp. 77–78.

53 Singh and Kamboj, 1996, Vol. II, p. 53.

54 Ibid., p. 87.

55 Ibid., p. 66.

56 *PH,* March 21, 27, and 29, 2003.

57 Singh and Kamboj, 1996, Vol. II, p. 65.

58 *PH,* May 30 and 31, June 1, 7, 8, 11, 12, and 13, 1996.

59 Mukhopadhyaya and Aiyar, 2002, p. 33.

APPENDIX 1

Glossary

Flora

Ber or Bor	*Zizyphus mauritiana*
Corindah or Karvanda	*Carissa carandas*
Dudhalo	*Wrightia tinctoria*
Jambudo or Jamun	*Eugenia jambolana*
Khakhro or Palas, Flame of the Forest	*Butea monosperma*
Khadira or Khair	*Acacia catechu*
Sawar or Semal, Silk Cotton	*Bombax malabaricum*
Sag, Teak	*Tectona grandis*
Udumbara	*Ficus glomerata*
Vad, Banyan	*Ficus benghalensis*

Fauna

Antelope, Indian (Blackbuck)	*Antilope cervicapra*
Four-horned (Chowsingha)	*Tetracerus quadricornis*
Ass, Indian Wild	*Equus hemionus khur*
Persian Wild (Onager)	*Equus hemionus onager*
Boar, Wild	*Sus scrofa*
Buffalo, Wild	*Bubalus bubalis*
Bustard, Great Indian	*Ardeotis nigriceps*
MacQueen's (Houbara)	*Chlamydotis maqueeni*
Caracal	*Caracal caracal*
Cat, Jungle	*Felis chaus*
Rusty-spotted	*Prionailurus rubiginosus*
Cheetah	*Acinonyx jubatus*
Chinkara	*Gazella bennettii*
Crocodile, Marsh (Mugger)	*Crocodylus paluster*
Deer, Hog	*Axis porcinus*
Spotted (Chital)	*Axis axis*
Swamp (Barasingha)	*Cervus duvauceli*
Dog, Indian Wild (Dhole)	*Cuon alpinus*
Eagle, Crested Serpent	*Spilornis cheela*
Elephant, Indian	*Elephas maximus*
Syrian	*Elephas maximus asurus*
Falcon, Peregrine	*Falco peregrinus*
Red-headed or Barbary	*Falco peregrinus babylonicus*
Shahin	*Falco peregrinus peregrinator*
Florican, Lesser	*Sypheotides indica*
Fox, Indian	*Vulpes bengalensis*
Gaur	*Bos gaurus*
Gharial	*Gavialis gangeticus*
Goshawk	*Accipiter gentilis*
Hangul	*Cervus elaphus*
Hare	*Lepus nigricollis*
Hippopotamus	*Hippopotamus amphibius*
Hornbill, Grey	*Ocyceros birostris*
Hyena, Spotted	*Crocuta crocuta*
Striped	*Hyaena hyaena*
Jackal	*Canis aureus*
Kite, Pariah	*Milvus migrans*
Leopard	*Panthera pardus*
Lion	*Panthera leo*
Merlin, Red-headed	*Falco chicquera*
Mongoose, Common	*Herpestes edwardsi*

Nilgai (Blue Bull)	*Boselaphus tragocamelus*
Partridge, Grey	*Francolinus pondicerianus*
Peacock	*Pavo cristatus*
Pigeon, Green	*Treron phoenicoptera*
Quail, Common	*Coturnix coturnix*
Rhinoceros, Great Indian	
one-horned	*Rhinoceros unicornis*
Asian one-horned	*Rhinoceros sandaicus*
Asian two-horned	*Dicerorhinus sumatrensis*
Sambar	*Cervus unicolor*
Sandgrouse, Painted	*Pterocles indicus*
Sangai	*Cervus eldii*
Shrew, Musk	*Suncus murinus*
Sparrowhawk	*Accipiter nisus*
Sunbird, Purple	*Nectarinia asiatica*
Tiger	*Panthera tigris*
Turkey	*Meleagris gallopavo*
Urial	*Ovis orientalis*
Vulture, King	*Sarcogyps calvus*
Wolf	*Canis lupus*
Zebra, Burchell's	*Equus burchelli*

Indian Words

arti	prayer performed with a lamp lit with clarified butter waved before the deity
arzi hakumat	government in exile
ashrafi	gold coin
baharvatia	outlaws
chakravartin	universal ruler
Charan	bard community
chhattra	umbrella over the head of a king sitting on a throne or carried over his head by a bearer, a traditional Indian insignia of royalty
dang	staff of a pastoralist
darbar	court of a ruler; often Darbar is used to denote a Rajput or Kathi
dhamma/dharma	teachings of the Buddha, religion, right behaviour
dharna	form of peaceful protest
hukk	right or entitlement
Kathi	caste of people who ruled many small principalities in Saurashtra, after whom the peninsula was called Kathiawar

Kathiawar; Kathiawari	Saurashtra; Gujarati dialect spoken in Saurashtra
Koli	tribe of hunters and food gatherers
kos or koss, kuroh	measure of length, approximately 2½ miles or 4 kilometres
machan	covered platform usually in a tree erected for shikar
Maldhari	cattle graziers of Saurashtra and elsewhere
mehmandari	hospitality
moongiya	colour of moong, a lentil, dull green or yellow, used in shikar for camouflage
ness	cattle pen of Maldharis
pagi	tracker
prant	administrative unit
Qamargah	mode of encircling and trapping game for hunting by an ever-decreasing circle of men, a procedure made famous by the Mughals
Rabari	cattle herders who make a living out of selling milk and its products
safa	turban of a type popularized in the 20th century, usually worn by Rajputs
Sidi	person of African descent
swapado	savage, ferocious, wild beast
tasu	measure of length, about 1.33 inches or 3.5 centimetres
thikana	fiefdom within a princely state
tilak	mark worn on forehead by a practising Hindu
zortalbi	tribute collected by Junagadh state from other states in Kathiawar

Kathiawari Words Relating to the Lion

sawaj/hawaj, sinh	male lion, lions
sinhan	lioness
janawar	in Gir the word is usually used for lions; in general usage: animals
pathdo, pathadi	immature lion, lioness
belad	pair of male lions
tolu	pride of lions; in general usage: group of animals, people
bhurio	lion with a light brown mane
danak	lion's roar
daro	lion's warning grunt or growl; in general usage: to frighten
dhodvun	lion's charge; in general usage: to run
gadhio	short-bodied/stockily built lion
ghamak	low grunt used by a lioness to call her cubs
ghor	lioness in oestrus
ghoro	mating of a pair of lions
huk	lion's roar
jamwo	male lion whose mane is very dark but not necessarily black, the body being a shade of grey; usually an old animal
kalo, kalio, kamho	black-maned lion; in general usage: black
kesarisinh	lion with a luxuriant mane
keshwari	mane of a lion; also of a horse
maran	kill of a lion; also of other carnivores such as leopard
pilo	lion with a light coloured mane; in general usage: yellow
radiyo	noisy lion given to roaring very often; in general usage: noisy person
sagad	footprint/spoor of a lion; also of other animals
untio	tall mangy lion, camel coloured lion, scantily maned
velar	long-bodied lion

WITH THE DECREASING numbers of wildlife, most of the vocabulary concerning wild animals has disappeared from common usage. Even dictionaries do not always give the correct meaning. There is an urgent need to record such words before some of them vanish forever. Given here are the words used for lions/lionesses, followed by terms used to describe them and their behaviour.

I have not come across a word for a maneless lion such as the common Gujarati words *taklo*, *bodo*, or *ganjo* which mean bald. The nearest word is *untio* used for a mangy lion. The word *untio wagh* (camel coloured tiger) is described as the word for a lion in use in Kutch and elsewhere in Gujarat in the literature of the British period (Rice, 1884, p. 138; Russell, 1900, p. 196). It is not in use in the Gir today. Rice also mentions that in the Gir the word *sooee* was used for a lioness. However, this name too is not in use today.

APPENDIX 3

The Size of Asiatic Lions

THE SIZE OF the Asiatic lion has been a subject of prolonged discussion during the British period particularly in comparison with the lions from Africa. For a long time it was believed that the animals from Africa were bigger. The present list was compiled with the sizes in descending order to compare it with records from Africa to arrive at a conclusion based on records of hunting trophies which were until recently the single most extensive source available. Usually, the length of the animal was considered.

The tenth edition of *Rowland Ward's Records of Big Game, African and Asiatic Sections* published in 1935, the ultimate authority on the subject, has twelve entries on the length of the trophies from Africa but only four for India (Dollman and Burlace, 1935, pp. 365–67). In order to expand the information base I undertook an extensive search through the shikar literature of the period since 1807, unpublished shikar diaries, personal interviews, etc. to produce the present list which has 73 entries for India. Such a compilation cannot ever be complete.

Measurements of large carnivores were of four kinds. Field measurements of the length were taken by the sportsman from the tip of the nose to the tip of the tail. The measurement was either taken along the curves of the body of the animal, or the animal would be suspended by its feet, pegs would be driven into the ground at the extremities of the nose and the tail, and then the distance between the pegs would be measured. The second method naturally gave a shorter length – the difference varying between 2 and 5 inches (M.K. Ranjitsinhji, pers. comm., 2003). This method appears to have come into vogue after the first world war though a definite date cannot be assigned. The third method was to measure the pegged down pelt after the animal was skinned. Such measurements could exceed the "along the curve" measurements by up to a foot (Ranjitsinhji, pers. comm.). This method appears to have gone out of use early in the 20th century. The last method was to measure the cured and dressed skin of the rug or trophy, which was usually done by the taxidermist. It may be noted here that since field measurements were taken by the sportsman himself, there was a tendency to maximize the length of the trophy so that it would look good in a record book or shikar diary. Which of the first two methods was used by a sportsman in a particular instance, is difficult to ascertain unless specifically noted by him.

Recently there has been a change in the approach, and now only skull measurements are taken. The 22nd edition of *Rowland Ward's Records of Big Game* published in 1989 has 325 entries for lions of Africa and only two for lions from Asia (Smith, et al., 1989). With such a dearth of information from India, the matter was not pursued further as it is now not possible to obtain such measurements from trophies of old.

TABLE I: SIZE OF ASIATIC LIONS FROM HUNTING RECORDS						
S. No.	Sportsman	Year	Sex	Size		Locality	Source
				LENGTH	SKIN LENGTH		
1.	Major General William Rice	circa 1850	Male	Over 10' 6" (length of mane 18")	11' 6"	Near Rajkot	Rice, 1884, p. 136; Newall, 1882–87, Vol. II, p. 445.
2.	Unknown	–	Male	–	11' 5"(tail 2' 10", height 3' 3")	Central India	Burke, 1920, pp. 11–12.
3.	"Collector"	1832	Male	–	11' 3"[A]	Banas, Gujarat	Anon., 1873A, p. 132.
4.	J.H. Du Boulay	1905	Male	–	11' 0"	Gir	Edwardes and Fraser, 1907, p. 176; Fenton, c. 1924, p. 9.
5.	Darbar Saheb Imammuddin Khanji Babi of Pajod	circa 1949	Male	–	11' 0" (dressed skin)	Waghania	K.S. Ayaz Khanji of Pajod, pers. comm., 1997.
6.	Colonel W.P. Kennedy	1905	Male	–	10' 10"	Gir	Edwardes and Fraser, 1907, p. 176; Fenton, c. 1924, p. 9.
7.	Lord Lamington	-do-	Male	–	10' 4"	-do-	-do- Stracey, 1963, p. 136; Dollman and Burlace, 1935, p. 367.
8.	M.K. Bhim Singh of Kotah	1935	Male	9' 2"	10' 4" (dressed skin)	Amrithal, Sasan Gir	Maharao Brijraj Singh of Kotah, pers. comm., 1997; Dollman and Burlace, 1935, p. 367.
9.	Princess Rajendrakunverba of Palitana	circa 1950	Male	10' 2"	–	Jamwala, Gir	Princess Rajendrakunverba of Palitana, pers. comm., 1997.

10.	H.H. Maharaja Sayaji Rao Gaekwad of Baroda	circa 1914	Male	About 10' 0"	–	Ghatwad, Amreli district	Carruthers, et al., 1915.
11.	Lieutenant [later Maj. Gen.] W. Rice	circa 1850	Male	9' 11"	–	Gir	Stracey, 1963, p. 136.
12.	Lieutenant Percy Hancock	–	Male	9' 10"	–	Gir	Burke, 1920, p. 11.
13.	Unknown[B]	–	Male	9' 0"	9' 11" (body 6' 10", tail 2' 10", mane 11")	Allahabad	Pocock, 1930.
14.	"Ignotus"	1830	Male	–	9' 6"	Pattan, Khandesh	Burton, 1933, p. 277.
15.	Lord Harris	1893	Male	9' 7"	–	Gir	Pocock, 1930; Dollman and Burlace, 1935, p. 367.
16.	H.H. Maharaja Ganga Singh of Bikaner	1942	Male	9' 7"	–	Gatraliadhar, Sasan Gir	Thakur Dalip Singh, pers. comm., 1997.
17.	Captain Habbert	circa 1900	Male	–	9' 6"	Gir	Edwardes and Fraser, 1907, p. 176.
18.	H.H. Maharaja Ganga Singh of Bikaner	1940	Male	9' 5½"	–	Billiat, Sasan Gir	Thakur Dalip Singh, pers. comm., 1997.
19.	Lieutenant Colonel L.L. Fenton	1886	Male	9' 5" (tail 2' 11")	–	Gir	Fenton, circa 1924, p. 9; Pocock, 1930.
20.	H.H. Maharaja Ganga Singh of Bikaner	1940	Male	9' 4½"	–	Gatraliadhar, Sasan Gir	Thakur Dalip Singh, pers. comm., 1997.
21.	Emperor Jahangir	1623	Male	9' 4"	–	Rahimabad near Agra	Thackston, 1999, p. 411.
22.	R.S. Nirmalkumarsinhji of Bhavnagar	1933	Male	9' 4" (height 38" girth 60")	–	Andhania, Gir	Dharmakumar-sinhji and Wynter-Blyth, 1951.
23.	Darbar Rawatwala of Bilkha	circa 1940	Female	9' 4"	–	Bilkha	Darbar Jaswantsinhji of Bilkha, pers. comm., 1997.

24.	Yuvraj Brijraj Singh of Kotah	1946	Male	9' 4"	–	Devalia, Gir	Maharao Brijraj Singh of Kotah, pers. comm., 1997.
25.	Unknown	–	Male	9' 3"	–	–	Burke, 1920, p. 12.
26.	H.H. Maharaja Ganga Singh of Bikaner	1941	Male	9' 3"	–	Booh Badli, Sasan Gir	Thakur Dalip Singh, pers. comm., 1997.
27.	-do-	1941	Male	9' 3"	–	Gatraliadhar, Sasan Gir	-do-
28.	R.K. Pushpendrasingh of Panna	1942	Male	9' 3"	–	Gir	Narayansingh Bhayal, pers. comm., 1997.
29.	Count F. Scheibler	–	Male	9' 3"	–	-do-	Pocock, 1930.
30.	Captain Leathers	Circa 1900 (?)	Male	–	9' 2"	-do-	Edwardes and Fraser, 1907, p. 176.
31.	H.H. Maharaja Ganga Singh of Bikaner	1916	Male	9' 2½"	–	Nana Mano Ness, Sasan Gir	Thakur Dalip Singh, pers. comm., 1997; Dollman and Burlace, 1935, p. 367.
32.	Colonel J.W. Watson	Circa 1890 (?)	Male	–	9' 1"	Gir	Edwardes and Fraser, 1907, p. 176.
33.	Lieutenant Colonel L.L. Fenton	Circa 1895	Male	9' 1"	–	Talala, Gir	Fenton, c. 1924, p. 9.
34.	A.S. Vernay	1929	Male	9' 1"	–	Gir	Pocock, 1930.
35.	Lieutenant Colonel L.L. Fenton	Circa 1895	Male	9' 0"	–	Khokhra, Gir	Fenton, c. 1924, p. 9.
36.	Colonel J.W. Watson	-do-	Male	9' 0"	–	Mytiala, Bhavnagar	Dharmakumar-sinhji and Wynter-Blyth, 1951.
37.	H.H. Maharaja Krishnakumarsinhji of Bhavnagar	1941	Male	9' 0" (tail 3' 1", girth 45¾", height 40")	–	-do-	-do-

38.	H.H. Maharaja Raj Mayurdhwajsinhji of Dhrangadhra	1950	Male	9' 0" (along curves) 8' 8" (between pegs)	–	-do-	Maharaja Raj Megrajji of Dhrangadhra, pers. comm., 1995.
39.	Presented to British Museum by H.H. Nawab of Junagadh	1934	Male	–	9' 0" (tail 2' 8", dressed skin)	Gir	Pocock, 1936.
40.	Major H.G. Carnegie	1905	Female	–	9' 0"	Gir	Edwardes and Fraser, 1907, p. 176.
41.	Colonel Founthorpe	1929	Male	–	8' 11" (dressed skin)	-do-	Pocock, 1930.
42.	M.K. Chandrabhanusinhji of Wankaner	1934	Male	8' 11" (girth 45")	–	Ranithav, Mendarda portion of Gir	Wankaner, 1952.
43.	R.S. Dharmakumarsinhji of Bhavnagar	1938	Male	8' 10½" (height 39")	–	Mytiala, Bhavnagar	Dharmakumar- sinhji and Wynter- Blyth, 1951.
44.	Captain Trother	1871	Male	8' 10" (tail 35", height 40")	–	Shane, Mytiala, Bhavnagar	-do-
45.	H.H. Maharaja Krishnakumarsinhji of Bhavnagar	1931	Male	8' 10"	–	-do-	-do-
46.	Captain W. Smee	Circa 1830	Male	8' 9½"	–	Ahmedabad	Pocock, 1930.
47.	H.H. Maharani Vijayakumari of Bhavnagar	1938	Male	8' 8½" (tail 37", height 37", girth 38")	–	Mytiala, Bhavnagar	Dharmakumar- sinhji and Wynter- Blyth, 1951.
48.	H.H. Maharaja Krishnakumarsinhji of Bhavnagar	1934	Male	8' 7½" (height 39")	–	Sasan Gir	-do-
49.	W. Kelsey and party	1866	Male	8' 7" (height 3' 3", girth 3' 10")	–	Putna near Allahabad	Burton, 1933, p. 274.
50.	R.S. Nirmalkumarsinhji of Bhavnagar	1935	Male	8' 7" (height 39")	–	Mytiala, Bhavnagar	Dharmakumar- sinhji and Wynter- Blyth, 1951.

TABLE II: SIZE OF AFRICAN LIONS FROM ROWLAND WARD'S RECORDS OF BIG GAME (AFRICA AND ASIA) 10TH EDITION, 1935

S. No.	Sportsman	Year	Sex	Size		Locality
				LENGTH	LENGTH OF DRESSED SKIN	
1.	Captain J.K. Roberts	–		10' 11"	10' 4" (tail 3' 3")	Sudan
2.	A.S. Vernay	–		9' 10½"	11' 7"	Kalahari
3.	Countess Münster	–		–	10' 8" (tail 3' 2")	Tanganyika
4.	H.H. Prince Youssouf Kamal	–		–	10' 7" (tail 3' 1")	-do-
5.	F. Edmond Blanc	–		9' 9"	10' 5" (tail 3' 4")	Uganda
6.	Major J.B. Browne	–		9' 8"	10' 9" (tail 3' 4½")	Bahr-el-Arab
7.	H.H. the Heir Apparent [M.K. Sadul Singh] of Bikaner	–		9' 6½"	10' 7½" (tail 3' 2")	Tanganyika
8.	Madame E. Edmond-Blanc	–		–	10' 1" (tail 2' 11")	-do-
9.	Captain C.E. Parker	–		–	9' 10" (tail 3' 2")	Nyasaland
10.	H.H. the Heir Apparent [M.K. Sadul Singh] of Bikaner	–		9' 1"	10' 9" (tail 3' 1")	Tanganyika
11.	D.D. Stewart	–		–	8' 10" (tail 2' 10")	Darfur
12.	Mrs Hamilton-Leigh	–		8' 2"	9' 3½" (tail 3' 1")	Kenya Colony

Rowland Ward's compilation of 1935 (table II) has only one animal from Africa measured by the owner which was over 10 feet, as against two instances from India (table I). On the other hand there are nine entries from Africa of dressed skins above 10 feet whereas only two of Ward's four entries for India show skins above 10 feet.

A critical look at the compilation of the records of Indian trophies reveals that the lion shot by Major General William Rice circa 1850 was by far the largest even if we were to knock off 3 inches from his estimate of minimum length of the animal before skinning since he does not record the exact figure. If one were to discard this record, though Rice was a renowned hunter and would have been careful of his measurements, then the largest lion shot in India and recorded, came a hundred years later circa 1950, by Princess Rajendrakunverba of Palitana whose lion measured 10 feet 2 inches. This conclusion is based on the lengths recorded before skinning as the lengths of skins depend on several factors and this would lead to many more inaccuracies. The lengths are recorded here exactly as they were in various sources, not converted to the metric measures. Only the measurement of Emperor Jahangir's lion has been converted into feet and inches in order to make it uniform with other trophies listed here.

It will be seen that almost all the lions from India for which we have measurements here are of the Gir forest and its environs, a very small geographical area when compared with the African continent. However, if one assumes that the levels of accuracy in measurements are similar, one may conclude that the sizes of lions from Asia and from Africa are more or less equal.

APPENDIX 4

Lord Curzon's Letter of 1902

*Letter of H.E. The Rt. Hon'ble George Nathaniel Baron
Curzon of Kedleston P.C., G.M.S.I., G.C.I.E.,**
*Viceroy and Governor-General of India in reply to
The Humble Memorial of The Burma Game Preservation
Association of 23rd September 1901[+]*

* Privy Councellor, Grand Master of the Star of India, and
Extra Knight Grand Commander of the Indian Empire.
[+] Source: NAI, Home Public, August 1904, No. 15. In all
probability, the letter was written in 1902. It bears no date
but at 4.15 pm on January 17, 1902 it was sent for filing by
the Personal Secretary to the Viceroy. The file in the NAI
bears the date of 1904.

Gentlemen,

Among the many memorials which the enterprising
inhabitants of Lower Burma and of Rangoon have
showered upon me, and to all of which it has not been
possible for me to give a verbal reply, I have selected yours
as one of those to which I should be sorry not to return
such an answer – owing to the great importance of the
subject which it raises.

The question of Game Preservation in India is one that
may appeal, in my judgement, not merely to the
sportsman, but also to the naturalist and the friend of
animal life. It is certainly not through the spectacles of the
sportsman only that I would regard it, though I yield to no
one in my recognition of the manly attractions of shikar.
Such considerations, however, might be suspected of a
selfish tinge and I think that in approaching the matter we
should as far as possible, put our own predilections in the
background, and view it in the public interest at large.

There are some persons who doubt or dispute the
progressive diminution of wild life in India. I think that
they are wrong. The facts seem to me to point entirely in
the opposite direction. Up till the time of the Mutiny lions
were shot in Central India. They are now confined to an
ever-narrowing patch of forest in Kathiawar. I was on the
verge of contribution to their still further reduction a year
ago myself: but fortunately I found out my mistake in
time, and was able to adopt a restraint which I hope that
others will follow. Except in Native States, the Terai, and
forest reserves, tigers are undoubtedly diminishing. This is
perhaps not an unmixed evil. The rhinoceros is all but
exterminated save in Assam. Bison are not so numerous or
so easy to obtain as they once were. Elephants have
already had to be protected in many parts. Above all deer,
to which you particularly allude in the case of Burma, are
rapidly dwindling. Every man's hand appears to be against
them, and each year thins the herds. Finally many
beautiful and innocent varieties of birds are pursued for
the sake of their plumage, which is required to minister to
the heedless vanity of European fashion.

The causes of this diminution in the wild fauna of India
are in some cases natural and inevitable, in others they are
capable of being arrested. In the former class I would
name the steady increase of population, the widening area

of cultivation, and the improvement in means of communication – all of them the sequel of what is popularly termed progress in civilization. Among the artificial and preventable causes I would name the great increase in the number of persons who use firearms, the immense improvement in the mechanism and range of the weapons themselves, the unchecked depredations of native hunters and poachers, and in some cases, I regret to say, a lowering of the standard of sport, leading to the shooting of immature heads, or to the slaughter of females. The result of all these agencies, many of which are found in operation at the same time and in the same place, cannot fail to be a continuous reduction in the wild game of India.

I cannot say that the Government of India have hitherto shown any great boldness in dealing with the matter. But there has been, and still is, in my opinion, very good reason for proceeding cautiously. There are some persons who say that wild animals are as certainly destined to disappear in India as wolves, for instance, have done in England, and that it is of no use to try and put back the hands of the clock. I do not attach much value to this plea, which seems to me rather pusillanimous, as well as needlessly pessimistic. There are others who say that in a continent so vast as India, or – to narrow the illustration – in a province with such extensive forest reserves as Burma, the wild animals may be left to look after themselves. This argument does not impress me either: for the distant jungles are available only to the favoured few, and it is the disappearance of game from the plains and from accessible tracts that is for the most part in question. I do, however, attach great value to the consideration that wild animal life should not be unduly fostered at the expense of the occupations or the crops of the people. Where depredations are committed upon crops or upon flocks and herds, the cultivator cannot be denied, within reasonable limits, the means of self-protection. Similarly, it is very important that any restrictions that are placed upon the destruction of game should not be worked in a manner that may be oppressive or harassing to his interests.

Hitherto the attempts made by Government to deal with the question by legislation, or by rules and notifications based on statute, have been somewhat fitful and lacking in method. In parts, as I have already mentioned, elephants have been very wisely and properly protected. A close season has been instituted for certain kinds of game. An Act has been passed for the preservation of Wild Birds: and I observe from one of the enclosures to your memorial that your ingenuity has not shrunk from the suggestion that a deer may reasonably be considered a wild bird. Under this Act, the possession or sale during the breeding season of the flesh of certain wild birds in Municipal or Cantonment areas is forbidden. Then again rules have been issued under the Forest Act, protecting certain classes of animals in certain tracts.

The general effect of these restrictions has been in the right direction. But I doubt if they have been sufficiently coordinated, or if they have gone far enough: and one of my last acts at Simla, before I had received or read your memorial, was to invite a re-examination of the subject, with the view of deciding whether we might proceed somewhat further than we have already done. We must be very careful not to devise any too stereotyped or Procrustean form of procedures; since there is probably no matter in which a greater variety of conditions and necessities prevails; and the rules or precautions which would be useful in one place might be positively harmful in another. Among the suggestions which will occur to all of us as deserving of consideration, are some greater restriction, by the charge of fees or otherwise, upon the issue of gun licenses, the more strict enforcement of a close season for certain animals; the prohibition of the possession or sale of flesh during the breeding season, penalties upon netting and sharing during the same period, restrictions of the facilities given to strangers to shoot unlimited amounts of game, and upon the sale and export of trophies and skins. I daresay that many other ideas will occur to us in the discussion of the matter, or may be put forward in the press and elsewhere, by those who are qualified to advise. My own idea would be if possible to frame some kind of legislation of a permissive and elastic nature, the provisions of which should be applied to the various provinces of India in so far only as they were adapted to the local conditions. The question of Native States somewhat complicates the matter. But I doubt not that the Government would, where required, most [meet?] with the willing cooperation of the Chiefs, many of whom are keen and enthusiastic patrons both of animal life and of sport. The subject is not one that can be hastily taken up or quickly decided; but I have probably said enough to show you that I personally am in close sympathy with your aims: and I need hardly add that if the Government of India finds itself able, after further study, to proceed with the matter, an opportunity will be given to those who are interested in each province to record their opinions.

The Origin and Legal Basis of the Indian National Emblem

A PERUSAL OF various sources relating to the emergence of the Indian Constitution and the coming into being of the Republic of India, in a search for the genesis and the adoption of the capital of the Ashoka pillar at Sarnath as the official seal/emblem of the Union of India, has been illuminating and rewarding but not conclusive.

An obvious start would be to study Indian Constituent Assembly Debates which have been recorded in fourteen volumes and published by the Government of India. The Constituent Assembly Debates are also easily accessible on the Government of India website. It would be noteworthy to remember that the National Flag was adopted after a lengthy debate by the Constituent Assembly and the same has been recorded in Volume 4 of the Constituent Assembly Debates. I have found that there are references to the incorporation of the Ashoka Chakra to replace the charkha in the erstwhile flag of the Indian National Congress. Pandit Jawaharlal Nehru's speech relating to the incorporation of the Ashoka Chakra does not make any reference to the present National Emblem.

I have spent hours on the internet at the Government of India site which hosts the Constituent Assembly Debates and have used various options on the search engines but there appears no mention of the present National Emblem.

Further, I have physically examined the Constituent Assembly Debates from the date of the adoption of the Indian National Flag till June 14, 1948 (the day the Gazette of India changed its emblem from the British signet to the lion capital) and have found no reference to the adoption of the present emblem. I hasten to add that the Constituent Assembly Debates were not held on a day-to-day basis and that I have not examined any debate figuring after June 14, 1948.

The next feature of my research was B. Shiva Rao's multi-volume work, *The Framing of India's Constitution (Select Documents)* published by the Indian Institute of Public Administration, 1966. This work contains working notes of the sub-committee which was formed to decide on the issue of the adoption of the Indian National Flag and National Emblem. There are but two instances in relation to the notes of the sub-committee which are of importance, i.e. the notes dated July 10, 1947, which record the agenda in respect of the National Flag and a possible National Emblem. The notes dated July 18, 1947, crystallize the pattern of the National Flag but put off the National Emblem to a later date, which is not mentioned.

Further, the Gazette of India by a notification dated May 12, 1948 has certain draft amendments in respect of the Indian Pilgrim Ships Rules, 1933. One draft amendment refers to the "new seal" (lion capital) in place of the British signet. It is thus probable that any proposed change in respect of the nation's emblems took place between July 18, 1947 and May 12, 1948.

As this research has originated in Bombay, I also referred to The Bombay Government Gazette and the Gazette of India extraordinary. I found that the last day on which the Bombay Gazette displayed the British signet was Thursday, June 3, 1948. On Friday, June 4, 1948, the Indian emblem was displayed for the first time. Interestingly, the Gazette of India displayed the British signet for the last time on Saturday, June 12, 1948. The first time the Indian emblem was displayed in the Gazette of India extraordinary was Monday, June 14, 1948.

I have found no notification in either of the Gazettes pertaining to the change from the British signet to the [new] National Emblem. Furthermore, it is apparent that there was no uniform notification for the change in display of the National Emblem as the Bombay Gazette moved from the British signet to the Ashoka capital ten days *prior* to the change in the Government of India Gazette.

I therefore find it pertinent to note that the Constituent Assembly Debates do not shed any light on the basis for the choosing of the symbol, its origins, or the reasoning behind the National Emblem. To the best of my knowledge, there is no gazetted notification in the above period pertaining to the adoption of the National Emblem, or any sub-committee notification in respect of the same. As a result, the research on the basis for adoption of the National Emblem or the reasoning behind why the Ashoka capital was chosen is inconclusive and is open to speculation.

Udaybhanusinh
Advocate, High Court, Bombay

Maps

Past and Present Distribution of the Lion in North Africa and Asia

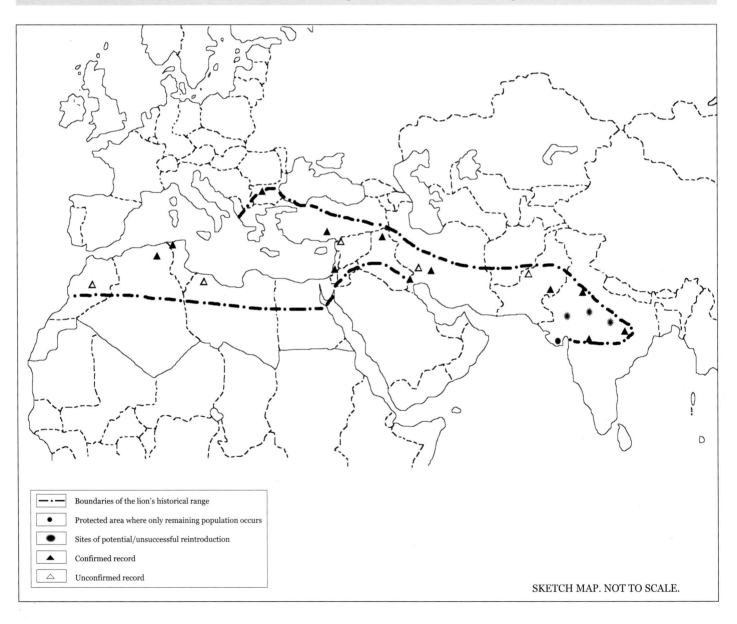

Boundaries of the lion's historical range

● Protected area where only remaining population occurs

✳ Sites of potential/unsuccessful reintroduction

▲ Confirmed record

△ Unconfirmed record

SKETCH MAP. NOT TO SCALE.

Courtesy Nowell and Jackson/IUCN 1996.

Past and Present Distribution of the Lion in India, R.I. Pocock's Map

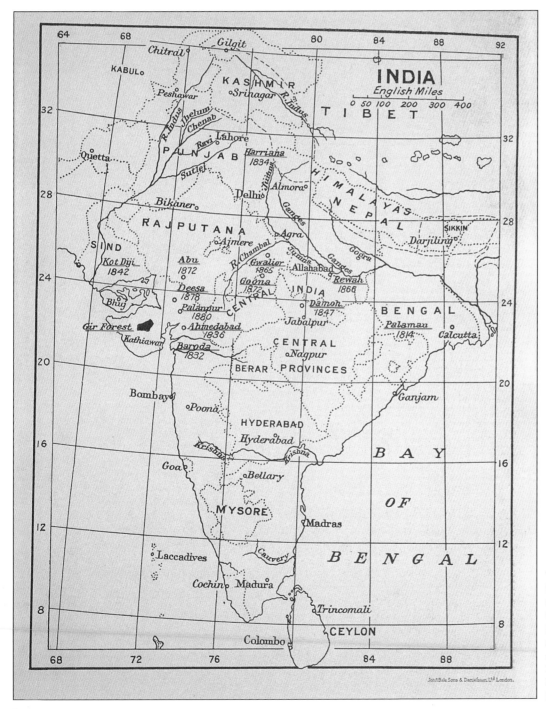

The dates indicate approximately the years when the lion became extinct at the various localities which are underlined in red. From R.I. Pocock, "The Lions of Asia". *Journal, Bombay Natural History Society*, Vol. 34, No. 3, 1930, pp. 638–65. Courtesy Bombay Natural History Society, Mumbai.

Junagadh State
at the Turn of the 20th Century

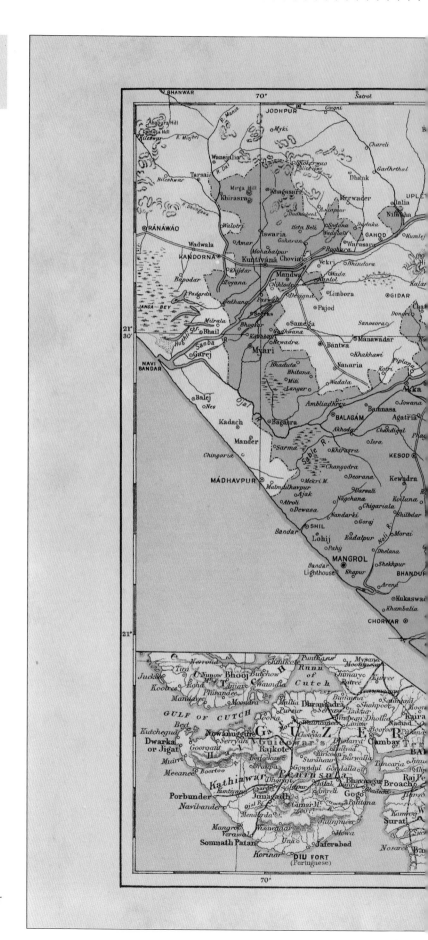

The boundaries of the state remained unchanged until 1947.
From *Ruling Princes of India: Being a Historical, Archaeological, Political and Statistical Account of the Premier State of Kathiawar* by S.M. Edwardes and L.G. Fraser, Bombay, The Times of India Press, 1907.

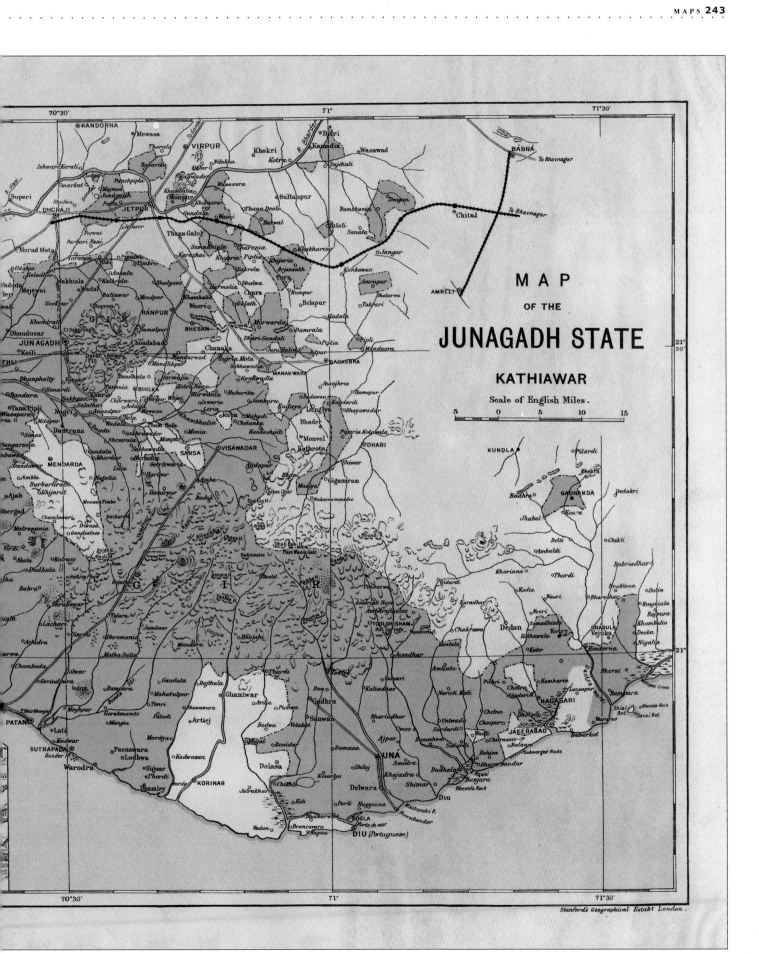

MAP

OF THE

JUNAGADH STATE

KATHIAWAR

Scale of English Miles.

DIU (Portuguese)

Stanford's Geographical Estab.^t London.

The Gir National Park and Sanctuary

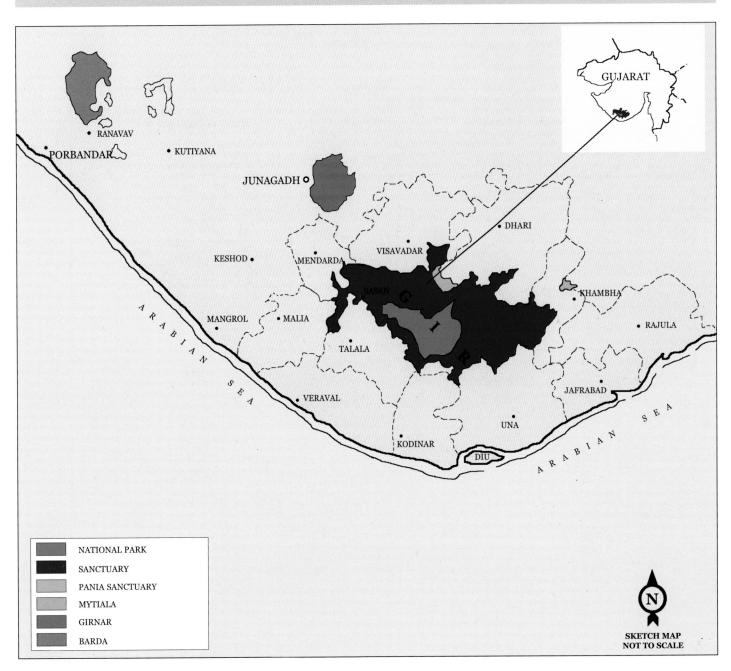

GUJARAT

RANAVAV

PORBANDAR

KUTIYANA

JUNAGADH

DHARI

KESHOD

MENDARDA

VISAVADAR

SASAN

G I R

KHAMBHA

MANGROL

MALIA

RAJULA

TALALA

A R A B I A N   S E A

VERAVAL

JAFRABAD

UNA

KODINAR

DIU

A R A B I A N   S E A

	NATIONAL PARK
	SANCTUARY
	PANIA SANCTUARY
	MYTIALA
	GIRNAR
	BARDA

N

SKETCH MAP
NOT TO SCALE

Courtesy Forest Department, Government of Gujarat.

Current Distribution Range of the Asiatic Lion

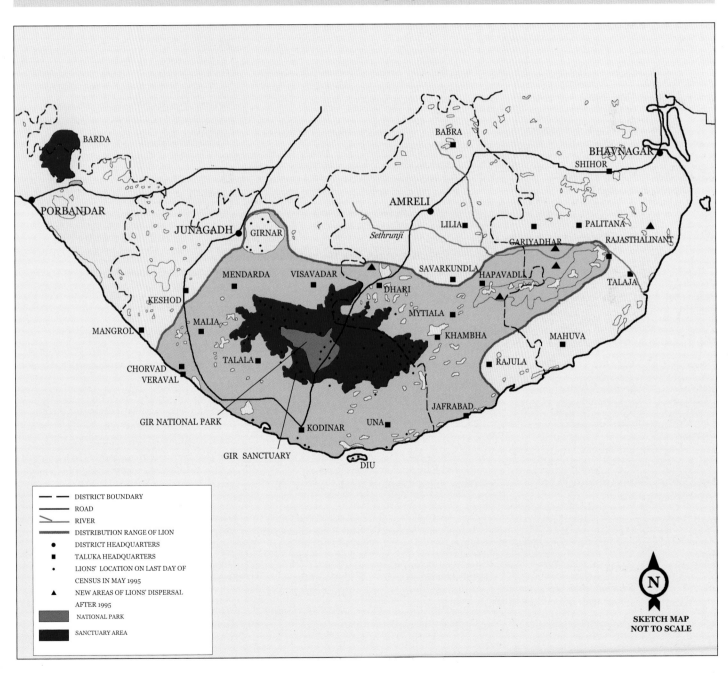

Courtesy Forest Department, Government of Gujarat.

bibliography

This bibliography includes some sources not referred to in the text. The reason for such inclusions is that they may be of relevance to readers interested in the history of Asiatic lions. Such references are identified by an asterisk.

In case of a reprint/revised edition, the original date of publication has been quoted for reference in the endnotes, while the date of the reprint/edition used by this author is also provided here.

The Gujarati sources remain untranslated into English. Quotations in the text from such sources have been translated by the author.

A

Aflalo, F.G. (ed.), 1904, *The Sportsman's Book for India*. Horace Marshall & Son, London.

Ahmud, Syud, 1864, *Toozuk-i-Jehangeeree*. Published by Author, Ally Gurh.

Ait. Br., 1931, *Aitareya Brahmana*, Anandasrama Press, Pune.

Albenda, Pauline, 1974, "Lions on Assyrian Wall Reliefs". *The Journal of the Ancient and Near Eastern Society of Columbia University*, Vol. 6, pp. 1–24. New York.

*Ali, Salim, 1927, "The Mughal Emperors of India as Naturalists and Sportsmen" Part I. *Journal, Bombay Natural History Society,* Vol. 31, No. 4, pp. 833–61. Bombay.

*———, 1928, "The Mughal Emperors of India as Naturalists and Sportsmen" Parts II and III. *Journal, Bombay Natural History Society,* Vol. 32, No. 1, pp. 34–63; No. 2, pp. 264–73. Bombay.

Allaby, Michael (ed.), 1985, *The Oxford Dictionary of Natural History*. Oxford University Press, Oxford.

Allan, John, 1936, *Catalogue of the Coins of Ancient India*. The British Museum, London, 1967.

Alvi, M.A. and A. Rahman, 1968, *Jahangir – The Naturalist*. National Institute of Sciences of India, New Delhi.

Anonymous, 1833, "Capt. Walter Smee on the Maneless Lions of Gujarat". *Proceedings of the Zoological Society*, Vol. I, p. 140. London.

———, 1873, *The Oriental Sporting Magazine From June 1928 to June 1833*, Vol. I, pp. 137–39. Henry S. King & Co., London.

———, 1873A, *The Oriental Sporting Magazine, From June 1928 to June 1833*, Vol. II, pp. 44, 200, 331–32. Henry S. King & Co., London.

———, 1903, *The Babi Rulers of Sorath, with a Short Account of Their Administration.* Junagadh State Press, Junagadh.

———, 1939, *Memorandum on the Indian States.* Government of India, New Delhi.

———, 1948, *White Paper on Indian States.* Ministry of States, Government of India, New Delhi.

———, 1950, -do-

———, 1959, *Stanley Gibbons Simplified Stamp Catalogue, 1960.* Stanley Gibbons Publications Ltd., London.

———, 1972, *The Gir Lion Sanctuary Project.* Revised Edition. Forest Department, Government of Gujarat, Gandhinagar, 1975.

———, 1980, *Stanley Gibbons Stamps of the World, 1981.* Stanley Gibbons Publications Ltd., London.

———, 2000, *India Eco-Development Project: Status Report 1999–2000. Gir National Park and Sanctuary.* Conservator of Forests Wildlife Circle, Junagadh (typescript).

*Ansari, Mohd. Azher, 1960, "The Hunt of the Great Mughals". *Islamic Culture,* Vol. XXXIV, pp. 242–53. Osmania University, Hyderabad.

Apte, Vaman Shivram, 1965, *The Practical Sanskrit–English Dictionary*. Motilal Banarsidass Publishers, Delhi, 1992.

Archer, Mildred, 1959, *Tipoo's Tiger.* Her Majesty's Stationery Office, London.

———, 1962, *Natural History Drawings in the India Office Library.* Her Majesty's Stationery Office, London.

———, 1969, *British Drawings in the India Office Library*, Vols. I and II. Her Majesty's Stationery Office, London.

Ashraf, N.K.V., R. Chellam, S. Molur, D. Sharma, and S. Walker, 1995, *Asiatic Lion: Panthera leo persica. Population and Habitat Assessment P.H.V.A. and Global Animal Survival Plan Workshops, 18–21 October.* Report, Municipal Corporation of Baroda/ Sayaji Baug Zoo, et al., Vadodra.

B

Bachkheti, N.D., 1995, "Introduction of Lions in Chandraprabha Sanctuary". *Cheetal, Journal of the Wildlife Preservation Society of India,* Vol. 34, No. 1, pp. 10–14. Dehra Dun.

Balachandran, G., 1998, *The History of the Reserve Bank of India (1935–51).* Oxford University Press, Delhi.

Balfour, Surgeon General Edward, 1885, *Encyclopaedia of India, Eastern & Southern Asia.* Third Edition. Bernard Quaritch, London.

Banerjee, S.C., 1980, *Flora and Fauna in Sanskrit Literature.* Naya Prokash, Calcutta.

Basham, A.L, 1954, *The Wonder that Was India; A Survey of History and Culture of the Indian Subcontinent Before the Coming of the Muslims.* Sidgwick & Jackson, London, 1982.

Beach, Milo Cleveland and Ebba Koch, 1997, *King of the World; the Padshahnama An Imperial Mughal Manuscript from the Royal Library, Windsor Castle.* Azimuth Editions/ Sackler Gallery, Washington, DC.

Beveridge, Annette Susannah (tr.), 1922, *Babur Namah (Memoirs of Babur)*, Vols. I and II. Oriental Books Reprint Corporation, New Delhi, 1979.

Beveridge, H. (tr.), 1904, *The Akbar-Nama of*

Abu-l-Fazl, Vol. II. Es Es Publication, New Delhi, 1979.

Bhavnagar, H.H. Sir Bhavsinhji, K.C.S.I., Maharaja of, 1911, *Forty Years of Rajkumar College*, Vol. I. Published by Author, Bhavnagar.

Bikaner, M.K. Sadul Singh of, 1928, *Big Game Diary* (unpublished).

Blochman, H. (tr.), 1873, *The A'in-i Akbari* by Abu'l Fazl, Vol. I. Second Edition, revised and edited by Lt. Col. D.C. Phillot. Oriental Books Reprint Corporation, New Delhi, 1977.

Bodenheimer, Dr F.S., 1960, *Animal and Man in Bible Lands*. E.J. Brill, Leiden.

Bole, P.V. and Yogini Vaghani, 1986, *Field Guide to the Common Trees of India*. World Wildlife Fund – India, Delhi.

Bopearachhi, Osmund, 1998, *Sylloge Nummarum Graecorum, the Collection of American Numismatic Society, Part 9, Graeco-Bactrian and Indo-Greek Coins*. American Numismatic Society, New York.

Bull, H.M. and K.N. Haksar, 1926, *Madhav Rao Scindia of Gwalior, 1876–1925*. Alijah Durbar Press, Gwalior.

Burke, W.S., 1920, *The Indian Field Shikar Book*. Fifth Edition. Thacker Spink & Co., Calcutta.

Burton, Brigadier General R.G., 1931, *A Book of Man-Eaters*. Hutchinson & Co. Publishers, London.

–––, 1933, *The Book of the Tiger*. Hutchinson & Co. Publishers, London.

Burton, Lt. Col. R.W., 1959, "The Voice of the Cheetah or Hunting Leopard (Acinonyx jubatus EREXLABEN)". *Journal, Bombay Natural History Society*, Vol. 56, No. 2, pp. 317–18. Bombay.

C

CAD, 1947–48, *Constituent Assembly Debates*. Government of India Press, New Delhi.

Cadell, Sir Patrick, 1933, "The Preservation of Wildlife in India, No. 5. The Indian Lion". *Journal, Bombay Natural History Society,*

Vol. 37, No. 1, pp. 162–66. Bombay.

Caldwell, Capt. Keith, 1938, "The Gir Lion". *Journal, Society for the Preservation of the Fauna of the Empire*, Vol. 34, pp. 62–65. London.

Campbell, Joseph, 1974, *The Mythic Image*. Princeton University Press, Princeton.

Caputo, Philip, 2002, *Ghosts of Tsavo: Stalking the Mystery Lions of East Africa*. Adventure Press, National Geographic Society, Washington, DC.

Carruthers, D., P.B. Van Der Byl, Lt. Col. R.L. Kenion, J.G. Millains, H. Frank Wallace, and Ford G. Barclay, 1915, *The Gun at Home & Abroad: The Big Game of Asia and North America*. The London & Counties Press Association, London.

*Chavan, Sanat and Dhun Karkaria, 2001, *Gir National Park: Handbook*. Tourism Corporation of Gujarat Limited, Gandhinagar.

Chattopadhyaya, U.C., 2002, "Researches in Archaeology of the Holocene Period (including the Harappan Tradition in India and Pakistan)". *Archaeology and Interactive Disciplines,* Vol. III, pp. 364–422. Indian Council for Historical Research and Manohar Publishers, Delhi.

Chellam, Ravi, 1993, "Ecology of the Asiatic Lion *(Panthera leo persica)*". Ph.D. thesis, University of Saurashtra, Rajkot.

*Chellam, Ravi and A.J.T. Johnsingh, 1993, "Management of Asiatic Lions in the Gir Forest, India". *Mammals as Predators. The Proceedings of a Symposium held by the Zoological Society of London and the Mammal Society, London, 22nd and 23rd November 1991,* No. 65, pp. 409–24. Edited by N. Dunstone and M.L. Gorman. Clarendon Press, Oxford.

Chellam, R., Justin Joshua, Christy A. Williams, and A.J.T. Johnsingh, 1994, *Survey of the Potential Sites for Reintroduction of Asiatic Lions*. Wildlife Institute of India, Dehra Dun (typescript).

COI, 2003, *Constitution of India with Short Notes*. Eighteenth Edition with Supplement. Eastern Book Company, Lucknow.

Constable, Archibald (tr.), 1934, *Travels in the Mughal Empire by Francois Bernier A.D. 1656–1668*. Second Edition, revised by Vincent A. Smith. Oriental Reprint, Delhi, 1983.

D

Dadhimatha, M.M. Pandit Sivadatta (ed.), 1915, *Namalinganusasana alias Amarakosa of Amarasimha*. Chaukhamba Sanskrit Pratishthan, Delhi.

Daljeet, Dr, 1999, *Mughal and Deccani Paintings of the National Museum*. Prakash Book Depot, Delhi.

Dalvi, M.K., 1969, "Gir Lion Census, 1968". *Indian Forester*, pp. 741–52. Forest Research Institute, Dehra Dun.

Daniell, William, 1836, *The Oriental Annual or Scenes in India*. Asian Education Service, New Delhi, 2000.

Das, Asok Kumar, 1978, *Mughal Painting During Jahangir's Time*. The Asiatic Society, Calcutta.

Deekshitar, Raja, 2004, "Discovering the Anthropomorphic Lion in Indian Art", *Marg*, Vol. 55, No. 4 (June), pp. 34–41.

Desai, Shambhuprasad Harprasad, 1983, *Gir*. Prabhas Prakashan, Junagadh.

*–––, 1995, *The Forest of Gir*. Prabhas Prakashan, Junagadh.

*Desai, Pradumna Kanchanrai, 1962, *Girna Bhitarma*. Sanskar Sahitya Mandir, Bhavnagar.

Dharmakumarsinhji, R.S., 1959, *A Field Guide to Big Game Census in India*. Ministry of Food and Agriculture, Government of India, New Delhi.

–––, 1969, "Story of the Lion Census". *Cheetal, Journal of the Wildlife Preservation Society of India*, Vol. XII, No. 1, pp. 48–56. Dehra Dun.

–––, 1979, "The Tiger 'Lionised'". *Swarajya*, Vol. XXIII, No. 39. Madras.

–––, 1992, *Reminiscences of Indian Wildlife* (written late 1970s). Oxford University Press, Delhi, 1998.

Dharmakumarsinhji, R.S. and M.A. Wynter-

Blyth, 1951, "The Gir Forest and its Lions" Part III. *Journal, Bombay Natural History Society*, Vol. 49, No. 4, pp. 685–95. Bombay.

Dharmakumarsinhji, R.S., Y.R. Ghorpade, Zafar Futehally, M. Krishnan, Hari Dang, V.B. Singh, and K.S. Sankhala, 1970, *Wildlife Conservation in India. Report of the Expert Committee, Indian Board for Wildlife*. Ministry of Food and Agriculture, Government of India, New Delhi.

Divyabhanusinh, 1986, "Earliest Record of a White Tiger". *Journal, Bombay Natural History Society*, Vol. 83, (Supplement), pp. 163–65. Bombay.

———, 1987, "Record of Two Unique Observations of the Indian Cheetah in Tuzuk-i-Jahangiri". *Journal, Bombay Natural History Society*, Vol. 84, No. 2, pp. 269–74. Bombay.

———, 1995, *The End of a Trail: The Cheetah in India*. Second Edition. Oxford University Press, 2002, Delhi.

———, 1999, "Hunting in Mughal Painting". *Flora and Fauna in Mughal Art*. Edited by Som Prakash Verma, pp. 94–108. Marg Publications, Mumbai.

Dollman, Guy and J.B. Burlace, 1935, *Rowland Ward's Records of Big Game, African and Asiatic Sections*. Tenth Edition. Rowland Ward, London.

D'Oyly, Sir Charles, 1810–15, *Indian Sports*, Vols. I and II. The British Library, OIOC, Acc. No. WD4405–4406 (unpublished album).

DUSJ, 1867 onwards, *Dusturul Umul Surkar Joonagudh*. (The Junagadh State Gazette published from December 1867, issued monthly.) Junagadh.

Dutta, Arun Kumar, 1976, "Occurrence of Fossil Lion and Spotted Hyaena from Pleistocene Deposits of Susania, Bankura District, West Bengal". *Journal of the Geological Society of India*, Vol. 17, No. 3, pp. 386–91. Calcutta.

E

Edwardes, S.M. and L.G. Fraser, 1907, *Ruling Princes of India. Junagadh: Being a Historical, Archaeological, Political and Statistical Account of the Premier State of Kathiwar*. Times of India Press, Bombay.

Elgood, Robert, 1995, *Fire Arms of the Islamic World in the Tareq Rajab Museum, Kuwait*. I.B. Taurus Publishers, London.

F

Falk, Toby and Simon Digby, 1983, *Paintings from Mughal India*. P.D. Colnaghi & Co. Ltd., London.

Falk, Toby, Ellen S. Smart, and Robert Skelton, 1978, *Indian Painting: Mughal and Rajput and a Sultanate Manuscript*. P.D. Colnaghi & Co. Ltd., London.

Fenton, Col. L.L., c. 1924, *The Rifle in India: Being the Sporting Experiences of an Indian Officer*. W. Thacker & Co., London.

Forbes, James, 1813, *Oriental Memoirs Selected from a Series of Familiar Letters Written during Seventeen Years in India*. Gian Publishing House, Delhi, 1988.

Foster, Sir William, 1926, *The Embassy of Sir Thomas Roe to India 1615–19 as narrated in his Journal and Correspondence*. Munshiram Manoharlal Publishers Pvt. Ltd., New Delhi, 1990.

Fox-Davies, Arthur Charles, 1909, *A Complete Guide to Heraldry*. Thomas Nelson and Sons Ltd., London, 1950.

G

GA, Gujarat State Archives, District Record Office, Junagadh. (Prior to 1947 it was called The Central Record Office, Junagadh State.) Records concerning lions are kept in *basta*s – bundles of documents tied in cloth – marked *Jungle Khatanu Daftar* – Forest Department Records.

Gee, E.P., 1956, "The Management of India's Wild Life Sanctuaries and National Parks". *Journal, Bombay Natural History Society*, Vol. 54, No. 1, pp. 1–22. Bombay.

———, 1962, "The Present Status of Four Rare Animals of India". *Cheetal, Journal of the Wildlife Preservation Society of India*, Vol. IV, No. 2, pp. 29–33. Dehra Dun.

———, 1964, *The Wildlife of India*. Collins, London.

Ghorpade, M.Y., 1983, *Sunlight and Shadows.*

An Indian Wildlife Photographer's Diary. Victor Gollancz, London and B.I. Publications, Bombay.

Gida, Bhanabhai, 1999, "Sinhni Dosti". *Gujarati Dhoran* 7, pp. 208–11. Gujarat Rajya Shala Pathyapustak Mandal, Gandhinagar.

Godrej, Pheroza J. and Firoza Punthakey-Mistree, 2002, *A Zoroastrian Tapestry. Art, Religion & Culture*. Mapin Publishing Pvt. Ltd., Ahmedabad.

Goetz, Hermann, 1950, *The Art and Architecture of Bikaner State*. Bruno Cassirer, Oxford.

*Gogate, M.G. (comp.), 1994, *List of References on Lion: Panthera leo Linnaeus* (typescript).

Gould, Brian, 1971, "Mathew Boulton and the Making of the Seringapatam Medal". *Coins*, Vol. 8, No. 9, pp. 23–24. Link House Group, Croydon.

Graves, Robert and Omer Ali-Shah, 1967, *The Rubaiyat of Omar Khayyaam: A New Translation with Critical Commentaries*. Cassell & Co. Ltd., London.

Guggisberg. C.A.W., 1962, *Simba: The Life of the Lion*. Bailey Bros. & Swinfen, London.

Guha, Ramachandra (ed.), 2000, *Nature's Spokesman: M. Krishnan and Indian Wildlife*. Oxford University Press, Delhi.

Guha, Sumit, 2001, *Health and Population in South Asia from Earliest Times to the Present*. Permanent Black, New Delhi.

*Gupta, S.P., 1980, *The Roots of Indian Art*. B.R. Publishing Corporation, Delhi.

H

Habib, Irfan, 1963, *The Agrarian System of Mughal India (1556–1707)*. Aligarh Muslim University, Aligarh and Asia Publishing House, Bombay.

———, 1982, *An Atlas of Mughal India. Political and Economic Maps with Detailed Notes, Bibliography and Index*. Oxford University Press, Delhi, 1986.

———, 1982A, "Population". *The Cambridge Economic History of India. Vol. I: c1200–*

c1700, edited by Tapan Raychaudhuri and Irfan Habib, pp. 163–71. Orient Longman, Hyderabad and Cambridge University Press, Cambridge, 1984.

Harrington Jr., Fred A., 1977, *A Guide to the Mammals of Iran*. Department of the Environment, Tehran.

Harting, James Edmund, 1883, *Essays on Sport and Natural History*. Horace Cox, "The Field" Office, London.

Hartner, Willy and Richard Ettinghausen, 1964, "The Conquering Lion, The Life Cycle of a Symbol". *Oriens*, Vol. 17, pp. 161–71. E.J. Brill, Leiden.

Hassan, Dr Zaky M., 1937, *Hunting as Practiced in Arab Countries of the Middle Ages*. Ministry of Education, Cairo.

Heaney, Lt. Col. G.F., 1944, "Occurrence of the Lion in Persia". *Journal, Bombay Natural History Society*, Vol. 44, No. 3, p. 407, Bombay.

Hemmer, Helmut, 1974, *Untersuchungen zur Stammesgeschiste der Pantherakatzen (Pantherinae). Teil III, Zur Artgeschiste des Lowen Panthera (Panthera) leo (Linnaeus 1758)*. Veraffenlichungen der Zoologischen Staatssamlung, Munchen. Translated by Uma Iyer (unpublished).

Heptner, V.H. and A.A. Sludskii, 1971, *Mammals of the Soviet Union. Vol. III Carnivores*. English translation edited by R.S. Hoffman. Smithsonian Institution and National Science Foundation, Washington, DC, 1992.

Houlihan, Patrick F., 1996, *The Animal World of the Pharaohs*. Thames and Hudson, London.

Humphreys, P.N. and E. Kahrom, 1995, *The Lion and the Gazelle: The Mammals and Birds of Iran*. Comma International Biological Systems, Lower Coed Morgan, Nr. Abergavenney, Gwent, U.K.

Hussain, Agha Mahdi (ed.), 1967, 1976, 1977, *Futuhu's Salatin or Shahnama-i-Hind of 'Isami, Vols. I, II, and III*. Asia Publishing House, Bombay.

Hussain, Maulvi Vilayat, 1891, *Shams Siraj 'Afif, Tarikh-i Firoz Shahi*. The Asiatic Society, Calcutta.

I

Ingalls, Daniel H.H. (tr.), 1965, *An Anthology of Sanskrit Court Poetry: Vidyakara's Subhasitaratnakosa*. Harvard University Press, Cambridge, Mass.

Irwin, John, 1973, " 'Asokan' Pillars: A Reassessment of the Evidence". *The Burlington Magazine,* Vol. CXV, November, pp. 706–20. London.

–––, 1974, " 'Asokan' Pillars: A Reassessment of the Evidence. Part II, Structure". *The Burlington Magazine,* Vol. CXVI, December, pp. 712–27. London.

–––, 1975, " 'Asokan' Pillars: A Reassessment of the Evidence. Part III, Capitals". *The Burlington Magazine,* Vol. CXVII, October, pp. 631–43. London.

–––, 1976, " 'Asokan' Pillars: A Reassessment of the Evidence. Part IV, Symbolism". *The Burlington Magazine,* Vol. CXVIII, November, pp. 734–53. London.

–––, 1983, "The True Chronology of the Asokan Pillars". *Artibus Asiae,* Institute of Fine Arts, New York University. Ascona, Switzerland.

–––, 1985, " 'Asokan Pillars'. Their Mystery and the Explanation" (typescript).

*Islam, Shuja Ul and Col. John H. Roush Jr., 2001, *Hunting Dangerous Game with the Maharajas*. Himalayan Books, New Delhi.

Iyer, K. Bharatha, 1977, *Animals in Indian Sculpture*. D.B. Taraporevala Sons & Co. Pvt. Ltd., Bombay.

J

Jacob, Capt. George Le Grand, 1842, *Report upon the General Condition, in the year 1842 of the Province of Kathiawar*. The Bombay Government, Bombay.

Jain, Manik, 1999, *Phila India 2000 Colour Catalogue: Indian Philately 1852–1998*. Philatelia, Calcutta.

Jain, Pushp (ed. and comp.), 2001, *Project Tiger Status Report*. Ministry of Environment and Forests, New Delhi.

Jamkhandikar, Dr M.M., 2000, *Of Homo sapiens and Panthera leo: A Diary of Experiences in Gir Forest of India*. Tolani Shipping Co. Ltd., Mumbai.

JAR, 1907 and 1908, *Sansthan Junagadh: Administration Report*. Junagadh Sarkari Chapkhana, Junagadh.

–––, 1908–09 to 1924–25 and 1929–30 to 1944–45, *Report on the Administration of Junagadh State*. The State Press, Junagadh.

Jarrige, Jean-Francis and Usman Hassan, 1989, "Funerary Complexes of Baluchistan at the End of the Third Millennium in the Light of Recent Discoveries at Mehrgarh and Quetta". *South Asian Archaeology 1985*. Edited by Karen Frifelt and Per Sorensen. Curzon Press, London.

Jepson, Stanley (ed.), 1936, *Big Game Encounters: Critical Moments in the Lives of Well-known Shikaris*. H.F. & G. Witherby, Ltd., London, 1937.

Jerdon, T.C., 1867, *Mammals of India: A Natural History of all the Animals known to Inhabit Continental India*. John Weldon, London, 1874.

Jha, Amiteshwar and Dilip Rajgor, 1994, *Studies in the Coinage of the Western Kshatrapas*. Indian Institute of Research in Numismatic Studies, Nashik.

Jhala, Y.V., Shoman Mukherjee, Nita Shah, Kartikeya Singh Chauhan, Chitaranjan Dave, and Yogendra Singh Jhala, 2002, "Monitoring Lions". *Impact Monitoring of Gir. A Technical Consultancy Report submitted to the Gujarat Forest Department under the GEF – India Eco-Development Programme*. Final Draft Report, pp. 55–72. Edited by Y.V. Jhala. Wildlife Institute of India, Dehra Dun (unpublished).

*Johnsingh, A.J.T., Ravi Chellam, and Diwakar Sharma, 1998, "Prospect for Conservation of the Asiatic Lion in India". *Biosphere Conservation, Journal of the Society for Conservation Biology*, Vol. 1, No. 2, pp. 81–90. Blackwell Scientific Publications, Malden, MA.

Jones, Horace Leonard (tr.), 1966, *The Geography of Strabo*. Harvard University Press, Cambridge, Mass.

Joslin, E.C., A.R. Litherland, and T.B. Simpkin, 1988, *British Battles and Medals*. Spink, London.

Joslin, P., 1973, *The Asiatic Lion: A Study of Ecology and Behaviour.* Ph.D. thesis, University of Edinburgh.

———, 1985, *Reintroduction Sites for Indian Lion* (typescript).

JRM, 1930, *Swasthan Junagadh: Revenue Manual. Vol. 3. Junagadh Rajyana Upayog Mate.* Compiled by Dalpatram Govardhan Vyas. State Press, Junagadh.

K

K.D. Kaur Singh, Amrit and Rabindra, 2003, *Images of Freedom.* Indialog, New Delhi.

*Kamboj, R.D., Mahesh Singh, and P.P. Raval, 1997, "Analysis of Threats to Gir Ecosystem". *Indian Forester*, Vol. 123, No. 10, pp. 964–72, Forest Research Institute, Dehra Dun.

Kangle, R.P., 1963, *The Kautilya Arthasastra,* Part II. Motilal Banarsidass, Delhi.

Kaul, H.K., 1979, *Travellers' India. An Anthology.* Oxford University Press, Delhi.

Khan, Saiyad Ahmad, 1882, *Ain-i Akbari.* Nawal Kishore, Lucknow.

Kincaid, C.A., 1905, *The Outlaws of Kathiawar and Other Stories.* The Times Press, Bombay.

———, 1935, *Indian Lions.* The Times of India Press, Bombay.

Kinnear, N.B., 1920, "The Past and Present Distribution of the Lion in South Eastern Asia". *Journal, Bombay Natural History Society*, Vol. 27, No. 1, pp. 34–39. Bombay.

*Klum, Mattias and Monika, 2000, *Den Sköra Träden: Berättelsen om de Sista Asiatika Lejonen.* Bokförlaget Prisma, Stockholm. (A pictorial book on the lion in Swedish.)

Kosambi, D.D. and V.V. Gokhale (eds.), 1957, *The Subhasitaratnakosa compiled by Vidyakara.* Harvard University Press, Cambridge, Mass.

Koch, Ebba, 1998, "Dara-Shikoh Shooting Nilgais: Hunt and Landscape in Mughal Painting". *Occasional Papers,* Vol. 1. Freer Gallery of Art/Arthur M. Sackler Gallery, Smithsonian Institution, Washington, DC.

Kossak, Steven, 1997, *Indian Court Painting 16th–19th century.* The Metropolitan Museum of Art, New York.

Kostioukovitch, Elena (ed.), 1996, *The St Petersburg Muraqqa: Album of Indian and Persian Miniatures from the 16th through the 18th Century and Specimens of Persian Calligraphy by 'Imad Al-Hasani.* Lenardo Arte srl, Milano & ARCH Foundation, Lugano.

Krishnadasa, Rai, 1999, *Anwar-e-Suhaili: Iyar-i-Danish.* Bharat Kala Bhavan, Banaras Hindu University, Varanasi.

L

Lal, Bharat, 2000, "Greater Gir Ecosystem: Ecorestoration of Girnar Forest & Recapture of Lost Territory by *Panthera leo persica* (Asiatic Lion)" (typescript).

Lavkumar, K.S., 1956, "Transferring of the Indian Lion to an Additional Locality". *Journal, Bombay Natural History Society*, Vol. 54, No. 1, pp. 173–75. Bombay.

Layard, Austen H., 1853, *Discoveries in the Ruins of Nineveh and Babylon.* John Murray, London.

Leipziger, E. von, 1888, *Sechs Monate Indien.* Adelbert Fischer's Verlag, Leipzig.

Liebert, Gosta, 1976, *Iconographic Dictionary of the Indian Religions: Hinduism-Buddhism-Jainism.* E.J. Brill, Leiden.

Low, Sir Francis (ed.), 1947, *The Indian Year Book 1947*, Volume XXXIII. Bennett, Coleman & Co. Ltd., Bombay.

Luckenbill, Daniel David, 1927, *Ancient Records of Assyria and Babylonia, Vol. II, Historical Records of Assyria from Sargon to the End.* The University of Chicago Press.

M

MA, Maharashtra State Archives, Mumbai.

Macdonald, David, 1992, *The Velvet Claw: A Natural History of the Carnivores.* BBC Books, London.

*Mahesh Singh; Punil P. Gajjar, and Badrish P. Mehra, 2002, *Gir National Park and Sanctuary: Bibliography.* Bishen Singh

Mahendra Pal Singh, Dehra Dun.

Mahadevan, Iravatham, 1977, *The Indus Script, Texts, Concordance and Tables.* Archaeological Survey of India, New Delhi.

Mbh., 1936–1966, *Mahabharata.* 19 Volumes, Bhandarkar Oriental Research Institute, Pune.

McCrindle, John Watson, 1877, *Ancient India as described by Megasthenes and Arrian.* Today & Tomorrow Printers & Publishers, New Delhi, 1975.

*———, 1892, *The Invasion of India by Alexander the Great.* Today & Tomorrow Printers & Publishers, New Delhi (year of publication of this edition not mentioned).

———, 1901, *Ancient India as described in Classical Literature.* Philo Press, Amsterdam, 1971.

Meghani, Jhaverchand, 1997, *Saurashtrani Rasdhara.* Prasar, Bhavnagar, 2000.

———, 1997A, *Sona-Navdi.* Prasar, Bhavnagar.

Mehta, Mahruq, 2001, *Cultural Mosaic of Gujarat.* Tourism Corporation of Gujarat Ltd., Gandhinagar.

Menon, V.P., 1956, *The Story of the Integration of Indian States.* Orient Longman, Bombay.

Minshull, Mrs E., 1937, "The Mysterious Man-Eater of Pachwara. Baby Seized from the Bed and Dropped". *Big Game Encounters: Critical Moments in the Lives of Well-Known Shikaris,* edited by Stanley Jepson, pp. 37–41. M.F. & G. Witherby Ltd., London.

Misra, Shiva Shekhar, 1966, *Somesvarakrta Manasollasa: Ek Sanskrtika Adhyayana.* Choukhambha Vidyabhavan, Varanasi.

Misra, V.N., 2000, "Climate as Factor in the Rise and Fall of the Indus Civilization – Evidence from Rajasthan and Beyond". *Decline and Fall of the Indus Civilization,* edited by Nayanjot Lahiri, pp. 239–51. Permanent Black, New Delhi.

Modi, Dr Sir Jivanji Jamshedji, 1932, "A Few Notes on Persian, African and Indian Lions in the First Century after Christ". *Journal, Bombay Natural History Society*, Vol. XXXV, No. 3., pp. 496–504. Bombay.

Mohan, Arun, 1990, *Princely States and the Reform in Hindu Law.* N.M. Tripathi Pvt. Ltd., Bombay.

Monier-Williams, Sir Monier, 1851, *English-Sanskrit Dictionary.* Munshiram Manoharlal, New Delhi, 1985.

———, 1899, *Sanskrit-English Dictionary.* Munshiram Manoharlal, New Delhi, 1988.

Mosse, Lt. Col. A.H., 1957, "The Lion of the Gir". *Journal, Bombay Natural History Society,* Vol. 54, No. 3, pp. 568–76, Bombay.

Moscati, Sabastino, 1960, *The Face of the Ancient Orient: Near Eastern Civilization in Pre-Classical Times.* Dover Publications, Inc., Miniola, New York, 2001.

Mukherjee, B.N., 1969, *Nana on Lion: A Study in Kushana Numismatic Art.* The Asiatic Society, Calcutta.

Mukherjee, B.N. and T.N. Raychaudhuri, 1990, *The Indian Gold: An Introduction to the Cabinet of Gold Coins in the Indian Museum.* Indian Museum, Calcutta.

Mukhopadhyaya, Jiban K. and Saritha Aiyar (eds.), 2002, *Statistical Outline of India: 2002–2003.* Tata Services Ltd., Mumbai.

Mundy, General Godfrey Charles, 1858, *Pen and Pencil Sketches in India. Journal of a Tour in India.* Third Edition, Asian Educational Services, New Delhi, 1995.

N

NAI, National Archives of India, New Delhi.

Negi, S.S., 1966, "Introduction of the Indian Lion in Uttar Pradesh". *Cheetal, Journal of the Wildlife Preservation Society of India,* Vol. 8, No. 2, pp. 49–52, Dehra Dun.

———, 1969, "Transplanting of Indian Lion in Uttar Pradesh". *Cheetal, Journal of the Wildlife Preservation Society of India,* Vol. 12, No. 1, pp. 98–101, Dehra Dun.

Newall, Maj. Gen. D.J.F., 1882–87, *The Highlands of India. Being a Chronicle of Field Sports and Travel in India.* Vol. II. Logos Press, New Delhi, 1984.

Nicholson, J.W., 1935, *A Census in Tigerland.*

Typescript from the Working Plan of the Palamau Division, Forest Department, Bihar Province.

Nizami, Khaliq Ahmad, 1997, *Royalty in Medieval India.* Munshiram Manoharlal, Delhi.

Nott, J. Fortune, 1886, *Wild Animals Photographed and Described.* Sampson Low, Marston, Searle & Rivington, London.

Nowell, Kristin and Peter Jackson (comp. and ed.), 1996, *Status Survey and Conservation Action Plan: Wild Cats.* IUCN World Conservation Union, Gland, Switzerland.

O

O'Brien, Stephen J., 2003, *Tears of the Cheetah and Other Tales from the Genetic Frontier.* Thomas Dunne Books, St Martin's Press, New York.

Oza, G.M.,1973, "Ban Experiments of Introduction of Asiatic Lions". *Indian Forester,* pp. 471–72, Forest Research Institute, Dehra Dun.

P

Pal, Pratapaditya (ed.), 1991, *Master Artists of the Mughal Court.* Marg Publications, Bombay.

Paul, E. Jaywant and Pramod Kapoor, 2003, *The Unforgettable Maharajas: One Hundred and Fifty Years of Photography.* Lustre Press/ Roli Books, New Delhi.

Parpola, Asko, 1994, *Deciphering the Indus Script.* Cambridge University Press, Cambridge, 2000.

*Patel, Chandrakant, 1997, *Sinh-Darshan.* Pravin Prakashan, Rajkot.

*Patel, Suleman, circa 1990, *Gir Lions.* Published by author.

Pathan, A.R., 1921, *Kolahpur Shikar Album: containing Beautiful Illustrations of Wild Beasts and Birds.* Pathan, Kolahpur.

Patterson, Lieut. Col. J.H., 1907, *The Man-Eaters of Tsavo and Other East African Adventures.* Macmillan and Co., London, 1952.

PH, Phulchchab. Gujarati daily newspaper, Rajkot.

Pilgrim, G.E., 1910, "Preliminary Note on a Revised Classification of the Tertiary Freshwater Deposits of India". *Records of the Geological Survey of India,* Vol. V, No. 40, Pt. 3, p. 199. Calcutta.

———, 1938, *The Fossil Carnivora of India. Palaeontologia Indica,* New Series, Vol. 18, pp. 138, 199. Geological Survey of India, Calcutta.

Pocock, R.I., 1930, "The Lions of Asia". *Journal, Bombay Natural History Society,* Vol. 34, No. 3, pp. 638–65. Bombay.

———, 1936, "A Pair of Indian Lions presented to the British Museum by H.H. Nawab of Junagadh". *Journal, Bombay Natural History Society,* Vol. 38, No. 2, pp. 382–84. Bombay.

———, 1936A, "The Lion in Baluchistan". *Journal, Bombay Natural History Society,* Vol. 38, No. 2, pp. 381–82. Bombay.

*———, 1939, *The Fauna of British India including Ceylon and Burma,* Vol. I. Today & Tomorrow Printers & Publishers, New Delhi, 1985.

Possehl, Gregory L., 1999, *The Indus Age: The Beginnings.* University of Pennsylvania Press, Philadelphia.

*Prakash, Ishwar, 1994, *Mammals of the Thar Desert.* Scientific Publishers, Jodhpur.

Prasad, Kamal, c. 1965, *A Preliminary Bibliography of Shikar and Wildlife in India and the Neighbouring Countries* (typescript).

Prater, S.H., 1948, *The Book of Indian Animals.* Bombay Natural History Society, Bombay, 1980.

Q

*Qammen, David, 2003, *Monster of God: The Man-Eating Predator in the Jungles of History and the Mind.* W.W. Norton & Company, New York.

R

RV, 1972–76, *Rgveda Samhita.* 4 Volumes. Vaidika Samsodhana Mandala, Pune.

Raghuvamśa, 1915, *Raghuvamśa of Kalidasa.* Edited by M.R. Kale. The Oriental Publishing Company, Bombay.

Rahim, Maulvi Abdul (ed.), 1879, *Akbarnama.* Asiatic Society, Calcutta.

Rajan, K.V. Soundera, 1985, *Junagadh.* Archaeological Survey of India, New Delhi.

Rangarajan, Mahesh, 1996, *Fencing the Forest: Conservation and Ecological Change in India's Central Provinces 1860–1914.* Oxford University Press, Delhi.

———, 2000, *India's Wildlife History: An Introduction.* Permanent Black, Delhi.

———, 2001, "From Princely Symbol to Conservation Icon: A Political History of the Lion in India". *The Unfinished Agenda: Nation Building in South Asia,* edited by Mushirul Hasan and Nariaki Nakazato, pp. 399–442. Manohar Publishers and Distributors, New Delhi.

Ranjitsinh, M.K., 1997, *Beyond the Tiger: Portrait of Asia's Wildlife.* Brijbasi, New Delhi.

———, 2001, "In Search of a Home". *The Express Magazine of the Indian Express.* New Delhi, December 9.

Rao, B. Shiva, V.K.N. Menon, J.N. Khosla, K.V. Padmanabhan, C. Ganesan, P.K. Krishna Mani, 1966, *The Framing of India's Constitution: Select Documents.* Vol. I. The Indian Institute of Public Administration, New Delhi.

Rapson, Edward James, 1908, *Catalogue of the Coins of the Andhra Dynasty, The Western Ksatrapas, the Traikutaka Dynasty and the "Budhi" Dynasty.* The British Museum, London, 1967.

Rashid, M.A. and Reuben David, 1992, *The Asiatic Lion (Panthera leo persica).* Department of Environment, Government of India, New Delhi.

Ratnu, Kavi Mavdanji Bhimjibhai, 1934, *Shri Yaduvamsaprakasa ane Jamnagarno itihas.* Jamnagar.

*Rawlinson, George, 1910, *Herodotus: The Histories.* Everyman's Library, David Campbell Publishers Ltd., London, 1997.

Rawlinson, George, 1898, *The Memoir of Major General Henry Creswicke Rawlinson.* Longman Green & Co., London.

Reade, Julian, 1983, *Assyrian Sculpture.* The British Museum Press, London, 1998.

Rice, William, 1884, *"Indian Game" (From Quail to Tiger).* W.H. Allen & Co., London.

Rizvi, S.A.A., 1987, *The Wonder that Was India. Vol. II: A Survey of the History and Culture of the Indian Sub-Continent from the Coming of the Muslims to the British Conquest, 1200–1700.* Sidgwick & Jackson Ltd., London.

Robinson, B.W., 1976, *Islamic Painting and the Arts of the Book.* Faber and Faber, London.

Rodrigues, Mario, 2003, *Batting for Empire. Political Biography of Ranjitsinhji.* Penguin Books, New Delhi.

Rogers, Alexander and Henry Beveridge, 1909–14, *The Tuzuk-i-Jahangiri or the Memoirs of Jahangir.* Munshiram Manoharlal, New Delhi, 1980.

Russell, C.E.M., 1900, *Bullet and Shot in Indian Forest, Plain and Hill.* W. Thacker and Co., London.

S

Saberwal, Vasant K., P. James Gibbs, Ravi Chellam, and A.J.T. Johnsingh, 1994, "Lion-Human Conflict in the Gir Forest, India". *Conservation Biology, The Journal of the Society for Conservation Biology,* Vol. 8, No. 2, pp. 501–07. Blackwell Scientific Publications, Malden, MA, USA.

Sankhala, Kailash, 1978, *Tiger! The Story of the Indian Tiger.* Collins, London.

Sanyal, Ram Brahma, 1892, *A Handbook of the Management of Animals in Captivity in Lower Bengal.* Bengal Secretariat Press, Calcutta.

Sarma, Sreeramula Rejeswara, 1991, "*Gajamuktika:* Poetic Convention and Reality". *Bulletin D'Etudes Indiennes.* Association Francaise Pour Les Etudes Sanskrites, Paris.

Śat. Br., 1940, *Śatapatha Brahmana.* 5 Volumes. "Laksmi Venkatesvara" Steam Press, Kalyan – Bombay.

Saunders, Nicholas J., 1991, *The Cult of the Cat.* Thames and Hudson, London.

Schaller, George B., 1972, *The Serengeti Lion, A Study of Predator-Prey Relations.* The University of Chicago Press, Chicago.

Scholfield, A.F. (tr.), 1959, *Aelian: On Peculiarities of Animals.* Harvard University Press, Cambridge, Mass.

Schwartzberg, Joseph E. (ed.), 1978, *A Historical Atlas of South Asia.* Oxford University Press, New York, 1992.

Sen, Geeti, 1984, *Paintings from the Akbar Nama.* Lustre Press Pvt. Ltd., Varanasi.

*Sen, Sri Sujit Narain, 1985, "Anecdotes of Kamargha and Fauna in Mughal Literature". *Indian Museum Bulletin,* Vol. XV, Nos. 1 and 2, pp. 41–48. Calcutta.

Seshadri, Balakrishna, 1969, *The Twilight of India's Wildlife.* John Baker Publishers, London.

Shaikh, G.A., 1936, *The Mahbat Album.* Junagadh.

Sharma, Arpan, Asmita Kabra, and Rumman Hameed, 2002, *Kuno Project, Madhya Pradesh. Progress Report V (November 2001–April 2002).* Samrakshan Trust, New Delhi (typescript).

Sharma, Diwakar and A.J.T. Johnsingh, 1996, *Impact of Management Practices on Lion and Ungulate Habitats in Gir Protected Area.* Wildlife Institute of India, Dehra Dun.

Sharma, Dr Ramdatta, c. 1970, *Sanskrit Kavyome Pashu Pakshi.* Devnagar Prakashan, Jaipur.

Shastri, M.M. Harprasad (tr.), 1910, *Syainika Sastram: The Art of Hunting in Ancient India of Raja Rudradeva of Kumaon.* Eastern Book Linkers, Delhi, 1982.

Shrigondekar, G.K. (ed.), 1939, *Manasollasa of King Someswara.* Vol. II. Oriental Institute, Baroda.

Singh, H.S., 1997, "Population Dynamics, Group Structure and Natural Dispersal of the Asiatic Lion PANTHERA LEO PERSICA". *Journal, Bombay Natural History Society,* Vol. 94, No. 1, pp. 65–70. Bombay.

———, 1998, *Gir Lion – Population Dynamics Predation Pattern, Dispersal and Management Issues* (typescript).

*———, 1998, *Wildlife of Gujarat.* Gujarat Ecological and Education Research Foundation, Gandhinagar.

———, 2001, *Natural Heritage of Gujarat (Forests and Wildlife).* Gujarat Ecological Education Research (GEER) Foundation, Gandhinagar.

———, 2001A, "Gir Lion – Present Scenario and Future Conservation Strategy". Paper read at *GEF – India Eco Development Project Initiative National Workshop on Regional Planning for Wild Life Protected Areas, 6th–8th August*, New Delhi (typescript).

Singh, H.S. and R.D. Kamboj, 1996, *Biodiversity Conservation Plan for Gir (A Management Plan for Gir Sanctuary & National Park).* Vols. I and II. Government of Gujarat, Gandhinagar.

Singh, M.K. Brijraj, 1985, *The Kingdom that was Kotah: Paintings from Kotah.* Lalit Kala Akademi, New Delhi.

Singh, Col. Kesri, 1959, *The Tiger of Rajasthan.* Robert Hale Ltd. London.

———, 1965, *Hints on Tiger Shooting (Tigers by Tiger).* The Hindustan Times, New Delhi.

Sinha, S.P., 1987, *Ecology of Wildlife with Special Reference to the Lion (Panthera leo persica) in Gir Wildlife Sanctuary, Saurashtra, Gujarat.* Ph.D. thesis, University of Saurashtra, Rajkot.

Sivaramamurti, C., 1974, *Birds and Animals in Indian Sculpture.* National Museum, New Delhi.

*Skelton, Robert, 1970, "Two Mughal Lion Hunts". *V & A Year Book*, No. 1, pp. 33–48. London.

Smith, S.J., P. Mcbee, and W.C. Mathews, 1989, *Rowland Ward's Records of Big Game XXII Edition.* Rowland Ward Publications, San Antonio, Texas.

Smythies, E.A., 1942, *Big Game Shooting in Nepal (with leaves from the Maharaja's Sporting Diary).* Thacker Spink & Co. (1933) Ltd., Calcutta.

Sodha, Jaisukhlal P., 2002, *Sorathna Antim Babi Shasak.* Pujam, Junagadh.

Soustiel, Joseph, 1973, *Miniatures Orientales de L'Inde: Les Ecoles et lurs styles Presentation d'un ensemble de peintures musulmanes et rajpoutes.* Librairie Leguettel, Paris.

*Spillett, J. Juan, 1968, "A Report on Wild Life Surveys in South and West India, November–December 1966". *Journal, Bombay Natural History Society*, Vol. 65, No. 1, pp. 1–46, Bombay.

Srivastava, Asheem and Suvira, 1999, *Asiatic Lion on the Brink.* Bishen Singh Mahendra Pal Singh, Dehra Dun.

Srivastava, T.N., 1969, "New Home for Lions in India". *Indian Forester,* pp. 706–10, Forest Research Institute, Dehra Dun.

*Stracey, P.D., 1959, "Lion Implanting in India". *Cheetal, Journal of the Wildlife Preservation Society of India,* Vol. I, No. 2. pp. 16–18, Dehra Dun.

———, 1963, *Wild Life in India: Its Conservation and Control.* Ministry of Food and Agriculture, Government of India, New Delhi.

Śubh., 1985, *Śubhasitaratnabhandagara.* "Shree Venkatesvara" Steam Press, Bombay.

Sunquist, Mel and Fiona, 2002, *Wild Cats of the World.* The University of Chicago Press, Chicago.

Sursinh, 1893, *Kalapino Kekarav.* Pravin Pustak Bhandar, Rajkot, 1982.

Suryakanta, Dr, 1962, *Kumarasambhava of Kalidasa.* Sahitya Akademi, New Delhi.

T

Taparia, Jaswantsinh, Harisinh, 1979, *Amar Charitra: Wankaner Maharana Rajsaheb Sir Amarsinhjinu Jeevan Vrutanta.* Wankaner.

Thackston, Wheeler M., 1996, *The Baburnama: Memoirs of Babur Prince and Emperor.* Freer Gallery of Art/Arthur M. Sackler Gallery, Oxford University Press, New York.

———, 1999, *The Jahangirnama: Memoirs of Jahangir, Emperor of India.* Freer Gallery of Art/Arthur M. Sackler Gallery, Washington, DC and Oxford University Press, New York.

Thapar, Romila, 1961, *Asoka and the Decline of the Mauryas.* Oxford University Press, Oxford.

———, 1966, *A History of India.* Vol. I. Penguin Books Ltd., Harmondsworth, Midddlesex, 1985.

Thapar, Valmik, 1992, *The Tiger's Destiny.* Time Books International, New Delhi.

———, 2002, *The Cult of the Tiger.* Oxford University Press, New Delhi.

———, 2004, *Tiger: The Ultimate Guide.* CDS Books/Two Brothers Press, New York.

Thomas, Elizabeth Marshall, 1994, *The Tribe of Tiger: Cats and their Culture.* Simon & Schuster, New York.

Thomas, P.K. and P.P. Joglekar, 1994, "Holocene Faunal Studies in India". *Man and Environment.* Vol. XIX, Nos. 1 and 2, pp. 179–203. Deccan College, Pune.

Thompson, Edward, 1999, "Mainly about Lions". *Oxford Anthology of Indian Wildlife: Watching and Conserving*, edited by Mahesh Rangarajan, Vol. II, pp. 96–99. Oxford University Press, New Delhi.

Titley, Norah M., 1983, *Persian Miniature Painting and its Influence on the Art of Turkey and India.* The British Library, London.

Tod, James, 1832, *Annals and Antiquities of Rajasthan.* Vol. II. K.M.N. Publishers, New Delhi, 1971.

*Tod, Neil B., 1965, "Metrical and Non-metrical Variation in the Skulls of Gir Lions". *Journal, Bombay Natural History Society*, Vol. 62, No. 3, pp. 507–20. Bombay.

Toynbee, J.M.C., 1973, *Animals in Roman Life and Art.* Cornell University Press, Ithaca, New York.

Trautman, Thomas R., 1982, "Elephant and the Mauryas". *India: History and Thought. Essays in Honour of A.L. Basham*, edited by S.N. Mukherji, pp. 254–81. Subernarekha, Calcutta.

Trivedi, K.K., 1998, "Estimating Forests, Wastes and Fields, c 1600". *Studies in History*, Vol. 14, No. 2, pp. 301–11. Sage Publications India Pvt. Ltd., New Delhi.

Turner, Alan, 1997, *The Big Cats and their*

Fossil Relatives: An Illustrated Guide to their Evolution and Natural History. Illustrations by Mauricio Anton. Columbia University Press, New York.

V

Vaidya, Suresh, 1958, *Ahead Lies the Jungle.* Robert Hale Ltd., London.

Van Buren, E. Douglas, 1939, *The Fauna of Ancient Mesopotamia as represented in Art.* Pontificum Institutum Biblicum, Roma.

Visaria, Leela and Pravin, 1982, "Population (1757–1947)". *The Cambridge Economic History of India, Vol. II, c1757–c1970.* Edited by Dharma Kumar and Meghnad Desai, pp. 463–532. Orient Longman, Hyderabad and Cambridge University Press, Cambridge, 1984.

*Vyas, Bhaskar N., 1997, *Girni Godma.* Published by author, Una, Gujarat.

*Vyas, Chintamani and Dr Daljeet, 1988, "Hunting Scenes in Indian Miniatures". *Indrama*, Vol. XIII, No. 3. Delhi.

W

Wallinger, W.A., 1913, *Report on Junagadh Forests.* Submitted to the Administrator of Junagadh State (typescript).

Wankaner, M.K. Chandrabhanusinhji of, 1952, *Shikar Diaries (Animals)* (unpublished).

Wankaner, Maharana Raj Saheb Pratapsinhji of, 1971, *Shikar Diary* (unpublished).

Watson, Col. J.W., 1884, *Statistical Account of Junagadh: Being the Junagadh Contribution to the Kathiawar Portion of the Bombay Gazetteer.* Bombay.

Weissert, Elnathan, 1997, "Royal Hunt and Royal Triumph in a Prism Fragment of Ashurbanipal (82-5-22.2)". *Assyria 1995. Proceedings of the 10th Anniversary Symposium of the Neo-Assyrian Text Corpus Project, Helsinki, September 7–11, 1995*, edited by S. Parpola and R.M. Whiting, pp. 339–57. The Neo-Assyrian Text Corpus Project, Helsinki.

Welch, Stuart Carey, 1978, *Imperial Mughal Painting.* George Braziller, New York.

–––, 1986, "A Lion-Kings' Lion". *Dimensions of Indian Art: Pupul Jaykar Seventy*, edited by Lokesh Chandra and Jyotindra Jain, Vol. I, pp 577–80. Agam Kala Prakashan, Delhi.

Wilberforce-Bell, Capt. H., 1916, *The History of Kathiawad from the Earliest Times.* William Heinemann, London.

Wildt, D.E., K.L. Bush, K.L. Goodrowe, C. Parker, A.E. Pusey, J.L. Brown, P. Joslin, and S.J. O'Brien, 1987, "Reproductive and Genetic Consequences of Founding Isolated Lion Populations". *Nature*, Vol. 329, No. 6137, pp. 328–31, September 24. Macmillan Magazines Ltd., London.

Williamson, Captain Thomas, 1807, *Oriental Field Sports; Being a Complete, Detailed and Accurate Description of the Wild Sports of the East.* Edward Orme, London.

Wolpert, Stanley, 1984, *Jinnah of Pakistan.* Oxford University Press, Delhi.

–––, 1993, *Zulfi Bhutto of Pakistan.* Oxford University Press, Delhi, 1994.

Wood, Ron with Meher, Vijay, 1998, *Soruth. Handbook of Indian Philately, Second Series – No. 3.* India Study Circle for Philately, London.

Wynter-Blyth, M.A., 1949, "The Gir Forest and its Lions". *Journal, Bombay Natural History Society*, Vol. 48, No. 3, pp. 493–514. Bombay.

–––, 1950, *Report on the Lions of the Gir Forest.* Published by author, Rajkot.

–––, 1956, "The Lion Census of 1955". *Journal, Bombay Natural History Society*, Vol. 53, No. 4, pp. 528–36. Bombay.

–––, c. 1961, *An Essay on the Geography of Saurashtra.* Rajkumar College, Rajkot.

Wynter-Blyth, M.A. and K.S. Dharmakumarsinhji, 1950, "The Gir Forest and its Lions" Part II. *Journal, Bombay Natural History Society*, Vol. 49, No. 3, pp. 456–70, Bombay.

Y

Ylla, 1958, *Animals in India.* Hamish Hamilton, London and La Guilde du Livre, Lausanne.

Z

Zeuner, Frederick E., 1963, *A History of Domesticated Animals.* Hutchinson, London.

Zimmermann, Francis, 1987, *The Jungle and the Aroma of Meats: An Ecological Theme in Hindu Medicine.* University of California Press, Berkeley.

index

Page numbers in bold refer to illustrations/captions